FUNDAMENTALS OF
PUBLIC SPEAKING

Edited by Dana Emerson and
Michele Dishong McCormack

FOUNTAINHEAD
PRESS

As a textbook publisher, we are faced with enormous environmental issues due the large amount of paper contained in our print products. Since our inception in 2002, we have worked diligently to be as eco-friendly as possible.

Our "green" initiatives include:

Electronic Products
We deliver products in non-paper form whenever possible. This includes pdf downloadables, flash drives, & CD's.

Electronic Samples
We use a new electronic sampling system, called Xample. Instructor samples are sent via a personalized web page that links to pdf downloads.

FSC Certified Printers
All of our Printers are certified by the Forest Service Council which promotes environmentally and socially responsible management of the world's forests. This program allows consumer groups, individual consumers and businesses to work together hand in hand to promote responsible use of the world's forests as a renewable and sustainable resource.

Recycled Paper
Almost all of our products are printed on a minimum of 10-30% post consumer waste recycled paper.

Support of Green Causes
When we do print, we donate a portion of our revenue to Green causes. Listed below are a few of the organizations that have received donations from Fountainhead Press. We welcome your feedback and suggestions for contributions, as we are always searching for worthy initiatives.

> Rainforest 2 Reef
> Environmental Working Group

Books may be purchased for educational purpose.

For information, please call or write:

1-800-586-0030

Fountainhead Press
Southlake, TX 76092

Web site: www.fountainheadpress.com
Email: customerservice@fountainheadpress.com

ISBN: 978-1-59871-612-2

Printed in the United States of America

TABLE OF CONTENTS

The Human Condition

After reading this chapter, you should be able to:

· Know the communication model
· List the rules of communication
· Identify the ten factors that affect communication
· Know the levels of communication
· Identify different careers available within various fields of communication

CHAPTER OUTLINE

· Introduction

· Defining Communication

· Rules of the Road

· Ten Factors that Affect Communication

· Levels of Communication

· Endless Opportunities

· Conclusion

· Chapter Review

Communication is not only the essence of being human, but also a vital property of life.
- John A. Piece

INTRODUCTION

As the mother of two grown children, Teresa Tyler had a great deal of trepidation about returning to school. It had been more than twenty years since she had stepped foot on a college campus let alone picked up a textbook for her own pursuit of knowledge. Her nerves did not get any better after she went for her advisement session. It was then that she learned she would have to take a course in communication her very first semester back. Whenever she would look at her schedule and saw the class's title, "Introduction to Communication," her stomach would immediately start doing flips. It did not take long for her family to pick up on her nervous reaction when they mentioned the class. When they finally decided to ask her about it, the only answer Teresa provided was that she was simply nervous about going back to school. She was too embarrassed to admit that she was deathly afraid of having to give speeches in class, especially after being out of the educational loop for so long.

After weeks of anxious waiting, the new semester arrived and Teresa headed back to school ready to face the monster in her head that was the communications class. As she arrived to the class and looked around, she found some consolation in the fact that several other students had the same look of worry on their faces that had been plastered across hers for the past month. When the professor came in, he introduced himself and then began to discuss the class and the syllabus in detail. Teresa became relieved with each passing minute as the professor told them that speaking was only a small component of the course. Following class, she raced to the bookstore to purchase the required text, anxious to see if the professor was telling the truth. Was communication and, in particular, a communications course about more than just public speaking?

How many of you reading this textbook had the same feeling of dread about talking a communications class because you thought that the only component of the course would be public speaking? You are most definitely not alone. Time and time again professors will see students who put their communications classes off until the last minute because they think that it will be nothing but continuous speaking exercises. While speech delivery is an important factor of communication, it is not the only one. Other components that are covered in the study of communication include: culture, stereotypes, ethics, and relationships, just to name a few. The following sections explore all of these concepts and more, debunking the myth that communication is only about public speaking.

DEFINING COMMUNICATION

Defining the term communication can be overwhelming because it calls to mind so many different ideas. When you mention communication to one person, images of cell phones and computers might pop into their head while others might think about relationships and the bonds that can be formed from communicating. Technically speaking, communication is the process of using

---

Communication
The process of using messages to create meaning.

Process
Any exchange or activity that happens over time

Messages
Ideas, emotions, or concepts that are exchanged from one person to another, either verbally or nonverbally

Verbal Communication
The use of language and vocal sounds to deliver a message

messages to create meaning. In order to make this definition perfectly clear, let's take a look at the three components that combine to make up communication: process, messages, and meaning. A process is any exchange or activity that happens over time. To define communication as a process is to say that it is ongoing without a definitive beginning or end. Messages can be ideas, emotions, or concepts that are exchanged from one person to another, either verbally or nonverbally. When done verbally, communication uses language and vocal sounds to deliver a message. Nonverbal communication, on the other hand, is the use of facial expressions, body language, and gestures to communicate. For example, a nonverbal message could include waving to a friend to say hello on the street. From this, your friend would conclude that your nonverbal message meant that you were saying hello. In other words, meaning is the understanding applied to a message.

The process that is communication follows a model that is used in delivering every message. This model starts with a sender. The sender is the origination point of a message. In the earlier example of waving to a friend, you would be the sender since you were the one who originated the communication. You, the sender, in wanting to say hello, translated that message into a wave, which is known as encoding. Your friend would be the receiver, or the person who gets the message. The way the communication is transmitted, by waving, is known as the channel. After receiving your message, the receiver gives meaning to the message, otherwise known as decoding, and gives a response to the sender, known as feedback. Anything that interrupts the transmission of the message from the sender to the receiver is known as noise. In case things got a bit confusing, take a look at the diagram below to help make better sense of things.

Nonverbal communication
The use of facial expressions, body language, and gestures to communicate

Meaning
The understanding assigned to a message

Sender
The origination point of a message

Encoding
The process of translating a message into a code

Receiver
The person who gets the message

Channel
The way in which a message is transmitted from sender to receiver

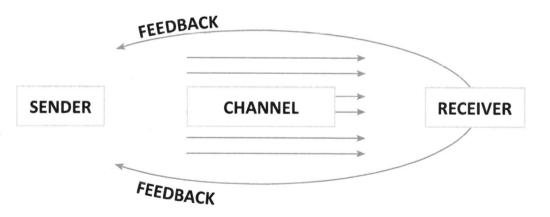

With the basic fundamentals under our belt, let's explore some rules that dictate communication and its function in the world.

RULES OF THE ROAD

Rule #1: Communication is dynamic.

For many of you, the term "dynamic" was first introduced in your high school English class when you learned about dynamic characters in literature. Like those same characters, communication is also dynamic. In other words, it is in a process of constant change and evolution. This should come as no surprise seeing as communication relies on a myriad of other things, including people and technology, that are constantly changing as well. Walther, Gay, and Hancock (2005) comment that the relationships that exist between these things are "reciprocal relationships between structures and rules imposed by any given communication tool, the social rules imposed by administrators, and the need for [people] to accommodate through their own innovative effort." In other words, a cyclical reaction occurs where people and technology affect and change the face of communication, and communication, in turn, affects the way people think and communicate, and so on. Without this dynamic quality and people's desire to change the way they interact with each other, we would be without many of the technological toys that make our lives so enjoyable and entertaining today.

Rule #2: Communication starts with you.

It is certainly no secret that we are all born communicating. Our first cries communicated to the doctor whether or not we were breathing properly. Nurses took our vitals, which helped to communicate our state of health. When we cried, our mothers knew that we were hungry. All of these things are examples of the communicative miracle that individuals take part in the moment we are born. This is the foundation of the second rule of communication: Communication starts with you.

As we mature, we begin to grow out of simply using our instinctive ways to communicate and begin to learn from the world around us how to get what we want and interact with others, building relationships and forming opinions from our experiences. These opinions can be broken down into three categories: attitudes, beliefs, and values. Simply put, an attitude is our predisposition toward something that causes us to act in a positive or negative way. In other words, you might maintain the attitude that a college education is necessary to succeed in the business world, which would cause you to oppose or act negatively toward those individuals who climb the corporate ladder without a college degree. Attitudes are rooted in our beliefs and, of the three categories of opinions, are the easiest to change because they tend to be a learned behavior. Beliefs are our convictions. If you believed that it pays to get a good education, then it would explain your attitude toward those individuals who did not go to college and their chances for success. This brings us to values, which are beliefs that are long-held and dictate our attitude toward people, ideas, objects, and events. Using this same example, it could be said that you valued education and hard work. Of the three, values are the hardest to change because of their long-standing tradition within an individual's life.

So, how does all of this relate to the second rule of communication? Well, these attitudes, beliefs, and values dictate the way that we take in information, how we assign meaning to it, and what we do as a result of this meaning. If we value patriotism and we believe that America is the greatest country in the world, our attitude might be that all of those individuals from other countries are not worth getting to know. Upon coming into a class with several international students, your actions, as a result of your attitude, would be to limit your communication with them or to treat them in a way different from other students. Therefore, your opinions impede you from getting to know other people and broadening your horizons by learning about other places and cultures. In this case, communication not only starts with you but it also ends with you and your close-minded way of thinking.

Rule #3: Communication happens in a context.

In watching any crime drama on television, you become familiar with the investigator's line of questioning that helps him or her solve the crime. These questions usually revolve around the who, the what, the when, the where, and the why of the incident. Communication is no different as it also has a who, what, when, where, and why, which we know as context. The context is the setting or set of circumstances in which communication occurs and has a huge bearing on how we communicate. For example, you are unlikely to communicate the same way at a funeral as you do a wedding, because the tones of these two events are vastly different and require you to act, and ultimately communicate, in a different way. The context can also include how many people that you are trying to reach through your communication. Contextually speaking, an audience of ten people and a lecture hall of 250 will require the speaker to tweak not only the message but also the way it is delivered.

Rule #4: Communication never happens the exact same way twice.

To understand the next rule of communication, let's take a look at the classes that you are enrolled in right now. In all likelihood, yours is not the only section of the course that your professor is teaching. As a result, he or she will have to repeat the same information several times throughout the day or week. The way this is done is never the same way twice. Your class, for example, might be first thing in the morning. If your professor has not had a morning cup of coffee, the delivery might be slightly unenthusiastic, and some details might be forgotten. Later in the day, the professor might be more awake and, therefore, lecture with more energy, making sure not to leave out anything. This same phenomenon can be seen all the time in live theater. Although the actors know the lines and have rehearsed countless times, each performance is slightly different. This is a result of the actor's own affect on communication as well as the audience's perception of what they are watching. Although it might be similar, it will never be the same.

Decoding
The process of assigning meaning to a message's code

Feedback
The receiver's response to a message

Noise
Anything that interrupts the transmission of a message from the sender to the receiver

Attitude
A predisposition towards something that causes us to act in a positive or negative way

Belief
A conviction

Value
Beliefs that are long-held and dictate our attitude towards people, ideas, objects, and events

Context
The setting or set of circumstances in which communication occurs

Rule #5: Communication is inevitable.

The next rule of communication can be a little bit frustrating for some because, try as you might to stop it, communication is going to happen. It is inevitable. Take for example your last argument. Were you trying to sit quietly not communicating anything about your mood or the way you felt about the topic at hand? Unfortunately, your silence and body language communicated as much about you as your words would have if you took a different argumentative approach. Communication is going to happen whether we like it or not, so it would be smart to pay better attention to it in order not to give off the wrong message.

Rule #6: Communication is irreversible.

It is imperative for us to recognize the inevitable quality of communication because it is equally irreversible, which could have disastrous results. There is no greater example of the irreversible nature of communication than the Internet. For many of you, the Internet, and, in particular, sites like Facebook, is your main outlet of self-expression and communication with friends, locally and globally. Although this is a great tool to keep in touch with the masses, posting updates and pictures of your late night escapades are dangerous. For example, after celebrating your friend's 21st birthday with a trip to Las Vegas, pictures of you acting foolishly appear on your profile thanks to a friend posting them on your wall. Although you deleted them a few hours after they were first posted, the damage has already been done. People are constantly connected to Facebook looking at status and picture updates. Even if one person saw the pictures of you, the message that they communicated cannot be reversed. Similarly, the things you say cannot be taken back either. That is why it is so important to weigh your words before speaking, because once you say something, whether or not you meant it, the words will not be forgotten no matter how much backpeddling and covering up you might try to do.

TEN FACTORS THAT AFFECT COMMUNICATION

Now that you know the rules that govern communication, it is important to understand the factors that affect the way that we communicate in our day-to-day lives. For the purposes of this text, we will be examining ten factors, although there are many more. The factors that we will be exploring include: age, gender, race, religion, educational background, socioeconomic background, political affiliation, sexual orientation, culture, and life experiences.

Age

Age is the first factor that we will examine because it is the one that we encounter first in our communicative lives. As we discussed earlier, the way we communicate evolves as we mature and grow older. The cries that once signified our need for food turn into requests for a "ba-ba" as a toddler. Eventually, we develop a vocabulary and style all our own. As a result, we are expected to communicate in ways that reflect our age. Standing in the middle of the grocery store and throwing a temper tantrum to communicate that we are upset over not getting the type of candy we want might work when we are four or five years old. Using this same channel of communication will get us several stares and a possible grounding when we are sixteen years old.

Not only does the way that we communicate evolve as we get older but the way in which the world communicates with us also changes. For example, the recent dispute over the use of cartoon characters to sell cereals high in sugar to children has recently been called into question. This is because the cartoon characters associated with these foods, which are believed to be linked to childhood obesity, communicate a fun-filled message that compels the child to want that particular cereal over the healthier choices that do not market their products with colorful characters. Similarly, advertisements for life insurance communicate to older individuals by discussing matters that are pertinent to their lives, such as funeral costs. Using a cartoon to advertise life insurance would be blatantly out of place in the same way that two adults discussing the health benefits of a kid's cereal would be.

Gender: Feminine and Masculine

Men and women communicate differently. If you are shocked by this news, please feel free to take a few minutes to recover and then continue with your reading. It should not, however, be all that surprising considering this concept has been drilled into our brains a countless number of times. The discussion of men and women's communication habits has become a thing of such curiosity in recent years that studies are even being done to evaluate the number of words men and women use daily. Liberman (2006) contends that these studies have not come up with any concrete number to assign to each group. Taking into consideration the various studies and their findings, men were designated with using a daily vocabulary ranging from 2,000 to 25,000 words per day and women using about 7,000 to 50,000 words daily.[4]

Although there is no agreement on the exact number of words used daily by each sex, there is no denying the fact that women do a great deal more talking on a day-to-day basis. Perhaps the clearest example of this in our lives is in the text messages we send and receive every day. When women send text messages, or any message for that matter, they tend to be very detailed and specific about what they want, using multiple lines of text if necessary. For example, the simple act of trying to determine if friends would like to go to the movies might go something like this: "Hey guys! I know we talked about it earlier this week, but I just wanted to make sure everyone was still interested in going to dinner and a movie tonight. I am not sure what you would like to get to eat, but I was thinking we could go for pizza or sushi because I have been craving that all week. As for the movies, there are a lot of good shows playing this week, but I know we were all really interested in seeing Iron Man 2, which is playing at 5:45, 7:30, 9:00, 10:15, 11:30 and 12:00. So, just let me know if you are interested, what you would like to eat, and what time you think we should go to see the movie. Can't wait to see you all tonight!" While some of the female recipients might respond with an equally lengthy message, the male response would generally be much shorter. It might go something like this: "Pizza and then movie at 10:15 works for me." What it took the female in this example 133 words to say, the male was able to respond in only nine. Although this might seem like an extreme example, it effectively illustrates just one of the differences that exist in even the most basic of communication styles between men and women. This kind of unbalanced conversation can lead to a great deal of frustration and miscommunication between the sexes.

Gender's affect on communication is deeply rooted in the early communication patterns developed by girls and boys as adolescent children searching for their identities and similarities among friends. Tannen (1991) comments on the communicative foundations of men and women writing:

> The research of sociologists and anthropologists...has shown that girls and boys learn to use language differently in their sex-separate peer groups. Typically, a girl has a best friend with whom she sits and talks, frequently telling secrets. It's the telling of secrets, the fact and the way that they talk to each other, that makes them best friends. For boys, activities are central: Their best friends are the ones they do things with. Boys also tend to play in larger groups that are hierarchical. High-status boys give orders and push low-status boys around. So boys are expected to use language to seize center stage: by exhibiting their skill, displaying their knowledge, and challenging and resisting challenges.[5]

The differences in early development of communication among peers certainly set the stage for vast communicative differences to emerge and expand among men and women. These differences call for a great deal of patience and care in order to ensure that misunderstandings and insults stay at a minimum.

Race

Race is another factor where stark differences, or the assumption of these differences, can have a massive impact on the way that people communicate. Just like with gender, the roots of these communicative variations are introduced at a very young age, shaping the way people communicate through their adolescence into adulthood. Berger (2006) addresses this saying:

> In 1963, Roger Abrahams, a folklorist, studied the patterns found in African American speech in an area of Philadelphia and found that this speech relied, to a considerable extent, on certain kinds of material that were familiar to the speakers from their childhood days.[6]

Clearly, the materials introduced during these early years differ largely based on the racial background of the child and are not strictly limited to the African American community. In 1963, race relations resulted in such stark contrasts in even the most trivial entertainment for children that a majority of people of all races were unable to adapt and communicate easily with one another. In 2010, it is perfectly acceptable and commonplace to turn on children's programming and find a variety of races and ethnicities represented, helping children to see the similarities in people from various backgrounds. Despite this, the fact still remains that race and the differences associated with it affect communication in a very real way.

Religion

There are over 40 religions with more than three million followers each around the world.[7] These religions are as complex and contrasting as the people who faithfully subscribe to them. Religion's effect on communication comes as a result of the long historical ties to communities of people and the way they lived, worked, and played. Berger (2006) writes:

> A study of the Middle Ages offers us an important insight into the mindset of people in this period of time – the fourteenth and fifteenth centuries, a period of powerful religious belief marked by extreme behavior, asceticism on one side and licentiousness on the other. In those days, people found meaning and significance in everything because, from their world view, everything was connected to God. If, in God, nothing is empty of sense, then everything is tied to God, and it is the duty of people to recognize this situation and thus find symbolic religious significance in everything.[8]

The way that God, or gods in some cases, is manifested in the hearts and minds of the followers of these religions plays a very important role in how they communicate with each other and with people of different religions. Many of the communicative differences that exist are the result of the various signs and symbols that are deemed significant from one religion to another. For example, members of the Roman Catholic Church use the Sign of the Cross as a way to communicate the beginning of prayer. For those who are not familiar with the Catholic faith or this tradition, the message that is communicated is one of confusion and even absurdity.

Educational Background

If you are reading this textbook, it is fair to assume that you are pursuing a degree in higher education. The things that you learn in college will shape your mind and life in ways that are unimaginable. The way that you communicate with those whose educational background is different than yours will often change. For example, you probably all know someone who pursued a career right out of high school rather than going to college. Your first inclination when talking to these people might be to "dumb" your language down as you might wrongly equate their fewer years immersed in studying with being less intelligent than you. Alternately, those same people who got a job right out of high school and have been working in the field ever since might not use technical terminology when talking about their job because they think you might not understand the jargon of their professional field. Both cases are assumptions that are usually always incorrect and can lead to insulting other people as a result.

Another aspect of educational background affecting communication deals with where one goes to school. Whether it be public and private high schools or Ivy League colleges and community colleges, there is a great deal of stress placed on where a degree comes from in today's society and what this automatically communicates to others. One educational avenue that bears an unworthy negative reputation is the GED. Comeford (2009) comments on this saying:

> Many people hear GED and automatically think "high school drop-out." The GED seems to have this stigma of a lower than high school diploma certification; that it is for those that were "not smart enough" to get their high school diploma. This is an unfair stereotype of the GED.[9]

The GED's origins as being an educational path for those individuals who dropped out of high school is largely what is still communicated to people today when they think of a GED. Unfortunately, those same individuals who attended prestigious schools or got their degrees in a more traditional way have not taken into account the circumstances surrounding a person dropping out of school or considered the countless numbers of entertainers, homeschoolers, and privately tutored children who choose a GED as a means to end one chapter of their lives successfully and begin another. A degree from a prestigious school might communicate to others an air of intelligence, but the people who earn them do not always use intelligence to communicate.

Socioeconomic Background

It is fitting to discuss the next factor, which is socioeconomic background, here after educational background as the two are often intrinsically tied to one another. The phrase "money talks" is very true because money has the power to communicate concepts of wealth and success or poverty and failure. We have seen the stereotypes played out time and time again in movies and television of the wealthy treating the poor badly and talking to them like a class of sub-humans. Alternately, we have seen the impoverished often portrayed as uneducated and lazy people enviously admiring the lives of the rich. These two extremes show how socioeconomic backgrounds are often communicated in the media, but what about in everyday life?

For those individuals who come from a wealthy family, it might not be how you communicate as much as it is what you communicate. For example, it would not be unusual for a person with money to discuss exotic vacations or extravagant shopping trips with their friends of the same monetary background. However, when they are with their friends who are not as wealthy, they might not discuss these things with such great detail or even at all. Similarly, those individuals who come from a poorer background might talk about how much they work or struggle to make ends meet around other friends in similar situations, but they would probably not discuss these same things with their wealthy friends. It is apparent that money does talk, but maybe sometimes it should remain silent.

Political Affiliation

In America, there are two major political parties: the Democratic Party and the Republican Party. Additionally, there are 35 other parties, called third parties, that include the Constitution Party, the Green Party, the Libertarian Party, and the Boston Tea Party, just to name a few.[10] Like religion, the differences in the people who subscribe to these various parties are as different as night and day. The concepts and topics in the political world are extremely personal and polarized often causing people to discuss them with a great deal more passion and fervor than they would more neutral topics. For example, one of the more polarized topics that people differ on based on their politics is abortion. Generally speaking, people who are affiliated with the Republican Party tend to be pro-life whereas those individuals affiliated with the Democratic Party tend to be pro-choice. Giving a speech in class persuading your audience to vote pro-life would communicate to them that your political background was one that was more conservative in nature and that you were probably a Republican. This, however, is not always the case as the lines of politics have become increasingly blurred over the past several decades. The person giving the speech might have, in fact, been a conservative member of the Democratic Party. Again, there is no hard and fast rule that governs the way that political affiliation is communicated or the way that it affects communication, especially since politics are as dynamic as communication itself.

Sexual Orientation

Out of fear, secrecy, shame, and bigotry, sexual orientation has long been held as a taboo topic that silently dictated the way people communicated with each other for decades. Fortunately, there has been a great deal of growth and acceptance within society to embrace people of all sexual orientations. Still, the preconceived notions and myths surrounding sexual orientation, and in particular those members of the gay, lesbian, bisexual, and transgendered community, still dictate the communication of those individuals to a certain extent. Gross (2005) writes:

> When lesbian and gay people in the United States began to organize in the 1950s and press for social change, they did so in an atmosphere that defined them as sinful, sick, and criminal... Another approach then began to surface, inspired by the argument that homosexuals should be seen, and should see themselves, as a minority community.

Because of the onslaught of negativity shown toward members of the gay, lesbian, bisexual, and transgendered community and their eventual relegation to a category of minority, they often communicated with the world in a way that kept their personal lives a secret in order to avoid rejection and segregation. At any rate, it is impossible to ignore the effect that sexual orientation has on communication of members of both the gay and the straight community.

Culture

Culture is a system of shared beliefs, values, traditions, and behaviors that are special to a given society or group of people. Culture is the overarching factor that affects communication, taking on an aspect of all of the preceding eight factors. Its place in society is pivotal because it shapes individuals day-in and day-out, dictating how they communicate with each another and the world. What is culturally accepted in one place is not necessarily the case in another. Consider the way that culture changes what the following two messages communicate:

- Eye contact – In several countries, including America, making eye contact is a show of respect and good communication skills. In Japan and Korea, however, making eye contact is a display of intimidation and can even be misconstrued as a sign of sexual intentions.
- The Peace Sign – Here in America, holding your index finger and your middle finger up in the shape of a "V" while your wrist is bent and your palm is toward you is a peace sign. For the English and Australians, this same sign is an obscene way to tell someone off.

> **Intrapersonal Communication**
> The transmission of messages to create meaning within one's self

Culture touches on everything in a society, including accents, dress, language, food, music, entertainment, and much more. As a result, its impact on communication is naturally very large and important. Although knowing about your own culture is extremely important to shaping your own identity and communicative style, it is equally important to know about other cultures as well to avoid communication blunders.

Life Experiences

We constantly draw on our frame of reference to determine how we are going to communicate. This frame of reference is made up of the jobs we have had, the places we have traveled, the movies we have watched, and so on. Without it, we would have to learn everything over again in order to communicate successfully. Consider this scenario: Following a nap, you wake up to find that your memory has been completely wiped clean while you slept. You look around and realize you do not know where you are let alone who you are. The most trivial things around you are foreign because the names that were assigned them in your memory are gone. How would you function or would you even be able to function at all?

Our memories are an invaluable communicative tool because they constantly tell us how to act and react to various stimuli in our environment. For example, seeing a hot stove would cause us to recall the time we burnt our hand

and thus communicate that touching the stove will result in getting hurt. This is only one small example of the way that life experiences affect communication. Nussbaum and Friedrich (2005) expand on this saying:

> Certain communicative behaviors and relationships serve us well at different points across the life span. The great diversity in the nature of relationship development and in the adaptability of our communicative behavior within numerous, simultaneously occurring relationships emerges from these investigations. Finally, and perhaps most importantly, these investigations have focused attention on the many environmental factors such as relationship experience, history, significant life events, parenthood, grandparenthood, work relationships, friendship networks, life crises, and health-related issues, just to name a few, that can significantly impact our communicative behavior.

In other words, our life experiences serve as a reference book that guides us in our interpretation of messages from others and, in return, helps us to deliver messages as well.

LEVELS OF COMMUNICATION

Just as there are different rules and factors that affect communication, there are also different levels on which communication takes place that play an important part in how messages are exchanged. These levels include: intrapersonal communication, interpersonal communication, public communication, and mass communication.

Intrapersonal Communication

The first level of communication is known as intrapersonal communication. Intrapersonal communication is the transmission of messages to create meaning within one's self. Examples of intrapersonal communication can include making lists in your head or thinking through the steps to a logic problem during a mathematics test. Intrapersonal communication does not always have to be an internal conversation. Singing aloud while alone in the car or reciting facts aloud when studying for a test are also both examples of intrapersonal communication.

Intrapersonal communication can be very powerful because it delivers messages in a very intimate way, positively and, sometimes, negatively. How many times have you looked in the mirror and spent countless minutes pointing out the imperfections you see? Do you ever psych yourself out before taking a test by saying that you do not know the material? These examples of intrapersonal communication can have detrimental effects because it molds our attitudes and ultimately our actions. Kaleimamahu (2003) writes:

> Within each person resides their own cultural heritage, parental lineage, and self-concept that is unique. As people constantly

Intrapersonal Communication
The transmission of messages to create meaning within one's self

Self-concept
How individuals perceive themselves

Self-talk
The conversations that we have with ourselves.

Interpersonal Communication
The exchange of messages to create meaning between at least two people

Dyadic Communication
Communication that occurs between two people

Small Group Communication
Communication that occurs between at least three people in a small group

Public Communication
The transmission of a message from a single sender to numerous receivers

Mass Communication
Communication where a single sender transmits a message to a great number of unseen receivers through a mediated system

debate and ponder life's every day questions, their thought and attitudes are influenced by many experiences and natural events… It is the silent thinking, the inner voice, and the self-talk that drives or prohibits each one of our thoughts and actions. It is the way man reasons out his thoughts and emotions, and the outcome of his intrapersonal communication can be seen in one's attitude, one's actions, and one's self-concept.[14]

Mentioned here are two terms that have a great deal of importance to intrapersonal communication: self-concept and self-talk. Self-concept is how individuals perceive themselves. Self-talk is the conversations that we have with ourselves. When your self-concept is negative, the way in which you speak to yourself will be negative as a result. Alternately, if your self-concept is positive, then your self-talk will be positive as well.

Interpersonal Communication

The next level of communication is interpersonal communication. This is the exchange of messages to create meaning between at least two people. It is on this level of communication that relationship building takes place. Interpersonal communication is composed of two sub-levels: dyadic communication and small group communication. Dyadic communication is communication that occurs between two people. Small group communication is communication that occurs between at least three people within a small group.

According to scholars at the University of Northern Iowa (2005) examining the function of communication in business, the role of interpersonal communication in an individual's life can take on many shapes. They write:

Interpersonal communication can occur in writing or by email, as well as in a face-to-face setting. Further, even total strangers who interact with each other respectfully could be said to be communicating interpersonally even though the topic of conversation might be trite or task related. In short, interpersonal communication is more about the content and character of the exchange than about the mechanics of how it happens or with whom. The successful member of a business organization will display a range of interpersonal skills whenever he or she uses communication to maintain relationships, share tacit knowledge, or exchange information about emotions, values and motivations.[15]

Of course, these truths do not strictly pertain to the business world alone because good interpersonal communication is the key to success of any relationship, professional or personal.

Public Communication

Public communication, which is also known as speech communication, is the transmission of a message from a single sender to numerous receivers. It is on this level of communication that we see a focus on public speaking. Generally, public communication tends to be formal in nature as one person is responsible for creating a message and delivering it to a large audience. This can take on many shapes including: classroom lectures, question and answer sessions, religious services, and so on. Whereas interpersonal communication aims at relationship building and maintenance, public communication is often used as a tool to inform or entertain. It can, however, be used for a myriad of other reasons, including to thank someone, to introduce, to dedicate, to honor, to memorialize, to entertain, to educate, to commemorate, to welcome, and to announce.

Mass Communication

Mass communication is the level of communication where a single sender transmits a message to a great number of unseen receivers through a mediated system. For example, advertisements on television are an example of mass communication because they are coming from a single source to multiple unseen receivers through the television, which serves as the mediated system. Mass communication has become a powerful tool over the last century as more and more people turn on and tune in to various mediums delivering messages. These individuals take in these messages both consciously and subconsciously. Postman (1985) comments on one form of mass communication, television, saying:

> Television has become…the background radiation of the social and intellectual universe, that all-but-imperceptible residue of the electronic big bang of a century past, so familiar and so thoroughly integrated with American culture that we no longer hear its faint hissing in the background or see the flickering gray light.[16]

Postman's words bring to light the new struggle that mass communication faces – standing out from the background. With the constant blur of media in the background becoming part of our every day lives, mass communication has to try now more than ever to jump off of the screen or out of speakers to deliver its message in a way that is not only heard but that is also understood and acknowledged.

ENDLESS OPPORTUNITIES

In case you have not figured it out so far, communication has limitless possibilities. It should come as no surprise, then, that the career opportunities that are possible within the field of communications are endless. Camenson (1995) expands on this saying:

Communications is all about getting the word out – and there are as many ways to do that as there are words…Communications opens more doors than any other major. With an understanding of how to penetrate public awareness and mold and respond to public opinion, communications can be public relations. With the knowledge of how to reach and influence consumers, communications can be advertising or publicity and promotion. Through the techniques of writing and editing, communications can be journalism. With problem-solving and group management skills, communications can be corporate troubleshooting or training. And for individuals working with communications disorders, communications can be speech-language pathology or audiology.[17]

Interested in a job in communications? Careers in communications can be broken up into four areas of concentration: corporate communication, consumer communication, media, and communications disorders. The following lists break down the various fields that communications is composed of and the jobs available in each. Notice that several jobs are repeated within the various fields, underscoring the expansive and versatile nature of communication.

Corporate Communication

Alumni Relations Coordinator

Business Development Manager

Civic Affairs Representative

Communications Consultant

Communications Specialist

Community Affairs Coordinator

Community Relations Specialist

Consumer Affairs Specialist

Copyeditor

Copywriter

Corporate Communications Director

Corporate Communicator

Director of Employment

Editor

Educational Affairs Director

Employee Publications Specialist

Event Coordinator

Fundraiser

Government Relations

Group/Regional Manager

Industrial PR Executive

Intercultural Communications Specialist

Intercultural Communicator

Interpersonal Communicator

Investor Relations Director

Management Supervisor

Patient Advocate

Press Secretary

Promotional Campaign Developer

Public Information Officer

Public Relations Assistant

Public Relations Manager

Public Relations Writer

Research Assistant

Researcher

Spokesperson

Staff Writer

Volunteer Coordinator

Consumer Communication

Account Coordinator
Account Director
Account/District Manager
Account Executive
Account Representative
Account Specialist
Account Supervisor
Account Trainee
Advertising Director
Advertising Photography
Art Buyer
Art Director
Broadcast Production Manager
Campaign Developer
Consumer Affairs Specialist
Convention Sales
Copyeditor
Copywriter
Creative Director
Demographer
Designer
Editor
Event Coordinator
Function Sales Manager
Fundraiser
Hotel Sales
Graphic Artist

Management Supervisor
Market Analyst
Market Research Manager
Media Buyer
Media Director
Media Evaluator
Media Placement Specialist
Media Planner
Media Supervisor
Membership Services Director
Print Production Manager
Producer
Production Assistant
Production Manager
Project Director
Promotion Manager
Publicist
Research Assistant
Researcher
Sales Assistant
Sales Planner
Sales Representative
Spokesperson
Statistician
Traffic Assistant
Traffic Manager
Travel Photography

Media

Print Media

Acquisitions Editor
Art Director
Assignment Editor
Assistant Editor
Associate Editor
Author
Book Editor
Bureau Chief
Bureau Reporter

Freelance Writer
International Publications Editor
Investigative Reporter
Journalist
Literary Agent
Managing Editor
News Editor
Newspaper Editor
News Writer

City Editor

Columnist

Contracts Assistant

Copyeditor

Copywriter

Correspondent

Critic

Desk Assistant

Dramatic Agent

Editor

Editorial Assistant

Editorial Writer

Editor in Chief

Electronic Publishing Specialist

Executive Editor

External Publications Editor

Feature Writer

Photojournalist

President

Production Editor

Publisher

Reporter

Researcher

Section Editor

Senior Editor

Senior Writer

Staff Writer

Story Editor

Stringer

Syndicated Columnist

Technical Writer

Wire Editor

Writer

Radio, Television, and Multimedia

Announcer

Associate News Director

AV Manager/Director

AV Producer

AV Technician

AV Writer

Broadcast Engineers

Broadcast Technicians

CAD Specialist

Correspondent

Director

Disc Jockey

Documentary Maker

Educational Film/Video Maker

Feature Film Director

Feature Filmmaker

Feature Film Producer

Filmmaker

First Assistant Director

Graphics Coordinator

Media Resource Director

Mixer

Music Director

Music Librarian

Newscaster

News Announcer

News Director

New Editor

News Writer

Operations Manager

Production Assistant

Production Manager

Production Sound Mixer

Program Manager

Public Services Director

Radio/TV Traffic Assistant

Radio/TV Traffic Supervisor

Scriptwriter

Station Manager

TV Director

TV Managing Editor

TV Producer

TV Production Assistant

TV Tape-Film Manager

Video Specialist

Communications Disorders

Audiology	Speech Language Pathology
Researcher	Teacher[17]

Conclusion

As you can see, communication goes a great deal deeper than just public speaking. The fact that speech delivery is often a graded component of a communications course and the one most dreaded by people probably has a great deal to do with this common misconception. Knowing what communication is and how it works can help an individual succeed both personally and professionally. Although Teresa's phobia of public speaking never completely went away, she did learn that communication was a multidimensional concept and that understanding it better helped her to work with her fear of speaking in front of a group rather than running away from it. While communicating might not always be easy, it is ultimately worth it.

Key Terms

Attitude	Feedback	Public communication
Belief	Interpersonal communication	Receiver
Channel	Intrapersonal communication	Self-concept
Communication	Mass communication	Self-talk
Context	Meaning	Sender
Culture	Messages	Small group communication
Decoding	Noise	Value
Dyadic communication	Nonverbal communication	Verbal communication
Encoding	Process	

Public Speaking, A Long Tradition

2

Practically SPEAKING

Imagine being tutored by one of the greatest minds ever to live. Imagine personal attention from a man responsible for some of the most important writings in history. Of course, such an opportunity is not really available today, but it was in the Classical World, and one person managed to receive such an education: Alexander the Great of Macedon. From his early teenage years Alexander was personally tutored by Aristotle, the man who wrote books that are still considered foundational texts for communication studies, philosophy, political science, and even the natural sciences. You might think that such an opportunity came about largely because of the wealth and power of Alexander's family, and in that you would be only partially correct.

In 343 B.C. Philip of Macedon, Alexander's father, approached Aristotle with an offer to tutor his son, then 13 years old. At the time, Aristotle had not written many of his works and only recently had finished 20 years of studies at Plato's Academy and had left Athens. In fact, he was little more than a roaming refugee in exile since Philip himself had ordered the complete annihilation of Aristotle's home city, Stagiros.[1] So, the fact Philip chose him is interesting. There was also a personal connection between Philip and Aristotle in that they knew each other from childhood when Aristotle's father, Nicomachus, was the personal physician to Philip's father. Perhaps the combination of the childhood connection, Aristotle's education under Plato, and Philip's possible desire to extend an olive branch to the remaining people of Stagiros led to the choice of Aristotle as personal tutor to Alexander.[2]

It did not take long for Aristotle to accept the offer and begin schooling Philip's son and a few other sons of nobles at Mieza, a spot of land west of the Macedonian capital of Pella.[3] While there Alexander learned about medicine, ethics, literature, Greek culture, and other subjects while sitting outdoors on stone benches. One can easily see the impact these lessons had on the young prince. When he became king and began his conquest of the known world at the time, Alexander would collect samples of flowers and animals and send them back to his former tutor for study.[4] He also carried a volume of Homer's *Iliad* with him that Aristotle had personally edited. Even more practical of an impact was the fact Alexander used his knowledge of medicine garnered from his time with Aristotle to personally treat wounded soldiers on the battlefield![5]

The education of Alexander by Aristotle provides us with an early example of what we now call a classroom and the broad outline of what we call a liberal arts education. Alexander was schooled in a wide array of subjects from ethics and philosophy, to rhetoric and politics, to medicine and physics, and today universities take a similar approach in designing a general education for students. The lasting impact of the way schools were structured and students taught in Classical Greece and Classical Rome can still be seen today.

In this chapter we will explore some of the great thinkers of Classical Greece and Rome and look at how their schools were structured. It is important to note that some of these great thinkers taught in schools, like Plato and Aristotle, but others were more like wandering tutors. All of these individuals and groups, however, understood the importance of education and the place of speech in it. To cover this much history in such a short space we will highlight aspects of classical education relevant to our focus on public speaking and introduce you to figures such as Aristotle, Cicero, and Quintilian, who we will revisit later in the book. We will conclude the chapter with a brief discussion of different contexts today where the lessons of these ancient Greeks and Romans are still relevant.

Education Then and Now

Right now, all across the country, students are sitting down, learning how to become an effective public speaker. They are taking a similar class to the one you are enrolled in right now; some courses are titled "Oral Communication," others may be "Introduction to Public Speaking," and others still perhaps refer to the class as "Speech Communication." The point is, you are not alone, and what you are doing is nothing new. In fact, public speaking instruction is rooted in a long tradition that we can trace back to at least Classical Greece (approximately 490–322 B.C.). There remain, however, two significant differences between your educational experience and that of the Greeks.

The first is in the nature of education. For our purposes, the Classical Period refers to Ancient Greece and the Roman Empire, and during that time education was not what it is today. Whereas today there is much government intervention and control over education (public schools, state-sponsored universities, etc.), in the Classical Period the state had very little influence over the nature of education. In fact, the two primary ways in which someone could receive an education were through hiring a teacher to essentially home-school a child, or, if the parents could afford it and the child showed enough promise, they could send their child to one of the few prominent schools. This model of education is nothing like what is available to students today.

The second major difference between education today and education in the Classical Period involves the curriculum. One of the fundamental tenets of an education in the Greek city-states or Roman Empire was rhetoric, which for them essentially meant the ability to speak well and persuade audiences. There were some who decried rhetoric in favor of philosophy, but there was no denying the importance placed on teaching people to speak well in the Classical Period. Today's education system, however, has moved away from this emphasis, and students are often only introduced to formal training in speech at the college level—and even there for only one semester. Education today does not emphasize the importance of speaking well, and one of our aims with this book is to show you how speaking well should be as important today as it was in the days of the Greeks and Romans.

To do that, we will first explore the different ideas several prominent Greek and Roman teachers had about rhetoric, as these concepts provide the foundation for how we still approach public speaking today. Then we will discuss ideas proposed by those who did not necessarily run schools in the Classical Period, but who still proposed ideas that have helped shape our understanding of the power of speech. Finally, we will explain why public speaking should be as important today as it was when the Greeks and Romans studied the craft.

PUBLIC SPEAKING AND CLASSICAL EDUCATION

We probably will never know with any amount of certainty who was the first formal public speaking teacher, but we do know that the Classical Greeks were the first to put quite a bit of emphasis on developing oratorical skills. For instance, the Greek poet Homer's *Iliad* and *Odyssey* contained quite a few long speeches by major characters. In this section we will describe the three different modes of education available during the Classical Period. First, we will look at the itinerant teachers known as Sophists. Second, we will investigate the more formal schools Greeks attended for training. Finally, we will discuss one Roman school made possible through state-sponsored efforts to promote education.

Sophists

The Greek democratic city-states often called for citizens to make speeches in order to discuss public policy and make cases for clients in the courts. Since no lawyers existed, people prevailed or failed in court and in the assembly purely on their ability to speak well, so some turned a profit from teaching others how to speak well.

Sophists
itinerant teachers who traveled from city-state to city-state in Classical Greece, training people in public speaking

These teachers, also known as *Sophists*, traveled from city-state to city-state selling their instruction to well-to-do Greeks. There was little to no consistency in the teachings of the Sophists as they all had a different degree of training. One might even say public speaking professors today are the modern day equivalent of Sophists—although they have more consistent training than the Sophists in Classical Greece!

One of the more notable Sophists was Gorgias (480–376 B.C.), who understood the relationship of speaker and audience as linear, whereby a speaker fills the audience with knowledge, or moves them to action. Gorgias was a foreigner in Athens who nevertheless developed a strong following. He believed audiences were passive and could be moved by elaborate and "magical" language that captured their attention. Language and words, according to Gorgias, accomplished things by encouraging human emotions, and so many of his teachings concentrated on different styles of language use. For Gorgias, the power of persuasion lay in style and the construction of creative linguistic phrases.[6] Gorgias's views on rhetoric and public speaking, however, differed from the views of other Sophists.

Protagoras (484–414 B.C.), another Sophist, taught a different understanding of rhetoric and public speaking to his students. For Protagoras, anything and everything could be argued. In fact, he taught his students to know both sides of an argument, because doing so was the only way to know which side they should believe. He asked his students to come with arguments for and against the same issue so they could better analyze which was stronger and, thus, more accurate. His critics, however, said that this approach merely instructed people to make the worse case look better in an effort to win the debate. The different views on rhetoric by Gorgias and Protagoras are contrasted in Table 2.1.

Table 2.1

Views on Rhetoric	
Gorgias's Views on Rhetoric	**Protagoras's Views on Rhetoric**
• Audience and speaker relationship is linear • Speaker fills the audience with knowledge/moves them to action • Audiences are passive and can be moved by language • Language can be used to stir emotions	• Anything and everything can be argued • Important to know both sides of an issue • Important to prepare argument for both sides of an argument to see which is best and more accurate

The "for-hire" nature of the itinerant Sophists, however, represented only one way in which instruction in the art of public speaking took place in the Classical Period. Many famous Greeks also opened schools designed to instruct those who could earn and afford entry. In the next section we will discuss several of these schools and their "headmasters," who had very particular views on speech.

The Formal Greek Schools

Classical Greece had several schools that many well-to-do citizens would send their students to for instruction. These schools often produced politicians and thinkers that defined the next generation. In some cases the schools competed with each other for students, but not to the degree universities and colleges do today. The first school we will discuss is generally regarded as the first school of rhetoric in Athens, and it was created by Isocrates. One of the first chief critics of Isocrates built another institution, which we know of as Plato's "Academy," and it is the second of the formal schools we will explore. Finally, we will discuss a school developed by a graduate of Plato's Academy, Aristotle, who was also employed as a tutor for one of the most successful conquerors in history.

Plato's Academy

The School of Isocrates

Isocrates (438–335 B.C.) shared several of the views held by Sophists; however, unlike the Sophists, he was an Athenian citizen. He opened a school where rhetoric and speech were core components of the education his students received. He charged quite a bit in terms of tuition, and even had very rigorous entrance requirements, accepting only the best and brightest students Athens had to offer.

Isocrates taught his students that a person's capacity to know things was limited, and so to expect to know the right course of action in every situation and on every issue was impossible. For Isocrates, only a well-educated man could determine the best course of action through a well-informed, yet incomplete, opinion. He believed that "it is much better to form probable opinions about useful things, than to have exact knowledge of useless things."[7] Essentially, Isocrates felt that good speakers were well-learned on a variety of subjects.

Isocrates also believed that good speakers were morally sound individuals who could discern right from wrong. He felt that education on many subjects was the best way to ensure ethical goals for a speaker. He also believed that ornate language and lofty sentence construction within a speech about a worthy topic—which could only be identified by well-informed individuals—evidenced an ethical, moral speaker. This emphasis on style and content represents a sort of fusion of the approaches taken by Gorgias and Protagoras.

Isocrates emphasized an amplified rhetoric that used many different rhetorical strategies (which will be discussed later in the book) to keep audiences focused on points for long periods of time. He did not, however, offer a set of rules and characteristics of a well put together speech like some of his contemporaries we will discuss in a moment.

kairos
....
Greek term meaning timing and recognition of the needs of the occasion

The one constraint to good speeches Isocrates recognized was ***kairos***, or timing and recognition of the needs of the occasion. He believed you could not teach this to people through a handbook, only through extensive repetition and exposure to civic life, which is where the speaking of his time took place. This almost constant involvement in social and political life was emblematic of the deep commitment to the strength of community felt by Isocrates. Despite his call for his students to immerse themselves in civic life, he himself never truly participated in the political arena.[8] That said, Isocrates influenced many great orators in his time and in the years that followed, especially those in the Roman rhetorical tradition.

Plato's Academy

A contemporary of Isocrates, Plato held a less than favorable view of Sophists and Isocrates. Plato was a student of Socrates, whom he used as a character in several of his writings that serve as the foundation for his understanding of rhetoric, government, and education. As these documents indicate, students at the Academy received very different instruction than those trained by Isocrates.

Plato derided the Sophistic approach for a variety of reasons. First, he believed it was dangerous and not conducive to living what he termed "a good life," where understanding justice and living a just life were the ultimate goal for an individual. Plato referred to rhetoric as "a knack" and felt that the Sophists trained people in how to achieve personal goals through the use of persuasion that used language to manipulate public opinion. He believed, instead, that education should focus on philosophy, or the search for truth, rather than persuasion, so that people could determine true knowledge. For Plato, rhetoric was a form of flattery, while philosophy was inquiry into the truth of things.

Plato and Aristotle in The School of Athens, by Italian Rafael

Additionally, Plato felt not everyone was capable of conducting the arduous task of seeking and knowing the truth. He believed that the only people capable of doing so, and thus the only people who could tell the difference between good and bad, were philosophers, and therefore they should lead the people. In his famous book *The Republic*, Plato argued that leaders of this kind might still need to employ the knack of rhetoric to deceive the public for its own good. Rhetoric in a just society, for Plato, was an advocacy tool for the philosopher, nothing more.

Several things can be said regarding Plato and his approach to education. The first is that he decried the Sophists and Isocrates for elevating rhetoric and devaluing philosophy. Second, he was skeptical at best regarding the use of rhetoric. He understood the way it was employed during his day as an evil, but when used properly in his vision of a just society, it became a utopian tool for philosophers. Regardless of the debate between which was better or more important (Rhetoric or Philosophy), Plato foreshadowed discussions about the power and purpose of speech that last to this day. He understood its power, and more importantly its relationship to shaping the world around us.[9]

One of Plato's brightest students, Aristotle, went on to tutor one of the world's greatest conquerors and eventually opened a school of his own. Aristotle, however, as we will see next, did not share his mentor's animus toward rhetoric and actually saw some redeeming value in the practice.

Aristotle's Lyceum

As we discussed at the very beginning of this chapter, Aristotle (384–322 B.C.), the most prominent of Plato's students, was hired by Philip of Macedon to tutor his son, the child we now know as Alexander the Great. Aristotle, like Plato, was also a contemporary of Isocrates, and like his mentor he regarded the teachings of Isocrates and Sophists as inadequate. Later, after his services for Alexander were completed, Aristotle opened his own school, the Lyceum, where he taught students a different conception of knowledge, philosophy, and rhetoric than his teacher had taught him.

Aristotle differed from his teacher in many respects, growing up when Athens was at the pinnacle of its power. He did not share Plato's mistrust of rhetoric and understood it as serving several beneficial purposes in a free society. Whereas Plato believed rhetoric was merely persuasion and philosophy was the only way to search for the truth, Aristotle disagreed. Aristotle, as we will see now, was very much a pragmatist.

Aristotle proposed three ways in which someone could know something, as opposed to the one way Plato advocated. The first of the three types of knowledge Aristotle described we will call experiential knowledge, or *techne*, because it comes from a person's own encounters. This knowledge is of particular things based on our interactions with the world around us, and although it is somewhat unreliable it is Aristotle's preferred form because, as he explained, we are aware that we know something because we have experienced it. That said, the Greek philosopher acknowledged that our senses, at best, see things differently and, at worst, can be easily deceived. Look at the optical illusion in Figure 2.1.[10]

techne
experiential knowledge; knowledge of particular events in the world around us; the least reliable form of knowledge

Figure 2.1
Optical Illusion

Is it a vase? A candlestick? Or two people about to kiss? Whatever your visual experience, we all see the same thing, but interpret it differently. Some of us see it as two faces, others see it as a vase or candelabra. So, we see the same thing, but can know it differently. Such is the unreliability of experiential knowledge.

The second form of knowledge taught by Aristotle is similar to the one true knowledge professed by Plato. *Episteme*, or universal knowledge, the understanding about the common characteristics of like materials, resembles Plato's idea of metaphysical forms, where he felt true knowledge existed.

episteme
universal knowledge, or understanding about the common characteristics of like materials

For Aristotle, knowing a particular thing comes from experience, and knowing universals comes from education and exploration. Public speaking allowed people to learn and search for universal characteristics by sharing knowledge of particulars with each other.

Aristotle's final form of knowledge represents an intermediate form. For Aristotle, this type of knowledge primarily concerned ethics, where neither the practical nor the universal worked. His idea of *intermediate knowledge*, or knowing what does not reflect an excess or a defect but instead what is intuitively correct to the person, is exemplified in his Golden Mean, where he claimed too much, or too little, of anything is a bad thing. Taken together, these three ways of knowing the world around us represent a huge departure from his teacher, Plato, who advocated a truth only one type of person—the philosopher—could know. In this way, Aristotle was much more democratic than Plato, and thus he saw significant uses for speech in a civil society for educated people.

intermediate knowledge
knowing what does not reflect an excess or a defect but instead what is intuitively correct to the person

Aristotle fundamentally disagreed with Plato on the nature of rhetoric and speech. He saw rhetoric as a creative process of determining what should be said, whereas Plato equated rhetoric with persuasion. While both understood rhetoric as relating to persuasion, they disagreed on how rhetoric and persuasion intersected.

SPOTLIGHTING THEORISTS: ARISTOTLE

Aristotle (384–322 B.C.)

Born in the village of Stagiros, near what was then considered Macedonia, in Northern Greece, this Greek philosopher and teacher was responsible for many contributions to rhetoric and public speaking. During his life he accomplished a great many things, including mentoring Alexander the Great of Macedonia.

Due to Aristotle's close connection to the kingdom of Macedon, many Greeks, especially those in Athens, probably viewed him with a great bit of suspicion. In 367 B.C. Aristotle moved to Athens to study under Plato at the Academy. Despite his fondness for Plato, Aristotle was much more realistic and practical in his approach to philosophy than his teacher. Aristotle used his education and exposure to great thinkers of his time while at the Academy to guide his academic pursuits. He was the first to outline what we refer to as formal logic, and he crafted an ethical code grounded in living a happy life rather than adhering to religious codes. Further, he developed a political philosophy vastly different from Plato's, that found as its inspiration the democratic and constitutional governments of his time— approaches Plato clearly held in disdain.

In the 350s Aristotle taught rhetoric at the Academy, largely as an attempt to compete against the school opened by Isocrates. Aristotle's rhetoric courses focused on logic, in direct contrast to what Isocrates and his Sophistic plan of study offered. In 347, just around the time Plato died, Aristotle left Athens and went abroad where he studied other subjects, like biology. Around 343, however, he moved back to his roots at the request of King Philip of Macedon in order to educate the prince, Alexander.

Within eight years, but well after his tutelage under Aristotle ended, Alexander conquered Athens and Aristotle returned to the home of his mentor. In 335 Aristotle opened the Lyceum, his version of the Academy, and taught students there until the death of Alexander the Great in 323 B.C. When Alexander passed, Aristotle gave his school over to his most prominent student, Theophrastus, and died a year later on the island of Euboea.[11]

Aristotle wrote extensively on a variety of subjects and remains one of the most influential philosophers on oratory, philosophy, logic and politics in all of history. He serves as an excellent example of the importance of education. Even today he is one of the most recognized of all Classical Greek thinkers and figures.

Aristotle noted that rhetoric, as a means rather than an end, fulfilled four functions in an open society. First, rhetoric through the application of speech allowed for true and just ideas to prevail, because he noted all things in public debate are not equal and capable speakers need to advocate for them to win out. In addition to the preservation of truth and justice, Aristotle also believed rhetoric offered the ability to instruct people on how to connect their ideas with the experiences of their audiences; in short, it allows us to teach others. Thirdly, Aristotle saw rhetoric as the means of analyzing both sides of a question—similar to the view taken by Protagoras as we saw earlier. Finally, Aristotle understood rhetoric as a means to defend oneself, noting that speech and rational thought are abilities unique to human beings.[12] He understood public speaking as one of the most important tools a person can possess for engaging in civic life. Table 2.2 notes how these four functions of rhetoric can pragmatically be used today.

Table 2.2

Aristotle's Four Functions of Rhetoric	
Function	Example
Upholding truth and justice	In a courtroom
	In a legislative body
	In a classroom
Teaching to an audience	Classroom
	Encouraging civic engagement
	Pulpit
Analyzing both sides of a question	Jury
	Voting decision
	Making a final decision
Defending oneself	Personal or public disagreement
	On the witness stand

Aristotle defined rhetoric not as a knack the way Plato did, but rather as the means of identifying probabilities inherent in an issue or interpretation. He focused on rhetoric as a persuasive process, and this is an approach still taken by scholars today. Despite his more favorable view regarding rhetoric than his mentor, Aristotle understood the dangers inherent in a purely sophistic understanding of speech, so he conducted an exhaustive analysis of how persuasion works. In this analysis he determined three sources of persuasion, two forms of proof for arguments, and stylistic virtues for speech.

ethos
······
the credibility of the speaker

logos
······
the logical dimension of the appeal

Aristotle taught his students about the interconnection of three component parts of persuasion. The first part he called *ethos*, or the credibility of the speaker. He felt that the more believable, honest, and learned on the subject a speaker was, then the more persuasive the message. In addition to ethos Aristotle proposed that *logos*, or the logical dimension of the appeal, contributed to a message's persuasive effect. Aristotle believed that persuasive messages must follow a logical order; without this orderly argument then persuasion is much less likely to occur. The third source of persuasion Aristotle called *pathos*, which referred to the emotional dimensions of the appeal that can influence an audience's disposition toward the topic, speaker, or occasion. He said that language can be used by a speaker to emotionally connect an audience with a topic and thus move listeners to an ethical and correct action. Ethos, pathos, and logos each focus on a

pathos
········
the emotional dimensions of the appeal that can influence an audience's disposition toward the topic, speaker, or occasion

different dimension of persuasion: the speaker, the audience, and the message, respectively. For a visual depiction of this, look at Figure 2.2.

Aristotle referred to ethos, pathos, and logos as *artistic proof*, or something created by the speaker for the presentation. The speaker's credibility is dependent on the occasion and topic, and the emotions of the audience are also directly related to the speech; thus both are crafted for the specific moment by the speaker. Likewise, you develop the logic in the speech that is meant to sway an audience. The other proof identified by Aristotle, *inartistic proof*, concerned all the evidence, data, and documents that exist outside of the speaker and the audience but nevertheless can aid in persuasion. Inartistic proofs are not manufactured by the speaker in the same way as artistic proofs.

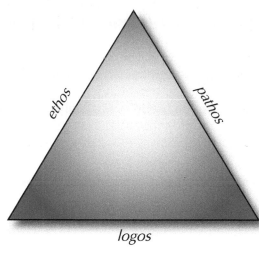

Figure 2.2
Three Parts of Persuasion

artistic proof
constructed by the speaker for the occasion; concerns ethos, pathos, and logos

inartistic proof
all the evidence, data, and documents that exist outside of the speaker and the audience, but nevertheless can aid in persuasion

Aristotle also understood that style played a part in the ultimate success or failure of persuasive appeals, and so he laid out three virtues of style by which *rhetors*, or speakers, should abide. The first stylistic virtue is *clarity*, or the ability of a speaker to clearly articulate what he or she wishes to say. Clarity manifests itself with simple, direct sentences, and we will discuss more about how to construct such messages in the chapter on language. Aristotle's second stylistic virtue, *correctness*, relates to the accuracy of information presented and the honest representation of the speaker. Quite obviously, this virtue is intimately tied to being an ethical speaker, which will be discussed later. Finally, Aristotle emphasized the virtue of *propriety*, or good behavior and faithfulness to what one considers moral and just. Propriety, therefore, relates to the idea that you should be both ethical and clear in your content, but also in your delivery. It is an overarching virtue that essentially encompasses both clarity and correctness.

rhetors
speakers

clarity
the ability of speakers to clearly articulate what they wish to say

correctness
the accuracy of information presented and the honest representation of the speaker

propriety
good behavior and faithfulness to what one considers moral and just

As we previously noted, Aristotle differed from Plato in many ways, but perhaps most importantly, he viewed rhetoric and speech as a potentially important component of civil society. He felt that through the use of ethical and proper speech people could continue to search for truth. Further, societies would become more open and therefore a sense of justice and fairness would be encouraged. He trained his students to examine arguments, defend themselves, and ultimately be able to teach the next generation these important skills. It is safe to say that Aristotle saw good public speaking skills as the foundation of a lasting productive civil society.

Isocrates's school, Plato's Academy, and Aristotle's Lyceum represented three important Greek schools. The Greeks, however, were not alone in writing and thinking about speech, rhetoric, and persuasion. Next we will examine two Romans, Cicero and Quintilian, who also had much to say on these subjects.

CICERO AND THE PRACTICE OF RHETORIC

Although schools in the Classical Period were sources of a significant amount of writings and information regarding rhetoric and speech, some notable contributions were made by those who did not operate schools or seek to train students. In this section we will discuss one individual whose major contributions to understanding speech and language came from his experience as a student and his implementation of those practices in his political life.

Cicero (106–43 B.C.), Speech and Politics

Cicero

Marcus Tullius Cicero is one of the most influential figures in the history of rhetoric. Born in 106 B.C. near Rome, Cicero received a strong education in Roman schools and began a career in the courts, later moving into the Senate. Eventually he rose to the highest position in the Roman Republic, that of consul, and developed a reputation as a well-spoken champion of the people.

Like Plato in Greece, Cicero lived during tumultuous times, watching the rise and fall of Julius Caesar and the subsequent establishment of the Roman Empire under Octavian. Throughout his career, Cicero fought against the nobility and the threat of military dictators, and it ultimately earned him the same fate as Plato's mentor, Socrates. Unlike Quintilian, Cicero lived and wrote during the waning days of the Roman Republic, not the Roman Empire, and thus he valued all uses of rhetoric.

While on one of his forced retirements from public life Cicero wrote *De re Publica* and *De Oratore*, two enormously influential books on speech and delivery, and these served as sequels to his earliest publication on speech, *De Inventione*. Whereas *De Inventione* was written when Cicero was in his late teens and is more of a compilation of educational approaches to teaching rhetoric at the time of his schooling, the two later works represent much more sophisticated and original thought on the subject.

invention
the first canon of rhetoric where you choose the best possible arguments for your case

In his works, Cicero did for the speech-making process what Aristotle did for persuasion: he broke speech down into its component parts, which he numbered at five (See Table 2.3). These five canons of rhetoric are the foundation for developing a strong speech. The first is *invention*, which is when you identify the best arguments for your case in a given situation. This is the creative dimension of speech where you find the best possible way to convince someone to agree with you. If you argued that Mickey Mantle was the best baseball player of all time, you would invent, or choose, certain facts that support your case.

The second of Cicero's five canons concerns organizing your arguments in the most effective manner. *Arrangement*, in which you determine the most effective way to organize your case for the topic and the audience, can be done in a variety of different ways. To arrange points in the best possible way requires that you understand your topic and your audience, because the most effective arguments on a given topic may not be the same for a different audience hearing a speech on the same topic. For example, political candidates make different arguments to different audiences when trying to get each group to vote for them. We will look at various arrangement options available to you when we look at how to craft the different types of speeches later in the book.

arrangement
the second canon of rhetoric where you determine the most effective way to organize your case for the topic and the audience

Cicero's third canon refers to how you design the specifics of your speech. *Style* involves your word choices, phrasing, and the level of formality in the language you use to present your case to the audience. All speakers have their own language style, and discovering yours will make this creative stage much easier and more enjoyable. Of course, style must also fit the situation and the audience. We cover the nuances of style in greater detail later.

style
the third canon of rhetoric; involves word choice, phrasing and the level of formality in the language you use to present your case to the audience

Today, people tend to place the most emphasis on the fourth of Cicero's five canons. *Delivery*, or the manner in which you physically and vocally present the speech, has now become erroneously equated with good public speaking. For Cicero, delivery was part of the speech, but not the sole determining element of its effectiveness. In this way he recognized the power of good delivery, but also by connecting it to the content itself cautioned against the dangers of emphasizing physical and vocal delivery.

delivery
the fourth canon of rhetoric; the manner in which you physically and vocally present the speech

The final canon of rhetoric proposed by Cicero is less important today than it was during his time but still remains a part of the speech process. *Memory*, according to Cicero, refers to one's ability both to use her or his memory to recall n̲ and important information in the middle of a speech as well as ̲gent speech without notes. The ability to speak without notes i̲ less of a concern today thanks to things like PowerPoint and Teleprompters, but in Classical Rome performing speeches without notes was a sign of eloquence and intelligence. That said, the ability to recall information relevant to a speech and incorporate it into the presentation is still a valued speaking skill.

me
n̲ canon of rhetoric; refers to one's ability to recall names and important information in the middle of a speech as well as to deliver a cogent speech without notes

Cicero contributed much to public speaking, and he himself was a gifted orator, but eventually his speaking ability got him into trouble. During the Roman Civil War between Octavian and Marc Antony which followed the death of Julius Caesar, Cicero vocally fought against a dictatorship and found himself at odds with Marc Antony. Eventually, Antony had him killed and nailed his tongue and hands to the door of the Senate as a sign to all those who might have aligned themselves with Cicero against him. The hands and tongue were symbols of Cicero's ability to persuade others, and the nails a warning to those who followed in his footsteps. Such was the sad death of Cicero.

Table 2.3

Cicero's Canons of Rhetoric	
Invention	Identifying the best argument or topic on which to speak
Arrangement	Determining the most effective way of organizing your speech
Style	Choosing the best words and phrasing to get your point across
Delivery	Physically and vocally presenting the speech
Memory	Your ability to recall important information during the speech

Quintilian's Public School

Roman education valued rhetoric, especially during the years of the Republic when Cicero lived. Rhetoric was such a core component of Roman education that even with the advent of the Roman Empire, speech training remained; however, it focused less on political speech and more on epideictic address, which focuses upon praise and/or blame. During the time of the Emperor Vespasian, who reigned from 69–79 A.D., rhetoric and public speaking rose in emphasis. Vespasian awarded grants to artists and teachers throughout the empire to encourage education and civic engagement in Rome. One of those to receive a grant from the Emperor was Marcus Fabius Quintilianus, or Quintilian (ca. 35–100 A.D.). Quintilian used the money to help fund his school and wrote *De Instituine Oratoria* (*On the Education of the Orator*), a manual for becoming the perfect speaker. This 12-book work spent a significant amount of time on every aspect of speech and evolved from the writings of Cicero.

In his book, Quintilian prescribes a definition of rhetoric that he felt encompassed all the ideas of those who came before him. He succinctly said rhetoric was simply "the art of speaking well."[13] He further argued that the art of rhetoric was only useful insofar as people applied it to practical and public affairs. To that end, he believed there were only five principle duties for any speaker:

- Defend Truth
- Protect the Innocent
- Prevent Criminal Behavior
- Inspire the Military
- Inspire the Public

Quintilian's approach mirrors the intense focus that the Greeks placed on the relationship between speech, politics, and civic engagement, be it in government or the courtroom. In fact, his five duties are an outgrowth of the functions Aristotle proposed earlier. Whereas Cicero's commentaries on public speaking emanated from his experiences, Quintilian's writings were essentially instructional tools developed for his school which he ran during the Roman Empire.

Early Scholars and Schools of Speech		Table 2.4
Early Scholars and Schools	**Ideas on Speech**	
Isocrates	• Believed good speakers were learned on a variety of topics • Believed good speakers were morally sound • Believed broad education helped ensure ethical speakers • Advocated ornate language and sentence construction • Emphasized an amplified rhetoric that used many different rhetorical strategies • Recognized kairos was a constraint on good speaking	
Plato	• Believed that Sophists used persuasive language to manipulate people • Felt that education should focus on philosophy and the search for truth • Felt that rhetoric was only about persuasion	
Aristotle	• Thought that rhetoric had value to a society • Believed rhetoric allowed true and just ideas to prevail • Believed rhetoric was useful for instruction of ideas • Believed rhetoric helped one see both sides of an argument • Believed rhetoric was useful to verbally defend oneself • Believed rhetoric was useful for finding probabilities • Identified three forms of artistic proofs: ethos, pathos, and logos • Argued that inartistic proofs were an additional form of persuasive evidence • Felt style was important	

Quintilian	• Saw rhetoric as the act of speaking well
	• Saw rhetoric as useful for practical and public affairs
	• Believed speakers had five principle duties:
	  Defend Truth
	  Protect the Innocent
	  Prevent Criminal Behavior
	  Inspire the Military
	  Inspire the Public
	• Saw rhetoric as useful in politics and civic engagement

Contemporary Scholars and the Speech Communication Process

Isocrates, Plato, Aristotle, Quintilian, and Cicero represent a small sampling of those who contributed to the rhetorical tradition, but they provided much of the foundation for the study and practice of speech. The ideas of four of these scholars are summarized in Table 2.4. Throughout this book we will introduce you to various other noteworthy figures and their contributions, some from the Classical Period and others from more contemporary times. The important thing to understand is that the practice of public speaking and our understanding of rhetoric, speech, and persuasion have evolved over time, but that evolution could not have taken place without these important individuals from Greece and Rome. That evolution has led us to understand and study the communication process from a variety of perspectives. In fact, contemporary scholars have developed various models that help explain the communication process that the Greeks and Romans taught. Let's take a look at these more modern models and explore the components of the speech communication process as we understand it today.

The Linear Model of Communication

sender
the person who desires to deliver a message to another person or group of people

encoding
the process of attaching symbols to ideas and feelings so that others may understand them

message
the actual content you send to an audience, both intentional and unintentional

Amazingly, the first modern model of communication came not from a member of the communication discipline, but from a research mathematician named Claude E. Shannon. Shannon designed this model in an effort to explain and train people on communication over telephone lines. As such, it concentrated on one-way, or linear, communication. Warren Weaver later added a component to Shannon's model, and so this linear model of communication became known as the Shannon-Weaver model of communication.

The Shannon-Weaver model essentially describes communication as a process much like injecting someone with a drug. There are essentially seven components to this model of communication. First, there is a *sender*, or the person who desires to deliver a message to another person or group of people. That person uses a symbol system, normally language, to encode the subject matter he or she wishes to send. *Encoding* is the process of attaching symbols to ideas and feelings so that others may understand them. The subject matter that is encoded is the *message* or the actual content sent to an audience, and it can be both intentional and unintentional. That message is then sent through a *channel*, or the mode through which the message is conveyed to another party. The traditional mode for transmitting messages is the voice or the written word; however, in today's society we also send messages through electronic channels like the radio, television, or Internet.

channel
the mode through which the message is conveyed to another party

As the message travels through its channel it competes with other forces that sometimes disrupt its transmission. These disruptive forces are broadly referred to as *noise.* This term constitutes anything that interferes with the encoding, transmission, and reception of a message, and it can take many forms. When you think about noise, don't simply assume it is auditory, or the result of some loud "bang" or "boom." Noise certainly can include sounds, but it also includes environmental distractions such as scenery and temperature, personal biases and predispositions, anxiety, and confusing word choice by the speaker. It is an umbrella term for elements outside the communication message that can hamper its transmission from one party to another.

noise
anything that interferes with the encoding, transmission, and reception of a message

The sixth and seventh components of the Shannon-Weaver linear model of communication involve the party opposite the sender of the message. The *receiver* is the person or persons who receive the encoded message sent by the sender. Receivers are not always those for whom the message is intended. Think about a toast at a wedding where the bride's father is celebrating the marriage of his daughter. You may think everyone in the room cares deeply for the bride and groom and is listening intently to the speech, but you would be wrong. The service staff who quietly shuffle through the room serving food to guests and the bartenders in the hall have no connection to either the bride or the groom, and the speech by the father is not meant for them—nevertheless, they receive the message! There are always unintended recipients to messages we send, which only underscores our duty to pay close attention to what we say.

receiver
the person or persons who receive the encoded message sent by the sender

Unintended receivers are only one of the potential issues that we need to be aware of when it comes to this part of the communication process. We also must understand that receivers decode messages using their own knowledge and experiences, and so they may not decode the same message you encoded for them. *Decoding* is the process of taking a message that has been sent and using one's own experiences and knowledge to give it meaning. Have you ever listened to a lecture in class and thought you heard the teacher say one thing, when she actually said something else? Sometimes this is due to words sounding alike, other times it is due to not paying close enough attention, and yet other times it happens when a speaker misspeaks or mispronounces something. Ultimately, though, we cannot control how an audience will decode the messages we send, but we can maximize our potential for them doing so accurately.

decoding
the process of taking a message that has been sent and using one's own experiences and knowledge to give it meaning

linear model of communication
communication process that involves a sender who encodes a message and sends it through a channel where it competes with distracting forces called noise while on its way to a receiver who then decodes the message

In summary, there are seven components to the basic *linear model of communication*: a <u>sender</u> <u>encodes</u> a <u>message</u> and sends it through a <u>channel</u> where it competes with distracting forces called <u>noise</u> while on its way to a <u>receiver</u> who then <u>decodes</u> the message[14] (see Figure 2.3). Now that we have laid out the model, let's briefly explore what it means for us in the context of public speaking and how this book will help illustrate that connection.

Figure 2.3
Linear Model of Communication

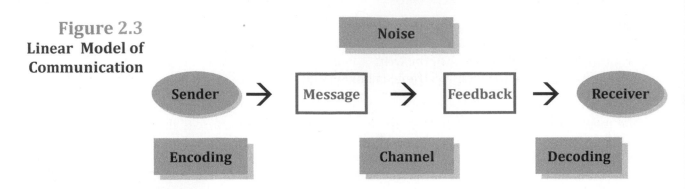

This model of communication is very speaker-centered, as it puts the onus of communication on the sender and places the receiver at the end of the process. Examples of communication situations where the linear model best explains what is happening include YouTube videos that broadcast a taped message or presentation. In this context, the speaker sends a message through two channels (voice and video) to you as a receiver and there is no further interaction. We will discuss mediated communication channels such as this when we cover the speaking environment later in the book, but it is important to know that the model for understanding presentations like these is the Shannon-Weaver, or linear, model of the communication process. This model also serves as the foundation for understanding the other models of communication developed by contemporary scholars.

The Transactional Model of Communication

transactional model of communication
∙∙∙∙∙∙∙∙∙∙∙∙∙∙∙∙∙∙∙∙∙∙
recognizes that we simultaneously send and receive messages; a cyclical model of the communication process

The linear model of communication, despite offering a clear explanation for the process of transmitting a message, does not adequately explain how all communication occurs—especially not even how most public speaking takes place. In fact, most public speaking does not occur in a one-way manner, but rather involves a constant exchange between the speaker and the audience. A more accurate model for public speaking as a process of communication, the *transactional model of communication*, expands upon the Shannon-Weaver model of communication by recognizing and incorporating the notion that we serve as sender and receiver of messages simultaneously.[15] To do this, the transactional model adds an eighth component to the communication process.

Figure 2.4
Transactional Model of Communication

SPOTLIGHTING THEORISTS: MARIE HOCHMUTH NICHOLS

Marie Hochmuth Nichols (1908–1977)

Marie Hochmuth Nichols's influential career covered more than three decades. She was one of the more preeminent rhetorical scholars, teachers, and leaders in the communication discipline during the twentieth century. She was the first female president elected by the entire membership of the Speech Communication Association in 1969 and shepherded the discipline through a tumultuous period of transition.[16] Nichols also served as editor of the most prestigious periodical of rhetoric and public address, *The Quarterly Journal of Speech*. In 1976 she was awarded the Speech Communication Association's Distinguished Award.[17]

Nichols was a scholar of both theory and criticism in the neo-Aristotelian tradition. She also was heavily influenced by the work of Kenneth Burke and I. A. Richards.[18] Nichols published many essays; two of the most prominent were "Lincoln's First Inaugural Address" in 1954 and "The Criticism of Rhetoric" in 1955. In these and other essays she argued in defense of the discipline of communication and called on people to focus less on developing models and paradigms, and more on the ends and purposes of speech. Specifically, she contended that the communication discipline is, and always will be, about understanding the uses and power of verbal symbols.

So highly regarded was Dr. Nichols that the National Communication Association (formerly the Speech Communication Association) named one of its most prestigious awards, The Marie Hochmuth Nichols Award, in her honor. It is awarded for published works in public address. In 1983 Kathleen Hall Jamieson issued the highest of praises for Nichols: "Some of us command an encyclical; some of us command a single rhetorical theorist; some of us command a rhetorical period. Marie Hochmuth Nichols commanded the tradition."[19]

This new component occurs after the receiver decodes a message, and is called feedback. *Feedback* consists of the responses and reactions to the messages transmitted by the sender and is itself a new message sent back to the original sender. The notion of feedback allows both parties in the message process to simultaneously serve as sender and receiver of messages (see Figure 2.4). Feedback can be verbal, nonverbal, or both, and it plays an important role in public speaking situations. Thus the transactional model of communication is a more appropriate explanation for communication in public speaking contexts.

feedback
the responses and reactions to the messages transmitted by the sender; is itself a new message sent back to the original sender

The feedback we provide in a communication situation can alter an unfolding interaction and can let senders know what our impressions are regarding the speaker and their message. Confused looks in an audience can tell a speaker to slow down and more thoroughly explain a concept, while head nods alert a speaker that an audience agrees with what he or she is saying. We will further explain audience feedback, what it means to you when delivering a speech, and how to adapt to it as a speaker when we cover audience analysis later.

There is one very important aspect to take away from the transactional communication model of communication as it relates to public speaking. We must always keep in mind that communication is an ongoing process, meaning that even as you give your speech the audience communicates with you just as much as you do with them. Paying attention to the dynamics of the communication process when delivering a speech will help you better adapt to the moment and increase your effectiveness at getting your messages across to an audience.

Both the linear and the transactional models of communication provide us with a logical way of understanding the communication process, but they cannot be understood as the "be all, end all" of the study of communication. In fact, several scholars have warned against emphasizing the development of models to the detriment of the more creative aspects of communication like language. Most notable among these contemporary thinkers is Marie Hochmuth Nichols, a former president of the Speech Communication Association (now the National Communication Association) who called on her colleagues to understand the power of the spoken word. Hochmuth Nichols can best be understood as someone who defended the roots of the discipline founded by Aristotle and the other classical figures we discussed earlier, but who also understood the potential of speech to change and affect the world around us. Her understanding of both the power of language and the models developed in the middle of the twentieth century provides important insight into how to craft and use speech today.

Thus far we have shown how essential rhetoric was in Classical Greek and Roman education. We explained that rhetoric resided at the heart of the curriculum, either as an element of the core (Isocrates and the Romans, for example), or as something to which the core responded (Plato's Academy, for instance). Today, training in speech is not as prominent a part of a student's education, and for many, their first exposure to rhetoric and speech education occurs in a dreaded required course in their first year of college. Speech training never used to be feared, but rather was welcomed as a means of participating in civic life. In the next section we will briefly explore a few moments in history where speech fundamentally altered civic life. These are key moments where the power of speech in the hands of those who knew how to wield it made an important and tangible impact on public life. After this discussion, we will then conclude by outlining the book and how it will help you get started in understanding how to become a better speaker.

SPEECH AS A FORCE IN OUR LIVES

Despite their different beliefs regarding how to teach speech and the definition and utility of rhetoric, the classical thinkers and practitioners we discussed earlier would agree on the important role speech serves in public life. They all knew public speaking could move people to action, change their beliefs, and educate the masses, and history has proven their understanding accurate. At key moments in our history speech has helped move us to war, aided in shaping public attitudes and policies, and enabled us to express a definition of our identity with each other. There also have been important technological advances that have affected our ability to use speech to accomplish those tasks. In this section of the chapter we will briefly discuss the power of public speaking as a means of civic engagement and address how technology has influenced that power, especially in today's hypermediated world.

Civic Engagement

The ability to use symbols to communicate with each other is what makes us human, and even neuroscientists recognize that speech, or put more formally, symbolic reasoning, is the one cognitive trait that separates humans from other animals.[20] Public speaking is also the way we negotiate and construct society's rules, values, and beliefs. The process by which we do this is called *civic engagement*, which can be defined as acting upon a sharp awareness of one's own sense of responsibility to his or her community. Unfortunately, our collective commitment to each other has seen a marked decline in recent years, despite enhancements in technology that make it easier than ever for us to communicate with each other.

civic engagement
acting upon a sharp awareness of one's own sense of responsibility to his or her community

For instance, Robert Putnam argued that our sense of community involvement and civic engagement has drastically decreased since the end of World War II as evidenced by low voter turnout, decreased membership in civic organizations like the Rotary Club and Knights of Columbus, and reduced subscription rates to newspapers.[21] These developments would shock the Greeks and Romans we discussed earlier who saw civic engagement, particularly through speech, as one of the most fundamental duties of a citizen.

Even though we may not experience it in the intense way the Greeks and Romans did, speech remains central to civic engagement. Have you ever wondered how to "have your voice heard" on a subject? Perhaps your state is thinking of raising tuition. How do you respond? Speech! Maybe your town wants to raise property taxes. How do you fight such an action? Speech! Or how do you let a congressman know that you don't like his behavior? Speech! Speech is central to understanding and participating in public life.

At a meeting of the G-20 in London, England, in March 2009, several thousand people rallied against the foreign leaders who gathered to talk about the world's economic troubles. How did they make their voices heard? They chanted, held posters, and gave speeches throughout the day in addition to marching. This is an example of civic engagement at its finest, and without speech all that would have happened was a bunch of people standing together in the middle of the street. Speech provided meaning for them, their purpose, and their protest. It allowed them to take an active role in the well being of their community.

Isocrates and Cicero, especially, recognized the relationship between speech and civic engagement. They understood that rhetoric and speech were central to a thriving democracy and that people needed to be taught how to deliver a speech, what to include in it, and how to ethically disseminate that information. Good people who spoke well could create a healthy and thriving nation. That belief still

Speech to the NAACP Comparing Improving Childhood Obesity to the Civil Rights Movement
by Michelle Obama

Delivered July 13, 2010, Kansas City, Missouri

First Ladies in the United States generally have a national agenda. Michelle Obama's cause is childhood obesity and she established a program entitled "Let's Move" to promote efforts to reduce childhood obesity.[23] She announced the program in early 2009 and it has remained a focus of her time as First Lady. She has delivered many speeches on the topic and in doing so she has kept a focus on the health of America's children. One of the reasons for her success is that she has what Aristotle would have termed strong ethos.

When Mrs. Obama spoke to the NAACP in Kansas City, Missouri, she had ethos, or credibility, not only due to the fact that she was the First Lady, but also because she was a working mother who had faced the task of feeding her children. She used this ethos effectively to reinforce her message.

Mrs. Obama noted some troubling statistics and spoke of the necessity to act immediately. She noted actions the government was taking but called on communities to get involved and individuals to exercise personal responsibility. Perhaps most importantly she told her audience that the battle could be won. In the speech conclusion Mrs. Obama called for action from the NAACP by linking the childhood obesity problem to the struggle for equal rights. Here is an excerpt from her address that shows how she did just that: "Surely the men and women of the NAACP haven't spent a century organizing and advocating and working day and night only to raise the first generation in history that might be on track to live shorter lives than their parents. And that's why I've made improving the quality of our children's health one of my top priorities."[24] Her speech in Kansas City is an example of ethos, but more importantly of how speech is central to civic engagement and can be a source of positive change in society.

holds true today, and many contemporary communication scholars continue to explore ways to speak well and encourage civic engagement.

Today, communication scholars and students explore speeches on a wide range of issues. Although many examine political figures and their comments, others analyze speeches by everyday folks because their words more than any others create the fabric of our society. For example, they look at how people discuss race, ethnicity, and even sports because these are the ties that bind us as a community. A good speaker in today's world, just like those in the days of Aristotle and Cicero, needs to be knowledgeable about the common characteristics of a community in order to effectively engage its members through speech.

Throughout this book you will encounter excerpts of speeches accompanied by a brief discussion of the issue being addressed by the speaker and how she or he approached it. The issues and speakers all vary, from the famous Dr. Martin

Luther King, Jr., to the contemporary and controversial Glenn Beck, to the classical Pericles of Athens. What they all have in common is a genuine appreciation of the power of speech to affect their community and the lives of their fellow citizens. Take a look at the *Speaking of Civic Engagement* box in this chapter that discusses a speech by First Lady Michelle Obama in which she seeks to motivate the NAACP to get behind her fight against childhood obesity.

As the Greeks and Romans taught, exposing yourself to a great many speeches is essential for learning how to become a better speaker yourself. These excerpts are designed to help you do that. Even though the importance of speech as a means of civic engagement has remained constant throughout history, there have been some developments that have changed the way we use it to enact change and send messages to audiences of which we need to be aware.

The Mediated World

Unlike Classical Greece and Rome, today we find ourselves bombarded with messages through a variety of different media, not just speech. We see billboards and magazine advertisements designed to persuade us to buy something; we watch occasional speeches and see television commercials; we listen to music and read social commentaries on the Internet. One might say all of these things are modern, and speech and rhetoric have thus become less important, if not obsolete. Nothing could be further from the truth!

Most messages we hear, read, or see are designed to persuade us in one way or another, and if we do not understand how persuasion works, then how can we defend ourselves from being manipulated? Knowing the fundamental tenets of persuasion allows us to not only critically analyze those messages sent to us but also craft messages of our own. Understanding how speech works, from invention to delivery, and recognizing that it gains its power from a fusion of both content and delivery allows us to become more critical listeners and more productive participants in our daily lives.

Today, training in speech, rhetoric, and persuasion is not defunct, but rather more important than ever because today we don't just have speeches that might influence us—we have commercials, articles, and images that attempt to move us to believe something or act in a certain way. The best way to counteract these influences is to learn about them yourself and then to employ the principles of persuasion in a just, ethical, and proper way.

SUMMARY

In this chapter we discussed how fundamental rhetoric and speech were to education in the Classical Period, and how scholars today define the communication process. We discussed the different ways in which rhetoric was taught and practiced by detailing five major contributors from Greece and Rome: Isocrates, Plato, Aristotle, Cicero, and Quintilian. We also explored several areas where rhetoric and speech education can help us in today's world; specifically, by making us more critical consumers of messages and allowing us to improve society through ethical and effective civic engagement.

arrangement	linear model of communication
artistic proof	logos
channel	memory
civic engagement	message
clarity	noise
correctness	pathos
decoding	propriety
delivery	receiver
encoding	rhetors
episteme	sender
ethos	Sophists
feedback	style
inartistic proof	techne
intermediate knowledge	transactional model of communication
invention	
kairos	

REVIEW QUESTIONS

1. What would be considered the major contributions of the Sophists to our understanding of speech and persuasion?

   _____

   _____

2. What are the three elements of persuasion identified by Aristotle?

   _____

   _____

3. What are the five parts of a speech as proposed by Cicero?

   _____

   _____

4. What are the five responsibilities of a speaker according to Quintilian?

   _____

   _____

5. What are the two major ways in which a greater emphasis on rhetoric and speech in today's curriculum would improve our abilities?

_____

_____

1. How are rhetoric and literature different disciplines if they both study the use of language?

_____

_____

_____

_____

2. Should rhetoric and public speaking be taught to young students and continued throughout their education, like it was for Classical Greeks and Romans?

_____

_____

_____

_____

3. Do speakers today still adhere to the principles and practices of the Greeks and Romans in this chapter? If so, how?

_____

_____

_____

_____

ACTIVITIES FOR ACTION

1. As noted in the chapter, there is a clear connection between the power of speech and civic engagement, but as Robert Putnam noted, people are less and less likely to join clubs and social groups in the community. Take a moment and consider this by doing an informal poll of those around you. How many clubs are they a member of? How faithfully do they attend meetings? What are the goals and what is the mission of that organization? Then ask the same questions of someone older. See if you notice any difference and think about what this means for the nature of the relationship between communication and civic engagement.

2. The chapter notes that we are constantly exposed to messages in society today, and that training in the art of persuasion is essential for being a critical consumer of those messages on a day-to-day basis. We often think, however, that speech is not that pervasive in society—that visuals are what we are exposed to most often. For one day keep a journal of the various messages you encounter by providing a brief description of how the message fits either the linear or transactional model of communication. Then, at the end of the day, look back at your journal and see how often you actually are exposed to messages through speech.

ENDNOTES

1. Peter Green, *Alexander of Macedon: A Historical Biography* (Berkeley, CA: University of California Press, 1991), 54-56.

2. Ibid.

3. Ibid., 54.

4. Paul Cartledge, *Alexander the Great: The Hunt for a New Past* (Woodstock, NY: Overlook Press, 2004), 84.

5. Philip Freeman, *Alexander the Great* (New York, NY: Simon & Schuster, 2011), 24.

6. James A. Herrick, *The History and Theory of Rhetoric* (4th Ed.) (Boston, MA: Pearson, 2009), 42-45.

7. Quoted in Thomas M. Conley, *Rhetoric in the European Tradition* (Chicago, IL: University of Chicago Press, 1990), 18.

8. Ibid., 20.

9. Herrick, 72.

10. http://www.123opticalillusions.com/pages/Facevase.php (accessed December 3, 2008).

11. All the information regarding Aristotle's life discussed here can be found in: George A. Kennedy (trans.), Introduction of *Aristotle: A Theory of Civic Discourse* (New York, NY: Oxford University Press, 1991), 5-7.

12. Herrick, 81-82.

13. Ibid., 39.

14. Claude E. Shannon and Warren Weaver, *The Mathematical Theory of Communication* (Urbana, IL: University of Illinois Press, 1949).

15. For example: Michael Dunne and Sik Hung Ng, "Simultaneous Speech in Small Group Conversation: All-Together-Now and One-at-a-Time?" *Journal of Language and Social Psychology* 13 (1994): 45-71.

16. Marie Hochmuth Nichols. http://www.natcom.org/Default.aspx?id=73&libID=94 (accessed June 11, 2011).

17. Marie Hochmuth Nichols, http://blog.umd.edu/ncapublicaddress/2011/03/09/call-for-nominations-2011-nichols-award/ (accessed June 11, 2011).

18. Ibid.

19. K. H. Jamieson, (November 1983). In honor of Marie Hochmuth Nichols. Paper delivered at SCA Convention, Washington, D.C.; As cited in "Marie Hochmuth Nichols," by Jane Blankenship. Available: http://www.natcom.org/Default.aspx?id=73&libID=94 (accessed June 25, 2011).

20. John Medina, *Brain Rules: 12 Principles for Surviving and Thriving at Work, Home and School* (Seattle, WA: Pear Press, 2008), 32.

21. Robert Putnam, *Bowling Alone: The Collapse and Revival of American Community* (New York, NY: Simon & Schuster, 2000).

22. http://blogs.suntimes.com/sweet/2010/07/michelle_obama_in_naacp_speech.html (accessed May 7, 2011).

23. As reported by Sunlen Miller of ABC News on July 12, 2010. For article where quotation was found see: http://blogs.abcnews.com/politicalpunch/2010/07/michelle-obama-to-the-naacp-now-is-not-the-time-to-rest-on-our-laurels.html.

The Practice of Public Speaking

CHAPTER OVERVIEW

- Covers the concept of fear and its relationship to the practice of public speaking
- Explains listening from the perspective of both the speaker and the listener

Practically SPEAKING

Many people suffer from phobias of one sort or another. For example, those who suffer from arachnophobia fear spiders of all shapes and sizes. Then there are those who fear animals, and they suffer from zoophobia. Perhaps you know someone with aerophobia, or the fear of flying. Maybe one of your friends has nyctaphobia, or the fear of the dark. There are other more unique fears, like triskaidekaphobia (the fear of the number thirteen) or the fear of older people (gerontophobia). One of the most debilitating fears happens to be agoraphobia, or the fear of public spaces that comes from a feeling of inescapability. People who suffer from this fear cannot even go outside their own homes without risking severe anxiety. For a list of the top 10 phobias, see Table 3.1.

Fear is as human an emotion as love or happiness, and so it is not a bad thing to be afraid of something. In fact, it can make you function better. Take the example of Oscar-winning actor Sir Laurence Olivier. Olivier, named to the American Film Institute's list of Greatest Male Stars of All Time,[1] suffered from debilitating anxiety attacks before performances.

From the age of five or six, Olivier demonstrated a penchant for drama and acting, creating a makeshift stage in his parents' house from window curtains and a wooden chest to perform for his sister, visiting neighbors, or even extended family members. Olivier's formative years took place during World War I, a time when England's image of itself as Europe's dominant force came under fire. Despite his commitment to the lines of each of the plays and roles he would perform, Olivier still suffered stage-fright, or performance anxiety.

One of the more poignant insights he offered to this fear was "it comes in all sorts of forms; I suppose it's always there, but most of the time it hovers unseen."[2] Olivier also suffered from fear right before going on stage, describing it as "nothing like first-night nerves...the breathing becomes affected: the breath becomes shorter when you want it to become longer and deeper...you try to calm down but the sweat breaks out again. The voice in the head starts to ramble."[3] Do any of these feelings and emotions sound familiar when you prepare to deliver a speech? Well, fear not, because Olivier mastered his fear, made it work for him, and went on to become a world renowned performer.

In this chapter we will first define and discuss exactly what performance anxiety is, as it goes by many names. We will then talk about the causes of it and provide strategies for managing it so it can help rather than hurt your efforts. We then talk about one of the skills we can develop as a speaker and an audience member that can help diminish our fear when we speak, as well as the fear of others when they speak: listening. If we can practice becoming courteous and effective listeners then we can create a more comfortable environment for speakers, no matter how nervous they are.

FEAR AND PUBLIC SPEAKING

Public speaking represents one of the most frightening experiences possible for a great many people and that fear is not abnormal. In this part of the chapter we will discuss the various ways in which the fear of public speaking is defined by the general public and academics. We will also explore the variety of factors that contribute to the anxiety associated with speech performances. Finally, we will provide several suggestions on ways to alleviate much of the trepidation associated with delivering a speech in front of an audience.

Top Ten Phobias/Fears
1. Arachnophobia: fear of spiders
2. Social phobia: fear of being evaluated
3. Aerophobia: fear of flying
4. Agoraphobia: fear of not being able to escape
5. Claustrophobia: fear of being trapped in a small space
6. Acrophobia: fear of heights
7. Emetophobia: fear of vomit
8. Carcinophobia: fear of cancer
9. Brontophobia: fear of thunderstorms
10. Necrophobia: fear of death
http://www.phobia-fear-release.com/list-of-the-top-ten-phobias.html

Table 3.1

Defining the Fear of Public Speaking

The fear of public speaking, also called performance anxiety or stage-fright, is a specific manifestation of *sociophobia*, or the fear of people and/or social situations. The fear of public speaking is essentially a combination of any of the following fears: fear of rejection, fear of criticism, fear of judgment, and fear of failure. In this section we will illustrate the academic definition of the fear of public speaking and then discuss what students fear most when they speak in front of audiences.

sociophobia
the fear of social situations and/or people

communication apprehension
the fear or anxiety associated with real or anticipated communication with another or others

Academics call the fear of public speaking *communication apprehension* and define it as "the fear or anxiety associated with real or anticipated communication with another or others."[4] Communication scholars apply this definition to more than public speaking situations, as it also helps to define shyness in interpersonal situations. Here you see why there are multiple ways of describing fear of public speaking. Fear and anxiety are synonymous, but one (anxiety) connotes a state that is easier to handle.

What is important to realize is that everyone has fear and everyone experiences anxiety in their lives. Perhaps things get really busy at work and you become easily agitated over things that normally do not bother you. This stress is a result of a heightened anxiety level. If you experience some level of anxiety before a speech, that is normal as it is a high stress situation. This level of anxiety is common.

anxiety disorder
abnormal mental outlook where individuals experience high levels of apprehension that keep them from living life

There are some individuals who experience abnormal levels of anxiety, or who become anxious for no reason at all. These people have what psychologists call an *anxiety disorder*. A perfect example of someone with an anxiety disorder is the fictional character Adrian Monk, formerly of the USA Network's award-winning

Tony Shalhoub plays TV's *Monk*

drama *Monk*. Adrian suffers from multiple phobias as well as obsessive compulsive disorder, significantly hampering his ability to function in mainstream society. His anxiety prohibits him from functioning, whereas normal anxiety does not do that, although it does cause a level of discomfort.

In the case of public speaking, the differences between anxiety and having an anxiety disorder are easy to identify. First, normal anxiety may result in sweating, a knot in your stomach, slightly elevated blood pressure, or the general "willies" before a speech. People with an anxiety disorder, however, would not go to class on the day of their speech simply to avoid being judged. The Mayo Clinic provides a list of several other defining characteristics of a social anxiety disorder:

- An intense and persistent fear of social or performance situations
- Avoiding the situations you fear
- Fear of being embarrassed or humiliated
- Fear that others will see your physical manifestations of nervousness
- The anxiety limits how you can live your life
- You recognize the fear is excessive[5]

Additionally, the Social Phobia and Social Anxiety Association reports that those who suffer from social anxiety disorder recognize the irrational and illogical nature of their fear, but nevertheless the fear remains with them.[6] Anxiety that results in these feelings or behaviors should be treated by a professional, but the fact is most people can find ways to manage or even overcome their fears—especially those with public speaking. Later in this chapter we will discuss how.

So, why do students experience communication apprehension, or a seemingly high level of anxiety about delivering a speech? What is it that they are afraid of? Some fear speaking too quickly, or too quietly. Some are afraid of boring the audience, or sounding as if they do not know what they are talking about. Others fear mispronouncing words, or having something on their teeth or face at which people will stare. Many people are afraid of making eye contact with those in front of them for fear that they will forget what they were going to say. Others erroneously believe that their nerves will be visible to the entire audience.

Ultimately, there is just something about the speaking situation that makes people worry and become anxious. In fact, just as the tradition of public speaking is a long one, so too is the history of fearing to give a public presentation. Isocrates, the Greek teacher whom we discussed previously, suffered from a fear of public speaking so intense he himself tried never to speak publicly. That didn't stop him from training some of the best speakers of his time, though!

In the next section we will discuss three major causes of speech-fright: environmental, psychological, and physiological factors. Following that we will provide some helpful suggestions on how to manage your performance anxiety.

Causes of Speech-fright

Speech-fright is often the result of a variety of factors, ranging from specific fears about the situation, aspects of a person's personality, or the physiological make-up of an individual. Environmental factors stem from the fact that speaking in public is different from speaking in a conversation with a friend or someone you know. We often see these differences and ignore the commonalities between the two situations, resulting in a fear of the one scenario and comfort with the other. Psychological factors that influence speech anxiety include your approach to everyday life and how you handle stress. Finally, different people have different physical reactions to stimuli, and sometimes these stimuli are present in a given speaking situation.

Three environmental factors influence a person's level of anxiety when delivering a speech, and each stems from fundamental differences in the nature of public speaking and conversation. The first two involve the audience. An audience for a speech is typically much larger than that of any conversation, and we often find this intimidating. That intimidation is only exacerbated by the fact that we are not as familiar with the people to whom we are speaking when we deliver a speech as we are with those we talk to over lunch. The third environmental influence is *spotlight syndrome*, or the perception encouraged by the room setup that all eyes are focused on you as the speaker.

spotlight syndrome
the belief encouraged by the room setup that all eyes are focused on you as the speaker

As those environmental characteristics illustrate, the public speaking environment is different from the atmosphere for most conversations. Public speaking uses more formal language, has a very structured format, and involves more than just a few people. Conversations are less structured, often employ slang, and typically involve only a few people. Differences aside, the two situations share certain characteristics as well, and understanding those common components can help reduce anxiety over speaking in public.

Conversations and public speaking share several elements that make them more similar than they are different (see Table 3.2). Both entail extensive nonverbal communication when delivering messages and receiving feedback. Both call on you to logically organize your thoughts. Public speaking and conversation also require you to adapt to audience feedback in order to tell a story in the most effective manner possible. Finally, in both situations you need to tailor your message to the audience. All told, conversations and public speaking have far more commonalities than differences! So, just think of public speaking as having multiple conversations at the same time and your anxiety will be dramatically reduced.

Table 3.2

Differences and Similarities in Conversation and Public Speaking	
Differences	**Similarities**
• Public speaking has more formal language • Format is more structured • Involves more than a few people	• Use of nonverbal communication • Logic is needed • Must adapt to feedback • Message is tailored to the audience

The environment is only one set of influences on a person's anxiety; the mental approach also can contribute to heightened stress in advance of a speech. Many people believe that public speaking is a talent and not a skill, and thus they enter into a speaking situation under the false assumption that they lack the tools necessary to effectively deliver a speech. The fact is public speaking is a skill, something that can be learned, and not a talent, something people are born with. Through practice and experience you can become a very effective speaker—just look at the example of Laurence Olivier from the beginning of the chapter.

self-fulfilling prophecy
believing that something will happen before it actually does, and then when it does come true reinforcing the original expectation

Psychological elements can also contribute to a person's reluctance to stand up and deliver a speech. Many people, especially as their performance draws near, allow worrisome thoughts to creep into their mind, creating a *self-fulfilling prophecy*. If you convince yourself that a speech will not turn out well, you will invariably not practice well and your performance will be poor, resulting in the original expectation coming to fruition. This and other forms of worrisome thoughts can cloud a speaker's mind to the point where it increases anxiety and gets in the way of a successful performance.

Nerves are not simply psychological, they appear in physical ways as well. When we get nervous our heart rate increases, resulting in potential blushing, we sweat, and we may even shake. These are some of the ways our bodies respond to stress, and often we believe people see them and immediately attribute them to nerves. Neither of those beliefs, however, are true. Often, people do not see us sweat, or our blushing, or even see our hands shake. The truth is that we can hide the physiological manifestations of nerves without even trying; the audience sees a fraction of what we feel.

Now that we are aware of the environmental, psychological, and physiological factors that affect speech-fright we can address how to manage performance anxiety and eventually make it work for us. In the next section we discuss several strategies for handling and reducing the anxiety present before and during a speech.

Managing Performance Anxiety

Fear is one of the most potent human emotions, and when you are afraid of something fear grips you and controls your thoughts and actions. It can be paralyzing, but it does not need to be so. One technique for overcoming a fear is to confront it head on and immerse yourself in the fear until you realize there is nothing to be fearful of. For example, if you were afraid of heights you could climb to the top of the tallest building and stare out over the edge of the roof until you got used to it. Although this immersion technique sounds logical, albeit a bit cruel, there is some truth to it.

Experience with that which is fearful ultimately will help you manage your fear. Unfortunately, this technique fails to address how you handle the fear while it is still there. Thankfully, overcoming performance anxiety entails both immersion and incremental management techniques. On the one hand, the more experience you get with delivering speeches, the less nervous you will become giving speeches in the future. On the other hand, there are several strategies for helping you manage the fear while delivering a speech, because you will not manage or master your fear overnight.

One of the ways you can combat worrisome thoughts and avoid creating a self-fulfilling prophecy is through visualizing success. Thinking positively about the speech and imagining yourself successfully delivering the speech will increase your belief in your ability to do so. Taking a positive approach and visualizing pulling off the presentation without any problems will also allow you to practice more comfortably.

Changing your mental approach also can minimize the influence of physiological factors on your anxiety levels. Understanding that people cannot see your nerves and acknowledging that there are a multitude of other reasons why you might sweat or blush alleviates the worry that people might "see that you are nervous" (see Table 3.3). You might be sweating because the room is hot, or blushing because of the same reason. Your shakes might be because you are sick, or the room is cold. Just because you know that you are anxious does not necessarily mean others know that too.

Table 3.3	Manifestations of and Reasons for Stress		
	Physical Manifestations of Stress	Could Be Caused by...	But It Might Be Caused by...
	Perspiring	Nervousness	Room temperature
	Blushing	Anxiety of embarrassment	Illness or room temperature
	Trembling	Apprehension	Room temperature or illness
	Breathing heavy	Anxiety	Physical exertion

Breathing can also help you combat nervousness and get more comfortable in front of an audience. You do not need to start your speech immediately upon getting behind the podium. If you are feeling tense, take a deep breath or two before you begin speaking. If you find your nervous state is still there, or that it returns during the delivery, do the same thing. Breathing increases your intake of oxygen and can reduce blushing and calm your nerves, so always remember that stopping and taking a breath is an option available to you when you get nervous during a presentation.

Finally, and perhaps most importantly, proper preparation and practice will undoubtedly make you more relaxed when you get to the point where you must deliver the speech. The easiest thing you can do to gain more confidence in your ability to speak is to practice, and practice often in advance of a speech. The more you practice, the more comfortable you get with the material, and the more comfortable you get with the material, the more you know it when you get in front of an audience. Practice and experience breed confidence, and confidence in your ability is the strongest tool you can develop to fight your fear. Realize that you do not have to present the speech using the exact same words each time. Focus on the content. As an example, a professor may deliver a lecture to one class, then leave and go deliver the lecture to a different section. He will not give the exact same lecture, as word choices may vary, but the content, or purpose, will be the same. See Table 3.4 for a summary of strategies for dealing with speech anxiety.

Table 3.4	Strategies for Dealing with Speech Anxiety
	• Directly confront it by presenting speeches • Visualize success • Realize the audience only sees a portion of what you feel • Take deep breaths for calmness • Adequately prepare and practice

So far we have covered performance anxiety, discussed several causes of it, and suggested some ways to combat the tension associated with preparing and delivering presentations. One skill we can develop to help create a more comfortable speaking environment—as both a speaker and an audience member—

SPOTLIGHTING THEORISTS: SOCRATES

Socrates (469–399 B.C.)

Virtually all we know of Socrates comes to us by way of his student, Plato, and his contemporaries Xenophon and Aristophanes, because he himself did not write any philosophical texts. Socrates perfected the art of listening to criticize through what we now call the Socratic Method and Socratic Questioning. In Ancient Greece, Socrates would wander through the marketplace questioning the political and moral positions of people in Athens. He did so by carefully listening to them talk and then asking questions about their statements. His questions almost invariably illustrated significant problems with the philosophies of his contemporaries. This would not have been possible had Socrates not carefully listened to and critically analyzed the positions they took. He can rightly be considered the father of modern logical intellectual inquiry, but even more to the point, he demonstrated the power and purpose of listening carefully to the messages of others.

Socrates was an Athenian who devoted his life to teaching philosophy, although according to Plato he did not accept payment for his educational services. He went through life poor in terms of money, but was highly regarded by his students. In addition to his teaching efforts he also served in the military during three Athenian campaigns.

Socrates lived in Athens during a time of turmoil, when neighboring Sparta and its allies defeated Athens. After this defeat, Athenians seemed to have doubts about democracy, and from Plato we can see how Socrates may very well have shared those doubts. One of his greatest roles during this time was as moral and social critic of the city he loved, leading to eventual problems with those in power at the time. Greeks at the time held a "might makes right" philosophy toward justice and governance and Socrates vehemently disagreed with this position.

Plato called Socrates the "gadfly of the state" because he spurred Athens into action through his various encounters with leaders, philosophers, and politicians. The story goes that one of Socrates's friends asked the Oracle at Delphi who was wiser than Socrates, and the Oracle responded that no such person existed. Upon hearing what he believed to be an erroneous statement, Socrates set out to show that there were wiser people throughout Greece by entering into dialogues with politicians and philosophers.

He used a dialectic method of discussion in these conversations whereby he would solve what he saw as problems by breaking problems down into a series of questions that eventually produced the answers sought by those around them. These discussions almost always centered on moral and social dilemmas and the concepts of justice and goodness.

Socrates's questioning agitated the leaders of Athens, because he often made them look foolish. They eventually had him arrested. When convicted he was sentenced to death, and despite the opportunity to flee and escape prison, he decided to stay and face judgment. Socrates was forced to drink a cup of hemlock, a poison, and died in his cell. His philosophy, however, has survived 2,400 years to this day and greatly influenced Western Thought.

is listening. In the next part of this chapter we will define the different types of listening, discuss some of the obstacles to becoming a good listener and how to overcome them, and illustrate how becoming a better listener when speaking and serving as an audience member can help minimize some of the factors that increase speech anxiety for some people.

LISTENING AND PUBLIC SPEAKING

hearing
the physiological process of processing sounds, conducted by one's ears and brain

listening
the psychological process of making sense out of sounds

People often confuse listening with hearing when, in fact, they are quite different. *Hearing* is the physiological process of capturing sound and it is conducted by one's ears and brain. *Listening* is the psychological process of making sense out of sounds and involves paying attention to the external world. Listening is an important skill for both speakers and audiences. For some rhetors, knowing that many people will be paying attention to them when they speak causes a high level of anxiety and contributes to their fear of public speaking. But like many things, once we understand what listening is and how people use it our level of discomfort will lessen. This part of the chapter will help you understand the complex nature of the different types of listening audiences employ, as well as discuss the importance of listening for the speaker as well.

Listening for Speakers and Audiences

Both speakers and listeners engage in listening, and it is key to understand the importance it holds for both parties. Speakers use listening as a means of measuring how well an audience is receiving their message, and how to adapt if they determine people are not getting it. Audience members use listening to gather information and form judgments; however, listening properly is far more difficult for them than for speakers.

Listening should be thought of as more than simply making sense of sounds, as it encompasses paying attention to nonverbal messages and processing them as well. Speakers both listen to the audience's verbal responses to statements—which can be as simple as making grunts of agreement or disagreement, or shouts of praise—and their nonverbal actions, which can include leaving the presentation, staring off at something else, or even nodding off. All of these actions indicate to a speaker who listens that changes need to be made in the speech to return the audience's attention to the message.

Socratic questioning
the process of asking questions of a speaker focused on the responses to previous questions; its ultimate goal is to uncover the truth

One way in which listening skills are exceedingly helpful for speakers is during a question and answer session. In fact, the questions that an audience asks are much more indicative of what they have learned than any statement they may make. Questions can be quite revealing in terms of an audience's retention of the message. In Ancient Greece, Socrates knew this all too well, as he developed a method of inquiry that balanced speaking with listening. *Socratic questioning* is the process of asking questions of a speaker focused on the responses to previous questions; its ultimate goal is to uncover the truth.

Audience members have a more difficult time listening than speakers because it is the only thing they are asked to do for the majority of the speech. Compounding this singular duty, the average human attention span is not very long and ranges anywhere from a few seconds to about 10 minutes, depending on the subject to which they are paying attention. When audience members do not pay attention to a speaker and the speaker notices, it may heighten the speaker's level of anxiety; convinced they are boring, they may lose confidence in their speaking ability. It is, therefore, an audience's ethical obligation to maintain attention to the speaker and his or her message as much as possible.

Types of Listening

One of the main reasons audience listening makes people nervous is because they are afraid the audience will catch them making a mistake or saying something inaccurate and call them on it. Although that is a remote possibility in some speeches, it is not common and only reflects one form of listening. There are, in fact, three listening purposes and two listening types audiences employ, and each engenders a response by the audience to the speaker and his or her message.

The first listening purpose is for appreciation. *Listening for appreciation* encompasses activities where you listen for enjoyment. Loading your favorite CD on your way to work or listening to the radio are examples of listening for appreciation. In these environments audiences are not waiting in the wings to pounce on an incorrect statement or to disagree with a speaker; they are listening to relax. Audiences do not employ high levels of cognitive commitment when they are listening for appreciation.

listening for appreciation
listening for enjoyment; not high in cognitive commitment

A second purpose of listening is *listening to comprehend*. When we try to understand a message or learn about something we do not know we listen to comprehend. This listening purpose involves a higher level of cognitive commitment than listening for appreciation because we pay attention to the message in order to gather and store information about a topic. Think of classroom lectures or news broadcasts as examples of listening to comprehend. We do not look for things to argue about in an instructor's lecture; rather, we take notes so we can learn about something with which we are unfamiliar. Like listening for appreciation, this type of listening by an audience is not combative.

listening to comprehend
listening to understand a concept or message

The final purpose of listening is the one we almost always ascribe to audiences, even when it is not what they are doing. *Listening to criticize* entails paying attention to the information and the argument presented by the speaker so that the audience can make a judgment about the message. Listening to a political candidate's speech is a prime example of listening to criticize. The word *criticize* holds such a negative connotation, however, that most people fear this type of listening. Unfortunately, that perception distorts the true benefits of this type of listening by audiences, such as encouraging debate and dialogue. Critical

listening to criticize
listening to make a judgment about a message; involves a high level of cognitive commitment on the part of the audience

listening is a fundamental part of any thriving democracy and is not something to fear. When we listen to criticize we are not looking to attack speakers or even make negative judgments about them. We are merely evaluating their message on its merits, and sometimes people simply must agree to disagree.

Both critical and comprehensive listening purposes require audience members to employ *active listening*. Active listening occurs when audiences have high cognitive involvement with the speaker's message and seek to understand the message. In other words, they are processing, storing, and potentially evaluating the message as it is being delivered. Active listening also involves some form of reaction by the listeners to demonstrate they are gathering the data being presented. This is not an easy process and takes much practice to develop, but it is an important skill to develop as both a speaker and an audience member.

active listening
listening to understand a message by processing, storing, and potentially evaluating a message. It also involves reactions by the listener in some form

There is also a difference between how you speak and how your brain functions. You speak at a rate of 150 words per minute, but your brain processes words at over 600 words per minute, resulting in lots of time for your mind to wander. This time is referred to as *spare brain time*, or the time available for your mind to wander due to your ability to process messages faster than it takes to construct them. Be aware that spare brain time makes it easy for your mind to wander to other things.

spare brain time
the time available for your mind to wander due to your ability to process messages faster than it takes to construct them

Passive listening is another type of listening. This is essentially listening without reacting, although the listener may well be receiving the information presented. Passive listeners do not raise hands or inquire during a presentation. This is the "sponge" approach to listening and can be risky if you do not understand something. This type of listening occurs more often when you are listening to comprehend, or listening for appreciation. When it takes place during the latter, then the sounds are often referred to as background noise.

passive listening
listening without reacting

Some noise, like background noise, does not affect a person's ability to concentrate or listen attentively; however, other noise can interfere with a person's ability to receive a speaker's message. These noises are distractions, and in the next section we will discuss several different types of distractions that can negatively impact someone's ability to listen and thus create a more uncomfortable atmosphere for a speaker.

Overcoming Three Types of Distractions

Distractions can engender an uncomfortable atmosphere, increasing a speaker's discomfort when delivering a speech. Some of these distractions occur because of a person's fear reactions, while others are external to the speaker. Nevertheless, all of these can inhibit a person's ability to listen. See Table 3.5.

Biological reactions to the environment in both speakers and audience members can distract people from listening. Think about a classroom situation in which you were too cold, or perhaps too hot. How hard was it to pay attention to the lecture in that room? Pretty difficult to be sure. Or perhaps you were ill, had a headache, or were hungry—all biological responses that diminish your capacity to pay attention to a message. So, how do we overcome these distractions?

Unfortunately, there are few remedies other than concentration and focus. You could try and eat or drink before a speech if you are hungry, and in fact if you are the speaker you should go into the presentation with a satisfied stomach. If you are ill, you could take medication, but even then the best course would be to acknowledge the illness to the audience at the outset so they are aware of it and do not spend time during the speech distracted by your reactions to the affliction.

In addition to biological distractions, there may be environmental occurrences that draw attention away from the presentation. Airplanes flying overhead, cars driving by, people coughing or sneezing, and even the howling of the wind can cause both speakers and listeners to turn their attention somewhere other than the message. Again, the best answer to these distractions is focus and acknowledging them to the audience.

The final type of distraction we will cover is also the rarest of them: hecklers. Hecklers are those individuals who seek to interrupt a presentation to inject their own viewpoint, either through insult, unsolicited questions, or unwarranted commentary. Heckling could quite possibly be the most unethical behavior an audience member can display. Hecklers have appeared at political speeches, guest lectures by faculty, and even during comedy shows. In fact, comedian Dane Cook called out a heckler during one of his live albums, explaining that the person was destroying the experience for everyone else.

Comedian Dane Cook

There are two ways speakers can deal with hecklers, and two ways audience members can help deal with hecklers as well. Speakers can choose to ignore hecklers in the hopes that they will eventually quiet down because they are not receiving attention. Rhetors also can acknowledge the hecklers and ask them to be quiet or face removal from the area. Audiences can help control hecklers by ignoring them, especially if this follows the lead of the speaker. They also can confront the heckler and express their displeasure with that person's behavior. Either way, hecklers can make both speakers and audiences uncomfortable for as long as they are making their unwanted contributions loud enough that people hear them. Choosing to be an attentive listener who allows speakers the opportunity to say their piece prevents this type of behavior from occurring and contributes to creating a more comfortable atmosphere for a presentation.

Table 3.5

Dealing with Distractions	
Type of Distraction	**Coping with Distractions**
Biological	Be sure to get enough rest, food, and water, and if ill, let the audience know
Environmental	Maintain focus and acknowledge distractions to the audience
Hecklers	Ignore them Directly address them The audience may support the speaker

Types of Nonlistening

nonlistening
....
providing the appearance of listening without actually paying complete attention to the message

Oftentimes we think we listen, when in fact we do not. What we are doing is called *nonlistening*, or providing the appearance of listening without actually paying complete attention to the message. Nonlistening comes in a variety of forms, and in each instance we believe, or pretend that, we are listening, but in fact we are not.

The first, and perhaps most common, form of nonlistening is called *pseudolistening*. This occurs when listeners attempt to hide their inattention to the message by appearing as though they are listening attentively to the speaker. Think about phone conversations you may have had where you take the phone away from your ear only to come back in time to say something like "uh-huh" to make it sound as though you were listening to the person on the other end. Or perhaps you went to lunch with someone and had to ask "are you listening to me?" because he or she seemed not to understand what you said. Finally, perhaps you have spent time sitting in class, looking at the professor, perhaps occasionally nodding your head, just pretending to pay attention. These are all examples of pseudolistening.

pseudolistening
....
when someone attempts to hide their inattention to the speaker's message

glazing over
....
daydreaming instead of hearing the message

A second form of nonlistening is *glazing over*. At some point in all our lives we have looked out the window or stared at a wall during a lecture in school, only to realize later that we missed important information. This daydreaming is a form of nonlistening common to situations where the audience is not enthralled with the topic. Although it may appear somewhat benign, speakers may internalize this as their poor speaking skills creating boredom in their audience.

ambushing
....
selective listening where the audience ignores the strengths of a message and hears only the weaknesses

Ambushing is a third form of nonlistening audiences may engage in. This involves selecting only the weaknesses of a presentation and ignoring the strengths of the speaker's argument. It is a negative form of nonlistening that can encourage a hostile atmosphere that increases a speaker's anxiety toward delivering the speech. It is important to listen to a speech with an open mind and judge the entire presentation on all its merits, not selected points that are made. This is the listening version of the strawman fallacy in crafting a logical argument, which we will discuss later.

Prejudging is the last of the nonlistening forms we will explore. It is dangerous and a potentially negative form that stems from an audience member's inability to enter the presentation with an open mind. Audience members have an ethical obligation to enter into any presentation with an open mind and allow the speakers to make their case. If you have already formed an opinion on the topic prior to the event, then the speech is pointless. For example: Suppose your university has been raising student fees quite often. An SGA representative is coming to your organization and you know she supports yet another increase in mandatory student fees. Your passion and attitude about the topic make it easy for you to already have a decision made before she even begins her speech.

prejudging
entering into a presentation with a judgment already formed about the message being delivered

Most times a speaker can easily determine whether people have prejudged the speech and the speaker before a word is spoken and this is not fair to the audience or the speaker. Listen for the evidence and the argument and then make your judgment.

Listening is an important skill for speakers and audiences and it should be treated as such. When both sides are attuned to the message then they create a more comfortable speaking situation and help to reduce speech anxiety on the part of the presenter.

Listening is a key component to any public presentation, and it is a requirement for an ethical speaker and audience member. In the next section of this chapter we will discuss four types of ethical public speaking and one form that violates the principle of a "good person speaking well."

ETHICAL CONSIDERATIONS IN SPEECH

Recall from our earlier discussion that the Greeks and Romans noted the importance of ethics in public speaking, although they focused their attention on providing speakers, rather than audiences, with guidance for ethical message construction. They understood the immense power speech had over the actions of the public, and so in their schools they often took care to teach not just the skills of speech construction and delivery, but how to wield speech for the public good. For them, and for us today, why you say something is just as important as what and how you say it.

The ethical principles and duties laid out by Isocrates, Quintilian, and other Classical thinkers still apply today. Just as with citizens during the time of Isocrates and Quintilian, when we speak to the public—be it our fellow students, our church congregation, or a rally—we are asking them for their time, attention, and trust. Whenever we speak we want someone's attention, thus we ask them to place value in our message by committing time to listen to us. That value rests on the principle that what we are saying is the truth that we know to the best of our ability. It also means that we have the audience's best interests in mind and that our goal is to achieve some good on behalf of the group.

The Struggle for Human Rights
by Eleanor Roosevelt

Delivered September 28, 1948, Paris, France

Former First Lady of the United States, Eleanor Roosevelt, lived a privileged existence. Despite her well-off origins, however, she witnessed much hardship and human suffering during her life: the Great Depression and World War II. To her, human rights were a fundamental issue worth fighting for. After her time in the White House alongside her husband, Franklin Delano Roosevelt, she confronted her growing concern over the expansion of the Soviet Union and how its policies infringed on human rights.

Mrs. Roosevelt became an advocate for human rights and delivered many speeches on the subject. One of the more notable of these speeches was given at the Sorbonne in France, where she noted: "It was here the Declaration of the Rights of Man was proclaimed, and the great slogans of the French Revolution—liberty, equality, fraternity—fired the imagination of man."[7] Speaking at virtually the front door of the Soviet Union and its allies on these issues would have been a risky proposition for any speaker, but Mrs. Roosevelt found it important and necessary to do so.

Mrs. Roosevelt noted that the charter of the recently formed United Nations concerned human rights and that the Human Rights Commission was working on language concerning those rights. She also commented on the objections of the USSR and a few other countries and outlined differences between the United States and the Soviet country.

Mrs. Roosevelt recognized that achieving universal human rights would be difficult, but she concluded her speech with a prayerful message of hope for the future of human rights: "I pray Almighty God that we may win another victory here for the rights and freedoms of all men."[8]

One such moment we can use to illustrate a speaker addressing a group with the global community's best interests in mind came following World War II when Eleanor Roosevelt spoke about human rights to a group in France. The issue of basic human rights is something that affects all of us, and speaking on behalf of protecting those rights represents a good and ethical goal. If we have good goals, we should also share our intentions with the audience honestly and acknowledge any personal interests or biases we may have related to the topic.

As a more current example, consider charity work in your community. A "good" that you may seek to achieve could be convincing your class to donate money to breast cancer research. We can all agree that the elimination of breast cancer is a good thing and that raising money for research to achieve that end is a noble and good pursuit. Using a speech to encourage support of this charity work would fit the characteristic of an ethical speaker because you are seeking a good goal, and as Isocrates and Quintilian said, good speakers must have good goals.

But ethical speaking is not just about achieving goals or ends, it is also about the means we use to achieve those ends. Let's look again at the previous example about a speech in which you seek donations from your classmates for breast cancer research. This time, as a piece of evidence in your speech, you state that there is a 75% chance that each audience member's mother will develop breast cancer—except this data is not accurate and you do not even provide a source for the information. In fabricating the statistic you would be violating the principles of ethical public speaking because you would not be, in Quintilian's words, defending the truth. Despite the fact this story may help your case and move the audience to donate to a noble cause such as breast cancer research, the ends would be achieved through deception and manipulation, two things not characteristic of a good person. Additionally, this behavior would damage your ethos.

Fabricating statistics and other forms of evidence is not the only way we can be unethical public speakers—and it is probably not even the most common or insidious. In fact, today speakers in society tend to rely primarily on demagoguery when crafting appeals, rather than outright mistruths. *Demagoguery* refers to speech that attempts to win over an audience through appealing to their prejudices and emotions, particularly those of fear, anger, and frustration. Unfortunately, the practice of demagoguery has become even more common with the advent of mediated communication and 24-hour news channels.

demagoguery

speech that attempts to win over an audience through appealing to their prejudices and emotions, particularly those of fear, anger, and frustration

Demagogues originally referred to leaders of the common people in Classical Greece, but like today, the term carried a negative connotation that implied deceit, selfishness, and a desire to create mischief in the population. Demagogues typically seek to gain power for themselves by activating and exacerbating the darker side of human emotions. For example, Huey Long, governor of Louisiana in 1928, won election by demonizing the wealthy and corporate interests while promising a utopian community where "every man is a king, but no one wears a crown." He referred to the wealthy as "parasites" and used them as a target for the anger of the Louisiana public that had begun to feel the effects of an economic downturn.

Perhaps the most famous demagogue in American history was Senator Joe McCarthy who, in the 1950s, accused high ranking officials, Hollywood celebrities, and even newsman Edward R. Murrow of being either communists or communist sympathizers bent on destroying the fabric of American society. This period, now referred to as the Red Scare, saw many people lose jobs and suffer damaged reputations that could not be repaired, even when McCarthy's accusations were discovered to be baseless and unfounded. His speeches and accusations created a public frenzy by playing solely on the public's fear of communism.

Ethical speech also requires that you stand up for what you believe to be right, just, and good. This may present an uncomfortable situation, but if your motives are to benefit the audience and not serve a personal interest, and if your ideas are sound, just, and logical, then you owe it to your audience and yourself to speak up,

Figure 3.1
The Ten Commandments of Ethical Public Speaking

The Ten Commandments of Ethical Public Speaking

1. Speakers will respect all audience members, including those who may advocate different opinions than the one which they are advocating.

2. Speakers will not claim to be informed or an expert on a topic when they are not.

3. Speakers will ensure research sources are accurate and will not use false, fabricated, or irrelevant information in their presentations.

4. Speakers will not use demagoguery to move the audience.

5. Speakers will not use material from sources without giving them credit.

6. Speakers will not manipulate the audience solely by playing on their emotions.

7. Speakers will have no agenda and will not advocate for something they do not believe in or would not do themselves.

8. Speakers will not deceive their audiences by concealing a hidden agenda.

9. Speakers will respect the amount of time they are given to deliver their presentation.

10. Speakers will not claim certainty when it does not exist.

like Edward R. Murrow did with McCarthy and like Cicero did in Rome. Cicero's speeches denouncing Julius Caesar and then Marc Antony cost him his life, but his ideas and the principles he espoused live on. Today such penalties for speaking out are protected in a variety of contexts, but consider this: Perhaps we are afraid to speak up or raise our hands in class because we are aware of the power of speech. Making good ethical decisions on the small things you encounter in your everyday life will best prepare you for speaking up on the more complex ethical challenges when they confront you.

Emotions are an important part of effective message construction, but it is when speakers use emotions to further their own ends or fabricate evidence to create particular emotional reactions in the audience that their use becomes unethical. There are plenty of emotional appeals that are both ethically constructed and designed to achieve ethical ends, but as a speaker we must be cognizant of both the means we use to move an audience to action, and the action toward which we move them. Demagogues violate both of these principles by capitalizing on an audience's emotions to achieve personal, rather than communal, goals. See Figure 3.1 for a summary of the ten commandments of ethical public speaking.

SUMMARY

Many people suffer from performance anxiety, or what we call fear of public speaking. It is only natural to be nervous in such a situation for a variety of reasons, ranging from environmental factors, to physiological reactions, to a person's psychological approach to the situation. Thankfully, there are a variety of ways to counter and manage this feeling so that it can work for you and make your speeches better in the long run. There are also ways in which audience members can contribute to making the atmosphere more comfortable, and one of the easiest ways is to be an ethical and effective listener. Avoiding nonlistening techniques and actively paying attention to the speaker's message will only serve to create a more open and relaxing environment for any speaker. Conversely, speakers have ethical responsibilities to their audiences to present the truth and be honest about their goals.

KEY TERMS

active listening	listening to criticize
ambushing	nonlistening
anxiety disorder	passive listening
communication apprehension	prejudging
demagoguery	pseudolistening
glazing over	self-fulfilling prophecy
hearing	sociophobia
listening	Socratic questioning
listening for appreciation	spare brain time
listening to comprehend	spotlight syndrome

REVIEW QUESTIONS

1. What is the difference between fear of public speaking and an anxiety disorder?

   _____

   _____

2. What are the three major factors that can cause speech-fright?

   _____

   _____

3. What are some strategies for combating speech anxiety?

_____

_____

4. What are the three listening purposes and two listening types?

_____

_____

5. What are the forms of nonlistening prevalent in an audience?

_____

_____

THINK ABOUT IT

1. If someone is deaf, can they listen?

_____

_____

_____

_____

2. At what point does general speech anxiety become an anxiety disorder?

_____

_____

_____

_____

3. How can you actually tell if a speaker is nervous or anxious?

_____

_____

_____

_____

4. As an audience member how can you aid a nervous speaker?

_____

_____

_____

_____

1. Take a moment and make a list of things that you fear. Now, take each one and write out an explanation of why you fear each of these things. Finally, look at the reasons and causes of your anxiety and write a plan that will help desensitize you to the fear.

2. Think of a song to which you like to listen. Write down the title, band, and what is appealing about the song. Now, find the lyrics to the song and write a description of what the song is about based upon the lyrics alone. Finally, think about what the speech is about and how you feel about the message within the song. Do you agree with the message? Why or why not? In doing this exercise you practice appreciative listening, listening for comprehension, and critical listening.

3. Find the lyrics to a song you like and deliver those lyrics as you would a speech. Do the same with a poem and page from a book. In practicing speaking with each of these texts you will become more comfortable in the speaking situation and reduce the anxiety public speaking can cause.

ACTIVITIES FOR ACTION

ENDNOTES

1. American Film Institute, "AFI's 100 Years…100 Stars," http://www.afi.com/tvevents/100years/stars.aspx (accessed June 25, 2008).

2. Laurence Olivier, _On Acting_ (Simon and Schuster: New York, NY, 1986), 181.

3. Ibid., 183.

4. James C. McCroskey, "Oral Communication Apprehension: A Review of Recent Research," _Human Communication Research_ 4 (1977) 78-96.

5. "Social Anxiety, Social Anxiety Disorder/Social Phobia: Symptoms, Types, Causes, Treatment and Support," http://www.helpguide.org/mental/social_anxiety_support_symptom_causes_treatment.htm (accessed June 25, 2008).

6. Ibid.

7. http://www.americanrhetoric.com/speeches/eleanorroosevelt.htm (accessed May 9, 2011).

8. Ibid.

Research and Preparation

CHAPTER OVERVIEW

- Addresses finding and developing a topic for a speech
- Discusses what it means to be information literate
- Identifies various research sources
- Explains the ethical importance of citing sources and provides examples of how to cite in CMS, APA, and MLA formats

Practically SPEAKING

Students today typically react to the necessity of venturing to the library with a mixture of dread, loathing, and reluctance; however, that has not always been the case. In fact, there was a time when libraries held an exalted status and represented more than simply storage facilities for the printed word. In the ancient world, libraries were castles of learning and homes to schools, zoos, museums, and the brightest minds of the day. They were, in point of fact, the backbone of empires and kingdoms.

The most famous library in history was located in Alexandria, Egypt, and its history is a mixture of both fact and myth. King Ptolemy I (Soter) and his son King Ptolemy II (Philadelphus) commissioned the Great Library at Alexandria and modeled it after Aristotle's Lyceum in terms of mission, but the Alexandrian library dwarfed the Lyceum in terms of size, structure, and content. This model, however, occurred for good reason.[1]

Ptolemy I was one of Alexander the Great's generals, and after the death of his leader and subsequent partition of the empire, Ptolemy ruled Egypt. Alexander was a student of Aristotle's, and so he made sure his generals were schooled in the same vein. Additionally, through his conquests Alexander attempted to Hellenize the world by spreading the value of the *enkyklios paideia*, or rounded education, which tiered instruction into the *trivium* (grammar, rhetoric, and logic), and *quadrivium* (arithmetic, geometry, music, and astronomy).

The Ptolemys sought to create a universal library, one where knowledge of all things could be found, not just a localized culture-specific repository of knowledge. The Great Library also contained a Museum and together they represented one of the greatest achievements in all of antiquity.[2] The Great Library and Museum worked in tandem to store and develop the wisdom of the ages. Scholars from around the known world lived and worked tax-free at the Library copying scrolls secured by the government. On several occasions, Ptolemy and his successors even brought scrolls on loan from Greek city-states and copied them only to keep both the original and the copy! It was the epicenter of scholarship and innovation because many of those holdings were original Greek works and translations of non-Greek texts of religious, poetic, and political significance.[3]

Unfortunately, nothing much remains of the Great Library and Museum and the histories of it are the product of researching letters and writings that reference it. No one is sure how it was destroyed, but destroyed it was, and many writings contained there are now lost forever. Ironically, we know about the ancient world's research mecca only through research, as it no longer exists and its documents are long gone.

Nowadays we think of libraries simply as places where knowledge is stored, and the university as a whole fits the model set forth by the Great Library. Nevertheless, the Greeks and Romans recognized that libraries and research skills are central to the development of a critical mind, and we should learn from that example.

In this chapter we will explore the very nature of research and illustrate the importance of becoming information literate. We will discuss different types of sources and how you can find the ones most appropriate to your project. Finally, we will detail the importance of properly citing sources you use and provide two examples of how to do so. A successful speech is predicated on good research and helps you determine your topic.

Topic Selection

In many situations speakers know their topic because someone provided it for them. There are, however, times when speakers need to pick topics on their own, such as in your public speaking class. Regardless of the speaking situation, determining one's own topic is the first step toward performing a successful act of public speaking. In this part of the chapter we will discuss ways to find a topic, develop a research question for that topic, and eventually refine the topic so it is clear for you and your audience.

Finding a Topic

There are three primary ways to determine a topic for a speech. One is easy, and takes little effort from the speaker; unfortunately, it is not always available. The second involves a person's familiarity or expertise in an area, and the final method for picking a topic hinges on a speaker's curiosity.

As we mentioned earlier, many times speakers are provided not just the opportunity to speak, but the topic on which to speak. This makes things relatively easy as they know what to research and what to say. Take, for instance, a business situation when a budget director must report on sales and earnings for the company at a shareholder meeting. The budget director knows his topic well in advance, but how he chooses to deliver the message and the data he uses rest largely with him.

Other times the specific topic is not provided, but speakers are given a general guideline for their presentation. This often happens when professors are asked to deliver guest lectures. In fact, the non-fiction book, *The Last Lecture,* by Randy Pausch (with assistance from Jeffrey Zaslow), is about a

enkyklios paideia
rounded education spread under the reign of Alexander the Great

trivium
grammar, rhetoric, and logic

quadrivium
arithmetic, geometry, music, and astronomy

Randy Pausch
at Carnegie Mellon

professor who, while dying of cancer, prepares to deliver a talk at Carnegie Mellon University during its "Journeys" series. The only direction provided was that Pausch must speak about his career and how he ended up doing what he did. He gave a speech that creatively addressed achieving your childhood dreams.[4] Tragically, Pausch lost his fight with pancreatic cancer on July 25, 2008, at age 47. His speech, however, remains a perfect example of how speakers use their own creativity to determine a specific topic when provided with only general criteria for a speech.

There are times when even this type of minimal direction is not provided for you. One easy option for you then is to select a topic with which you are very familiar, or perhaps one in which you are an expert. Consider this fictional case involving Donald, a freshman in a public speaking class who needs to deliver an informative speech. Donald loves baseball, and so he chooses to inform the class about the rules of the game. He knows exactly where to go to find the proper sources, knows of several easy-to-find anecdotes to support his speech, and feels confident that he knows the material. Donald's prior knowledge and familiarity with the topic make it easy for him to pick this topic.

Perhaps you do not wish to speak on a topic with which you are familiar; such topics bore you and you want to actually learn about something new in the process of developing your speech. Let's look at Phyllis, who has always wanted to know more about the Dow Jones Industrial Average because she has invested so much money in it over the years. Unfamiliar with the topic, Phyllis's curiosity leads to her discovery of a wealth of knowledge about the Dow Jones Industrial Average she never would have known had she not chosen the topic. Choosing topics on which you know little but wish to know much can be a valuable tool in expanding your knowledge. It also exemplifies how rhetoric and public speaking cut across disciplines and require knowledge of many subjects, not just skill at delivery.

Crafting a Research Question

research question
the question about your topic you seek to answer

Once you determine your topic, you need to focus your research around a question about that topic. This question is called your *research question*, and it guides you through the rest of your preparation for your speech. Regardless of whether you are delivering an informative, persuasive, or epideictic address, a research question is essential for providing you with a focus for your presentation. There are three characteristics of every quality research question.

Bob Dylan

First, a research question is an open-ended question and cannot be answered with a simple "yes" or "no." The answer to the question is complex and requires a level of detail and description that are not necessary for a "yes" or "no" question. If your general topic is an informative speech about a famous musician, and your specific topic is Bob Dylan, then your research question might be, "What inspired Bob Dylan to write his song "Hurricane"?" Answering such a question calls for you to talk about who Bob Dylan was, discuss some history of the song, provide some background on its topic, and perhaps discuss some cultural issues at play during the time he wrote the song. Of course, you could craft a myriad of different research questions from the specific topic of Bob Dylan, and each would need different data and information to answer, but any question you seek to answer must be open-ended.

In addition to being open-ended, the research question must be tailored around the topic. In other words, it must be relevant to the general and specific topic of the speech in some way. Using the Bob Dylan example again, some other successful research questions might be, "What was Bob Dylan's childhood like?" "Why did Bob Dylan choose music as a career?" or even, "How has Bob Dylan influenced contemporary musicians?" What would not work in the framework of this general and specific topic would be persuasive questions like, "How can I convince people to listen to Bob Dylan?" or this informative example of a question unrelated to the topic: "Who else was a successful speaker at the time of Bob Dylan?" This question, though it mentions Dylan, is not about Dylan, thereby violating the requirement that the research question be tailored around the specific topic of the speech.

Finally, the answers to strong research questions will inevitably become the thesis statement or argument for your entire presentation. Look at the Dylan example from a few moments ago. Let's say that your research indicates that Dylan wrote his hit song "The Hurricane" because of a personal sense of social justice, the desire to right a wrong perpetrated on a minority, and to shed some light on the situation in which Rubin "Hurricane" Carter found himself. That presents a strong thesis for an informative speech about the song and how it reflected the plight of Carter, a former boxer who was accused, convicted, and later exonerated for the murder of three people at a bar in Paterson, New Jersey, in 1966. This topic is

Rubin "Hurricane" Carter

obviously complex and warrants further explanation, hence the need for a longer speech built on the foundation provided by the answer to your initial research question. See Table 4.1 for some examples of poorly and properly worded research questions.

Table 4.1

Wording Research Questions	
Poorly Worded Research Questions	**Properly Worded Research Questions**
Who is Barack Obama?	What is the history of Barack Obama's political career?
Is it easy to pass Calculus 1?	What are some study strategies to successfully pass Calculus 1?
What is an easy way to break up with someone?	What is an ethical method to end a romantic relationship?
Why do service learning?	What benefits can students receive from engaging in service learning?
Are you a healthy eater?	What are the factors to consider for a healthy diet?
Why did Germany start WWII?	What were the historical, economic, and social events that led to Germany's military aggression leading to WWII?
Why play video games?	How can playing video games improve hand and eye coordination?

Refining Your Topic

As you search for the answer to your research question you also must adapt to the results of your research. To do this, you must be prepared to refine your specific topic and even your research question to better guide you on your quest for information. First and foremost, when you begin you must be prepared to discover that the focus of your speech when you finish researching may very well not be the focus you wanted or had in mind when you began. This is only natural and is the result of good research skills.

One of these skills is note-taking. Good researchers have a method of note-taking that works best for them. This may involve note cards, photocopying information to better write margin notes, keeping a research notebook, or even using post-it notes to label where you found information. Regardless of how you choose to take notes, you need to develop a categorizing system that makes sense to you so that when it comes time to organize the information into meaningful points for the speech you can easily do so. Taking good, organized notes while you research will help you refine your topic and focus your speech even more.

Good researchers seek information with an open mind and do not simply look for data that supports their original idea. It is important to allow contrary information to count as much as material that supports your ideas when conducting research. There are multiple interpretations of a variety of different data, from statistics to events to the lives of people, and good researchers find as many of these as possible to better balance their results. The more relevant information you collect, the stronger your speech will become. Let the information be your guide, rather than you guiding the research.

It is tempting for any student to simply go and locate the minimum amount of sources to complete the assignment, but that defeats the purpose of expanding your knowledge base and contributing to the research field. If you research properly, sometimes it can take you to places you never thought about. Many students have lost track of the time, reading through newspaper articles from long-ago, interesting times, only to realize they spent far more time in the library than they had planned! Remember, those who used the Library at Alexandria lived there, they did not just visit. Follow the information, don't simply collect it, and you might just find the experience enjoyable and enlightening.

One final tip for conducting research and developing your topic is to think big initially, then reduce your topic down to something more precise. There is a reason why we talked about a general topic, then a specific topic, and finally a research question. Each step gets progressively more specific and thus smaller than the previous one. As you gather more information you can fine-tune your focus and make it more specific, thus helping you determine what you need in your quest for information. When you know your topic, you then have a better idea of where to look for information; however, you also must be able to distinguish useful and reliable information from useless and unreliable material.

INFORMATION LITERACY

Literacy refers to the ability to read, while information literacy is the ability to read information. Specifically, *information literacy* is the ability to figure out the type of information you need, find that information, evaluate it, and properly use it. There are five characteristics of an information literate person, and in this part of the chapter we will explain each of them, paying particular attention to the last: understanding the issues regarding the use of information. We will then differentiate between three different types of information researchers encounter and eventually use.

information literacy
the ability to figure out the type of information you need, find that information, evaluate it, and properly use it

Characteristics of Information Literacy

Just as literate people can read properly, information literate people can successfully research material they need. There are five characteristics of information literate people. First, they are able to determine what they need information for. Second, they are able to go out and find that information. Third, they can evaluate the information for accuracy, bias, and relevance as it relates to their purpose. Next, they can use the information they find to create new knowledge for themselves and/or others. Finally, the information literate person understands the issues relevant to using information, such as plagiarism.

Once you have a topic and purpose you are ready to begin to research, but what will you look for? Good researchers take an intermediate step between determining the topic and researching material. They determine their information need. Are they seeking background information? A strong anecdote for an attention-getter? Or evidence for their claims? Knowing the type of information you need will determine where you look, because not all types of information can be found in the same place. Depending on your need, you will look at different sources to find the information that best suits your need.

In today's media-rich environment we tend to believe we can find anything we need on the Internet, but the Internet is not a cure-all to the difficulties of research. In fact, it presents some disadvantages along with all the advantages it provides for researchers. Because it is rife with biased and sometimes false information, the Internet should be considered only one of several options for researching materials. Libraries, specifically the ones on your campus, hold vast stores of potentially useful information that might not even be available on the Internet, such as articles from a remote British newspaper during the Nazi's London Blitz of World War II. Knowing where the information is, however, is only one part of finding the information you need. The second part is recognizing which tool will net you the best results in your quest. Is it the Internet? The library? A book? A journal?

accuracy
the truthfulness or correctness of a source

As an information literate researcher, when you find information you think might help with your project you need to evaluate it for accuracy, bias, and relevance. *Accuracy* refers to the source's correctness or truthfulness. *Bias*, or the attempt to unfairly influence someone's perception of something, is also a concern. Accurate information can be presented in a manner that unfairly influences how one side is perceived by, among other things, excluding certain pieces of relevant material that might dispute a claim. Information also must be judged for relevance to your topic. Researchers able to evaluate material they find for accuracy, bias, and relevance will create stronger presentations and contribute more to the world around them.

bias
presenting information in a way that unfairly influences someone's perception of something

The fourth characteristic of an information literate individual, using the material garnered through research to create new knowledge for others, is associated directly with the contributions produced by research. Information literate researchers use the information they discover to educate and enlighten themselves and those around them. They make connections from work by others and information they find that others did not see to create a new perspective on a topic or issue. They also may be providing valuable information about something to a group of people who were unaware of what they needed to know about it. Building new knowledge from old research and information is one of the chief aims of research. Doing so without committing plagiarism is a chief component of the final characteristic of an information literate researcher.

Nevada Congressman Jim Gibbons

Plagiarism and Accountability in Information Use

In addition to the four characteristics we just discussed, information literate individuals understand the gravity of the issues involved with information use. The most important of these issues is giving credit where credit

SPOTLIGHTING THEORISTS: MELVIL DEWEY

Melvil Dewey (1831–1931)

Although computers, and more specifically the Internet, have eased the difficulties inherent in research, there still remains no greater influence on the research process than the development of the Dewey Decimal Classification System. Although not a communication scholar per se, Melvil Dewey changed the way in which scholars of any discipline conducted research. His classification and indexing system changed the way libraries operated, making the Great Library at Alexandria seem more like a warehouse than a library.

Melvil Dewey was born in New York and attended Amherst College in Massachusetts. From 1874–1877 he worked as assistant librarian at that college's library. It was during his time at Amherst College that he developed the now famous cataloguing system that bears his name.

In 1883 he took the position of chief librarian at Columbia University in his native state only to go on and be named director of the New York State Library in 1888. While in New York he championed the development of state and local libraries and was the first to instruct young librarians. He also managed to convince the state that the library system should be supported through the same tax revenue used to support public education, as public libraries, he argued, were a logical extension of public education.

These contributions to the creation of a modern library system and public education system greatly influenced the development of contemporary scholarship. Dewey helped make access to books and research materials easier through his coding scheme and efforts to link libraries to state and local educational efforts.

---

is due. Not to give credit to people whose work you use in a report or speech is *plagiarism*, or presenting another person's work or ideas as your own. It is important to understand that intent is irrelevant with plagiarism (e.g., "I didn't mean to do it" carries no weight). It is best to overcite sources than not to cite them enough.

plagiarism
to present another person's work or ideas as your own

Plagiarism comes in three different forms, but all are equally wrong. The first is *incremental plagiarism*, or failing to give credit for parts of a speech borrowed from a source. Incremental plagiarism is the most common form of plagiarism, as many people fail to reference parts of a speech they have paraphrased or even lifted directly from a source. In 2005 Congressman Jim Gibbons (R-NV) ran for governor and delivered a speech that seemed to rail against liberals. In this speech he delivered 15 paragraphs that were taken directly from a speech delivered by Alabama Auditor Beth Chapman two years earlier.[5] This is a perfect example of incremental plagiarism.

incremental plagiarism
failure to give proper credit for parts of a speech that are borrowed from others

patchwork plagiarism
⋯⋯⋯⋯⋯⋯⋯⋯
stealing ideas from two or three sources without referencing them

Another form of plagiarism is called *patchwork plagiarism*, or stealing ideas from more than one source and pawning them off as your own. Patchwork plagiarism involves lifting whole sections of information from several sources and linking them together without referencing any of them. This may appear to be using various forms of information to build new knowledge, but it is not, as there is little to no integration of the sources to an argument. This type of plagiarism occurs most often when students list information within a speech without referencing where the data has come from.

global plagiarism
⋯⋯⋯⋯⋯⋯⋯⋯
taking an entire speech from a single source and pawning it off as your own

The final form of plagiarism, *global plagiarism*, is the one most people are familiar with. Global plagiarism involves stealing an entire speech or paper from a single source and calling it one's own. Global plagiarism takes many forms, from cutting and pasting, to having someone write a speech for you, to buying a paper off a website. None of these give proper credit to the source of the ideas and information that have become the speech and, as such, they represent plagiarism.

Perhaps the greatest problem with plagiarism, aside from the fact it is an ethical and moral affront, is the fact that it destroys the fruits of researching. No longer are you able to learn about something, build new ideas, or expose yourself to things you may never have explored if not through research. You lose the opportunity to expand your own knowledge and help others do the same. Plagiarism attacks the very heart of a university's mission and thus is typically punished harshly; it is the worst academic crime possible. An information literate researcher is aware of all of this and avoids plagiarism at all costs by properly citing information found through research. There is one exception to the rule when it comes to presenting someone else's ideas as your own—but it does not apply in the classroom.

ghostwriting
⋯⋯⋯⋯⋯⋯⋯⋯
to write for and in the name of another person

Ghostwriting, or to write for and in the name of another person, is a fairly common practice among politicians and business leaders. In fact, presidents employ an entire speechwriting staff to write their speeches because they simply do not have the time to do so. Business executives also employ staff members who research and write many of their presentations because of time constraints.

The difference between ghostwriting and plagiarism is that ghostwriters are professionals who still abide by the rules of research and expectations for citations and allow the speaker to take credit and accountability for what is eventually said in the presentation. Most importantly, their participation in the speech's development is not hidden from the audience. In short, we all know the president uses speechwriters, but in the case we discussed earlier about Jim Gibbons of Nevada, there was no ghostwriter and the material was appropriated from a source without letting the audience know from whence it came.

Ghostwriting is also not a new phenomenon. In Classical Greece, citizens often hired professionals to help them write speeches. The Sophists whom we mentioned earlier sometimes fulfilled this role and made a pretty penny doing so! Clients often sought out professionals to help them write speeches to use in assemblies or in court, in much the same way business leaders and politicians use ghostwriters today.

Ghostwriters are examples of people who are information literate. A little earlier in the chapter we mentioned that information literate people know their information needs. Specifically, they know what material they need to research. In the next section we discuss the three main forms of information used within a speech: background, "adding flavor," and evidence.

Using Information

Information contributes to speeches in a variety of ways. Researchers sift through the data they find and determine if and how that material can be used. One way information can be used is to provide background for the speech topic. Another way it can help a speech is by "adding flavor" or color to the presentation. The third and final form of useful information is evidence, or information that supports main points within a speech.

Background information provides context for your topic. It covers things such as definitions of key concepts, dates of events, and the key players or moments related to the topic. This type of information helps you further narrow your speech topic and point you in the direction of evidentiary information for your topic. Despite the fact you will undoubtedly not use all of the background information you gather in early drafts of your speech, you should hold onto it until you deliver the speech as it may be useful later.

background information
material that provides context for a topic

A second form of useful information is information that may capture the audience's interest in your speech. This type of information may be only slightly related to your topic but, it is nevertheless interesting and can be used to draw an audience in as an attention-getter. It also includes tangential anecdotes that can be placed in the body of a speech to illustrate a point. The more popular forms of *tangential information* include startling statistics, famous quotations, and unique stories; all should be related to the speech in some way, but not necessarily directly linked to the topic. Each of these may not support main points within a speech, but they do help make the speech more enjoyable, creative, interesting, and effective by adding unique data to the presentation.

tangential information
evidence used to provide color and capture an audience's interest

The third most common and most important use of information is to support main points. *Evidentiary information* is information that supports main points within a speech and is directly related to the topic. It allows us to bring the voices of experts to bear through building on their research findings. Without evidentiary information there would be little support for any points in a speech. It is, essentially, the "meat and potatoes" of a speech. This information can take the form of personal accounts, newspaper stories, or statistics, but all of it has to be directly connected to the main point it is intended to support. One example of the effective use of evidentiary information in a speech can be seen in an address given by the Reverend Billy Graham to the Empire Club in Canada in 1995 (see the nearby box).

evidentiary information
information that supports main points within a speech and is directly related to the topic

So far we have discussed both how to determine a topic and what type of information to seek to support a topic. In the next part of this chapter we will cover how to find information, because knowing how to find information is an essential characteristic of an information literate researcher.

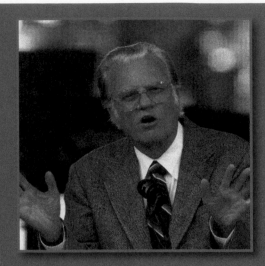

Leadership in the Third Millennium by the Reverend Billy Graham

Delivered June 6, 1995

The Reverend Dr. Billy Graham presented an invited speech to the Empire Club in Toronto, Canada.[6] Reverend Graham is a well-known author and evangelical Christian minister who has promoted a message of redemption through Jesus Christ since the late 1940s. In this address Graham spoke of the importance of leadership in a world fraught with challenges. Graham utilized multiple different sources of information to support the main points in his speech—all of which emphasized what he saw as the five attributes needed for contemporary leaders: integrity, personal security, sense of priority, sacrifice, and commitment.

Graham quoted numerous people throughout the address, ranging from Alexander Solzhenitsyn and George Washington to Queen Elizabeth. He quoted the Bible several times, particularly passages in the New Testament. Additionally, he quoted writers and reporters, as well as data on suicide rates in Canada. All of these various forms of evidentiary information provided data in support of his claims.

Graham's conclusion included a quotation from Sir Edmund Hillary, the famous mountain climber, who during a London speech when he reflected on his latest attempt to climb Mount Everest stated: "'I tried to conquer you once and you beat me. I tried to conquer you the second time and you took the lives of two of my best friends. But Everest, you will not be victorious. I will be victorious because you can't get any bigger, but I can." This piece of information fit perfectly with Graham's message of what it takes to be a leader in the third millennium and serves as an example of how speakers can wield information in different ways to maximum effect within a speech.

FINDING SOURCES

Finding information is no longer as difficult as it was during the days of the Great Library of Alexandria. Advances in technology and access now allow researchers to gather plenty of materials for projects without even leaving the comfort of their own office. In this section of the chapter we will discuss three places the contemporary researcher can explore when seeking information: libraries, personal correspondence, and the World Wide Web.

Libraries

Even with the advent of the Internet, the library still represents the largest and most reliable source for research materials. Every college and university still maintains a library, and many towns and cities also have public libraries that are easy to access. Libraries store books according to the Dewey Decimal System, and many allow for searches according to that classification system or by identifying other search criteria. Libraries also typically hold subscriptions to many different research databases that can help researchers find the information they seek. Above all, however, the most practical and useful tool in a library for assisting in research is the staff of the library. Many libraries provide the service of library tours. Signing up for a tour can save a novice researcher many hours of frustration. It will help you when you research because you will become more familiar with where libraries store the information you seek.

Libraries catalog and store books, magazines, and journals using the *Dewey Decimal Classification System*. This system has been revised 22 times since it was developed by Melvil Dewey in 1876. It organizes information into 10 major classes, which are then divided into 10 divisions which each have 10 sections. Except for fictional books, information is categorized by subject, and then further labeled according to relationships to time and place. Fictional books are coded differently and are not listed with nonfiction books. This system allows researchers to find several sources relating to the same subject just by initially finding one. When the Dewey Decimal Classification System first appeared it was a physical card catalog and took time to search. Now, most libraries allow for electronic searches of their holdings according to subject, author, keyword, and even publisher in some cases, making researching even easier.

Dewey Decimal Classification System
the coding system for books, magazines, and journals used in libraries

The same types of searches are also available for databases to which a library subscribes. These databases allow for specified searches of discipline- or source-specific material. For example, databases such as *JSTOR* allow a researcher to explore only academic journal articles related to politics. *Communication/Mass Media Complete* allows the same for journals and mainstream references related to communication and journalism. While those are examples of discipline-specific databases, *Lexis-Nexis* is a source-specific database available to many researchers. Lexis-Nexis allows people to sift through newspaper and magazine articles from publications around the world, thereby limiting its reach to newspaper and magazine sources. There are many, many more databases of which researchers can avail themselves, and the best way to find out which one best fits your needs is to make use of the most approachable tool in the library.

JSTOR
an electronic database for political journals

Communication/ Mass Media Complete
an electronic database for academic journals and popular sources related to communication and journalism

Lexis-Nexis
an electronic database for newspapers and magazines

Even with the advances in organization and technology that have revolutionized the research process, it is important to remember that librarians remain one of the best resources for locating information. Librarians know where to go to find information on many different topics, and the chances are high they know how to help you as well. They also have that human knack for thinking on their feet and trying different tactics if initial lines of thought do not prove fruitful. It is important to talk to librarians when starting your project because they will be able to cut down on your research time and assist you in finding the most accurate, unbiased, and relevant information for your project. They also will counsel you on how to find information from more places than databases and the full-text information found there. They will open doors to print sources not uploaded on the web but just as relevant to your project, sometimes even more so.

Personal Correspondence and Interviews

Libraries often carry special collections of materials previously owned by private citizens. Within these collections are personal correspondence such as letters and diaries. These materials, as well as more structured personal correspondence such as surveys, make up yet another potential resource for researchers. Additionally, less scientific, but equally useful, communications such as interviews and emails can be used for background or evidentiary information. They also can sometimes be used to provide a colorful anecdote or clever attention-getter.

formal survey
time-consuming way of gathering data on a population that employs randomized sampling to ensure reliability and validity

Researchers survey groups of people to find out the moods, feelings, or characteristics of them. These surveys can take two forms, the first being formal surveys. A *formal survey* employs scientific methods to ensure random sampling, reliability, and validity. These take time to administer, and oftentimes in preparing for a speech, a person will not conduct an original formal survey, but rather find the results of one conducted by someone else that provides insight into the topic on which they are speaking. The second form of surveying is an *informal survey*, whereby the person preparing a speech asks a handful of people their opinions on a topic to add context to a topic. These surveys are not reliable or valid, but can still yield useful information for a speech.

informal survey
polling a few people based on convenience

Informal surveys sometimes morph into another method of gathering information, especially when conversations become deeper than the planned survey questions. This method, *interviewing*, allows for more information from an individual than a survey, which aggregates group responses. Interviews follow a specific format that respects both the needs of the interviewer and the rights of the interviewee.

interviewing
a direct method of gathering information from a human source that allows for questions to adapt to responses

When conducting an interview it is important to first identify what you hope to learn from the interview. After developing these goals, then set out to find the person to interview who will best help you achieve those information-gathering goals. Once the person is contacted and agrees to the interview you develop the questions in advance for the interview. During the interview, you must allow for the possibility of asking questions you did not initially plan for based upon the responses provided by the interviewee. Following the interview it is important to take your notes from the conversation and translate them to source material as quickly as possible, because memory fades and becomes unreliable the longer you wait to record information from the interview.

undercover interviewing
when the interviewer disguises either himself or his purpose in an effort to trick someone into sharing more information than they may have if the interviewee knew to whom he or she was speaking

One ethical issue related to interviewing concerns undercover interviewing. *Undercover interviewing* is when an interviewer either disguises himself or his purpose in an effort to trick someone into sharing more information than they may have if the interviewee knew to whom he or she was speaking. Many reporters and researchers use this technique to gather information, but it raises ethical questions. Is it right to disguise your motives or identity to gather information? Are there other, more honest, options available to get the information you seek? Researchers must weigh these questions when thinking about hiding their identity and/or purpose during an interview.

Interviews are not limited to face-to-face interactions and can take place through email or letters; however, these interactions, especially emails, must be viewed carefully. Research indicates emails are often read with a negative bias, and that plays a role in how researchers may interpret information they receive through email. People also write emails in a more informal style than letters, where letters typically follow proper rules of grammar. Some emails also contain disclosure notices at the end that may prohibit researchers from using the information contained within the message. It is important when sifting through such messages that you take care to see if this is the case with an email you are considering using.

Internet

Email occurs on the Internet, but websites are far more commonly used as sources by researchers than email correspondence. Unfortunately, for the many benefits the Internet affords researchers, there are still many pitfalls of which researchers must be aware. There are different types of websites, each providing information on various subjects with varying degrees of accuracy. Credibility, therefore, is a significant issue when it comes to using the Internet to find information on a topic. Researchers must take care when evaluating information found on websites.

All websites have a form designation at the end of their URL. For example, government-produced websites end with ".gov," for-profit companies end with ".com," educational institutions end with ".edu," organizations end with ".org," and sites affiliated with a network are labeled ".net." International websites use abbreviations to identify their country of origin, as with the

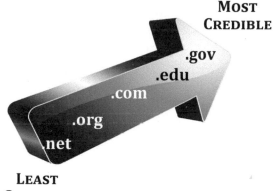

Most Credible

.gov
.edu
.com
.org
.net

Least Credible

Figure 4.1
Ranking URLs by Credibility

United Kingdom, which is labeled ".uk," or Canada, which goes by ".ca." The domestic labels each carry different levels of accuracy, bias, and credibility. See Figure 4.1.

The most reliable websites are ".gov" because they are government produced and easily verified. A close second in reliability is ".edu" because educational institutions have lower levels of bias on a wider range of issues than any other website designation except ".gov." Typically placing third in terms of reliability are the ".coms," which represent the interests and biases of companies. Most financial, historical, and organizational information found about the company on these websites is usually accurate; however, other information may not be as reliable. ".Org" is the next on the list, and only slightly more reliable than ".nets" because both of these URL designations can be obtained by almost any group or individual, making it more likely their biases will bleed through onto their websites. This is not to say all of these URLs are untrustworthy, just that researchers should take care to check the authorship of the website before citing it and using information contained on its pages.

Researchers should also pay attention to the timeliness of the website. Sometimes websites never remove information, and if you are not careful you might use outdated statistics, quotes, or data by citing a website that has not cleaned out old material. This may not always be the way the timeliness problem manifests itself, however. Consider giving a speech on the election of 2000. Blogs and postings from 2000 would be very relevant. However, those from beyond that year would not be. It is important to pay close attention to when the material you find was produced.

Authorship of a website also matters. A few moments ago we discussed websites designated with ".org" and how they can be questionable sources. Most organizations pursue an agenda, and looking at the mission statement of the organization or the biography of the author that produces the website will give you greater insight as to the biases inherent in the information found on that site. The harder authorship is to determine, the less credibility the researcher should attribute to the information.

Two popular resources on the web are Wikipedia.com and About.com; however, entries on these websites can be unreliable. Anyone can post, edit, or delete information within entries on these websites, thus causing one to question the veracity of the material found there. A good researcher will not use these as references, rather as initial places to get an idea of potential research questions that direct them toward alternative sources of information. See Table 4.2 for tips on how to use these websites.

Table 4.2

Using Wikipedia and Other Online Encyclopedias	
Improper Uses	Proper Uses
Citing in paper or speech	Background information that can direct you to other sources
Believing its accuracy is always reliable	Ideas for speech topics

The web provides many benefits in terms of access to information, but it also makes determining the quality of that information ever more important. An information literate individual can both find the appropriate information and determine its quality, especially when it comes from the Internet.

CITATION GUIDES

Referencing sources is a must for all researchers. When you deliver speeches it creates an added component to the process of identifying sources in that not only must you reference sources in the written outline, you must verbally attribute sources when you speak as well. This attribution is a matter of good ethical behavior because it lets the audience know what is your original work and what you have borrowed from someone else. Properly attributing sources adds to your ethos, or credibility, by demonstrating you give credit where credit is due. When you do not cite your sources or verbally attribute them in your speech, then you call yourself and your information into question and raise the possibility that you may appear to be manipulating your audience. So, to avoid such impressions, always reference your sources in your written and oral work.

Within the field of communication there are two preferred forms for references, each one slightly different from the other. Most who conduct rhetorical research follow the *Chicago Manual of Style (CMS)*, while those who utilize a social scientific approach to exploring communication follow the *American Psychological Association (APA)* manual. You may also encounter a third citation style, that of the *Modern Language Association (MLA)*, when you research in other fields within the liberal arts and humanities. In addition to formal written bibliographies and in-text citations, when speaking students must also verbally attribute their sources. In this part of the chapter we will provide a cursory guide for all three manuals when referencing some common resources, and then we will provide some useful tips for verbally attributing sources within a speech.

The Chicago Manual of Style (CMS)

The Chicago Manual of Style requires the use of footnotes in addition to a bibliography at the end of a manuscript. The CMS publishes a manual that covers all the specifics of citations and bibliographical references, and it is available here: http://owl.english.purdue.edu/owl/resource/717/01/. Here are nine different types of sources and how they are to be cited using the CMS:

Chicago Manual of Style (CMS)
preferred reference manual for rhetorical studies

American Psychological Association (APA)
preferred reference manual for social scientific communication scholars

Modern Language Association (MLA)
a citation style used in disciplines within the liberal arts and humanities

MAGAZINE/NEWSPAPER ARTICLE WITH SINGLE AUTHOR:

Footnote:

> 1. John A. Smith, "Proper Bibliographical Form," *U.S. News and World Report,* April 12, 2006, 30.

Bibliography:

> Smith, John A. "Proper Bibliographical Form." *U.S. News and World Report* vol. 189, issue 6 (12 April 2006): 30.

MAGAZINE/NEWSPAPER ARTICLE WITH MULTIPLE AUTHORS:

Footnote:

> 2. John A. Smith and Joanne Doe, "Proper Bibliographical Form," *Financial Times of London*, June 1, 2000, 17.

Bibliography:

> Smith, John A. and Doe, Joanne. "Proper Bibliographical Form." *Financial Times of London* (1 June 2000): 17.

Magazine/Newspaper Article with No Author:

Footnote:

> 4. "Footnoting Correctly," *The Economist,* December 7, 1999, 19.

Bibliography:

> "Footnoting Correctly." *The Economist* (December 1999), 19-22.

Journal Article:

Footnote:

> 4. John Smith, "The Works Cited Page Is Awesome," *Geopolitics* 9, no. 4 (2002): 38.

Bibliography:

> Smith, John. "The Works Cited Page Is Awesome." *Geopolitics* 9, no. 4 (2002): 35-60.

Chapter in an Edited Volume:

Footnote:

> 5. John Smith, "Footnoting in Alphabetical Order," in *Proper Citations and Works Cited Pages,* edited by S. Clark, J. M. Thompson & P. L. Jones (Boulder, CO: Westview Press, 1987), 8-14.

Bibliography:

> Smith, John. "Footnoting in Alphabetical Order." In *Proper Citations and Works   Cited Pages,* edited by S. Clark, J. M. Thompson & P. L. Jones. Boulder, CO: Westview Press, 1987. 8-14.

Book:

Footnote:

> 6. John A. Smith, *The Value of Footnotes* (Wilmington, DE: Scholarly Resources, 1981), 212.

Bibliography:

> Smith, John A. *The Value of Footnotes.* Wilmington, DE: Scholarly Resources, 1981. 212

WEBSITE:

Footnote:

> 7. "Health and Pregnancy," *WebMD*, http://www.webmd.com/baby/guide/amniocentesis.

Bibliography:

> "Health and Pregnancy." *WebMD.* http://www.webmd.com/baby/guide/amniocentesis.

A LETTER TO THE EDITOR IN A NEWSPAPER:

Bibliography:

Smith, John. "Why I Love Citations." *Las Vegas Review-Journal* (14 August 2007): 12.

GOVERNMENT REPORTS:

Bibliography:

U.S. Department of the Treasury. *Citations and Taxation, 2006.* Washington, DC: U.S. Government Printing Office, 2007.

> Note that there is a difference when citing a letter to the editor and any other article found in a newspaper. CMS also uses footnotes in the text, rather than parenthetical citations. These are identified by a number superscripted at the end of a sentence. Footnotes allow for the use of "ibid" which can be used in place of a full reference when the source is the same as the one in the previous citation. Additionally, if you have already used the full citation for a source in a previous footnote you need only list the author's last name and the page number on all subsequent references to that source. Of course this is just an abbreviated guide for CMS, but it should enable you to get started on citing material properly.

American Psychological Association (APA)

Unlike the CMS, the APA uses in-text parenthetical citations instead of footnotes. These occur at the end of sentences or after an author's name that is referenced in the sentence. In the event the source does not have an identifiable author then it is referenced using a truncated form of the title and the year of publication. In this section we will offer some brief guidance for some common reference types using APA style. First, let's look at some examples of in-text citations using APA:

- One author, not directly quoted: (Smith, 1990)
- Multiple author, not directly quoted: (Smith, Jones & Thompson, 1998)
- With author, directly quoted: (Johnson, 1981, p. 242)
- Multiple author, not directly quoted: (Smith, Jones & Thompson, 1990, p. 461)

- Website with author, not directly quoted: (Stevens, December 1, 2008)
- Website with no author, not directly quoted: ("The sky is blue," April 2, 2003)
- Website with author, directly quoted: (Morris, June 1, 2001, para. 2)
- Website with no author, directly quoted: ("Great sea," February 2, 1991, para.1)

There are some idiosyncrasies to keep in mind as well. For instance, if a work has more than six authors, you should use the last name of the first author and then the phrase "et al." to refer to the rest of the authors. Additionally, if the authors name is written in the sentence then the parenthetical citation needs only to have the year or the year and page number if it is directly quoted from the source. Finally, when a works author is credited as "Anonymous" cite the word anonymous followed by the date in the parenthetical citation.

In addition to the in-text citations, APA calls for a "Reference List" page, which is conceptually the same as the Bibliography in the CMS. Just as is the case with the CMS bibliography page, it is organized alphabetically and contains only the sources referenced within the project. If there is no author, the title is treated as author when it comes to placing it in the proper alphabetical spot in the works cited list. Following are the APA forms of the same references used for the previous CMS examples:

MAGAZINE/NEWSPAPER ARTICLE WITH SINGLE AUTHOR:

Smith, J. (2004 November 9). Proper bibliographical form. *The Toronto Star*, A8.

*Magazine articles only require the month, and not the specific date of publication, so they would appear (2004, November) in the above example.

MAGAZINE/NEWSPAPER ARTICLE WITH MULTIPLE AUTHORS:

Smith, J., Johnson, S. & Morris, M. (2000 January 21). Proper bibliographical form. *Winnipeg Free Press*, A9.

MAGAZINE/NEWSPAPER ARTICLE WITH NO AUTHOR:

The bibliography must be correct. (1987 March 1). *The New York Daily News*, A14.

JOURNAL ARTICLE:

Smith, J. (1993). Studies show bibliographies are easy to do. *European Journal of Communication, 19* (1), 89-114.

*Include the issue number only if the journal is paginated by issue.

CHAPTER IN AN EDITED VOLUME:

Smith, J. & Morris, E. (2008). Bibliographies difficult to master. Tom Johnson, Cedric Phillips, and Maurice Jones (Eds.), In *Citing correctly,* pp. 101-121. New York, NY: Routledge.

BOOK:

Jones, B. (2007). *The power of citing correctly.* Chicago, IL: University of Chicago Press.

WEBSITE:

Simpson, H. (2007 April 1). A letter to John Smith. Retrieved on: January 12, 2008. http://www.xgtsfjmnouiyh.com/jstr/htm/070908

A LETTER TO THE EDITOR FROM A NEWSPAPER:

Smith, J. (2008 June 1). Citations are important [Letter to the editor]. *Miami Herald,* p. A9.

GOVERNMENT REPORTS:

S. Rep. No. 207-294, at 9 (2003).

Pay close attention to the capitalization and punctuation schemes in both APA and CMS as they can be tricky. Citations in either form allow readers and audience members to know where you found the information you used so they can verify it or even use it for their own work. It also is designed to give proper credit to the person whose ideas you are using. Personal interviews do not need to appear in either the CMS or APA reference pages, but must be cited in text by listing the initials and last name of the interviewee and as exact a date as possible for the interview.

Modern Language Association (MLA)

The MLA is a third option for properly citing research within your outlines, manuscripts, or essays. It can be best described as a combination of both CMS and APA in many respects. For example, although footnotes and endnotes can be used to expound upon certain points in the text, the proper way to reference materials in the text is with parenthetical citations just like APA. Unlike APA, the MLA guidelines call for the page number in every parenthetical reference, not simply the ones where you attribute a direct quotation. Here are some examples of in-text citations using MLA guidelines:

- With author: (Smith 3)
- Multiple authors: (Smith, Jones and Thompson 15)
- Unknown author: ("Lakes and Mountains" 72)
- Website: (Stevens, "Lakes and Mountains")

In some ways MLA allows for a simpler method of citing sources within your outline or essay because it calls for the same information regardless of whether or not you used a direct quotation.

In addition to the in-text citations, MLA calls for a "Works Cited" page just like APA. It is organized alphabetically and contains only the sources referenced within the project, just like the bibliography in CMS and the "list of references" in APA. The "Works Cited" page for MLA, however, is closer to that of CMS's bibliography in terms of style. The following are the MLA forms of the same references used for the CMS and APA examples given above:

MAGAZINE/NEWSPAPER ARTICLE WITH SINGLE AUTHOR:

Smith, John. "Proper bibliographical form." *The Toronto Star,* 9 Nov. 2004: A8. Print.

MAGAZINE/NEWSPAPER ARTICLE WITH MULTIPLE AUTHORS:

Smith, John, Johnson, Stephanie O. & Morris, Melvin. "Proper bibliographical form." *Winnipeg Free Press,* 21 Jan. 2000: A9. Print.

MAGAZINE/NEWSPAPER ARTICLE WITH NO AUTHOR:

"The bibliography must be correct." *The New York Daily News*, 1 March 1987: A14. Print.

JOURNAL ARTICLE:

Smith, John. "Studies Show Bibliographies Are Easy to Do." *European Journal of Communication* 19.1 (1993): 89-114. Print.

CHAPTER IN AN EDITED VOLUME:

Smith, John A. & Morris, Eugene. "Chapter 5." *Citing Correctly.* Eds. Tom Johnson, Cedric Phillips, and Maurice Jones. New York, NY: Routledge, 2008. 101-121. Print.

BOOK:

Jones, Bridget. *The Power of Citing Correctly.* Chicago, IL: University of Chicago Press, 2007. Print.

WEBSITE:

Cool Stuff and Things. East Western University, 2007. Web. 12 Jan. 2008.

A LETTER TO THE EDITOR IN A NEWSPAPER:

Smith, John. "Citations are important." Letter. *Miami Herald.* 1 June 2008: A9. Print.

GOVERNMENT REPORTS:

> United States. National Institute of Health. *Citations Are Good for You.*
> DHHS Publication No. ADM 88-788867. Washington: GPO, 1998.
> Print.

Notice that there are some aspects of the MLA works cited entries that make it unique. For instance, titles of articles are placed within quotation marks while names of journals, newspapers, books, and magazines are in italic. Also, with regard to journal entries, their volume and issue numbers are depicted using decimals rather than parentheses.

Each of these three citation styles have their place in academic work and under most circumstances you will be instructed as to which style to use. Your instructor may prefer one form, a journal or magazine may require another—but more often than not you will be informed as to which style to use. If you are not, then use the style you are most comfortable with, but be sure to use it consistently and accurately.

Verbal Attribution

In a speech you not only need to cite sources within your manuscript or outline, but you must verbally do so as well. This is much easier than it sounds and helps you build credibility with your audience. Some common ways speakers verbally attribute sources is to preface the information being cited with "according to" or "so-and-so says," but here are a few more examples to use when constructing a speech that gives proper credit to source material:

- According to a recent Gallup Poll, Senator John McCain is seen as more knowledgeable on foreign policy than his opponent.

- In his book, *Perilous Times*, Dr. Geoffrey Stone argues that the First Amendment should not be suppressed during wartime.

- Some people, like Dr. Johann Strauss, argue the Motion Picture Association of America should think about the intentions of the moviemaker when rating films for public consumption.

- Many major league baseball players used steroids in the 1990s, according to the Mitchell Report produced by former Senator George Mitchell and his investigative team.

Each of these examples provides verbal attribution to the sources where the information was obtained. It is essential for a researcher to give credit like this when speaking because it helps the audience differentiate between the speaker's ideas and ideas that came from someone else.

Oral Source Citations

Adapted from James Madison University School of Communication (2009).

Using information from a website, book, journal article, newspaper article, television program, radio broadcast, or any other written or spoken source, without giving credit to the original source is considered unethical and an act of plagiarism.

**When using significant statistics or facts…
you must cite where you got them!!!**

Your audience does not expect you to have developed all of the ideas contained in your speech. Accordingly, during your speech, you will need to provide oral citations. Such citations are not difficult to include as long as you have completed your research and recorded the information so that you can include it in your speech.

Tips for Oral Citations

Adapted from Holladay, S. & Marsahll, R. (2006). *Using the University Rubric to Assess Individual and Group Presentations.* Eastern Illinois University

You are generally expected to include oral citations of sources in your speeches. Oral citations demonstrate that the presenter has conducted research. It also allows the audience to evaluate the credibility and timeliness of the information. When you are required to prepare a written outline, citations should be included in the outline and a page of listed of references should also be included.

Make certain that you know if you are required to provide written citations in APA or MLA style. Generally in the discipline of Communication, APA format is used. Although there is no APA or MLA citation style for oral citations, there are two styles, formal and casual, that can be used. The formal style of oral citation includes the author(s) (assuming that is available), the publication, the specific publication date and year, and any other pertinent information. The casual style, which some instructors prefer, includes the author and the date.

Other General Tips:

- Tell the audience your source before you use the information (the opposite of in-text citations).

- Do not say, "quote, unquote" when you offer a direct quotation. Use brief pauses instead.

- Provide enough information about each source so that your audience could, with a little effort, find them. This should include the author(s) name, a brief explanation of their credentials, the title of the work, and publication date.

- If your source is unknown to your audience, provide enough information about your source for the audience to perceive them as credible. Typically we provide this credentialing of the source by stating the source's qualifications to discuss the topic.

- Provide a caption citation for all direct quotations and /or relevant images on your PowerPoint slides

Some examples of formal and casual oral citations are provided below.

For a magazine article:

"According to an article by Ben Elgin in the February 20th, 2006 issue of *Business Week*, we can expect Google and Yahoo's supremacy as the search engine giants to be challenged by new U.S. startups. Elgin reports that ..."

Or

"As reported in the February 20th, 2006 issue of *Business Week*, many new companies are getting into the search engine business. This article explains that ..."

Or

"A February 20th, 2006 *Business Week* article reported that Google and Yahoo will face stiff competition in the search engine business ..."

Or

"A 2006 *Business Week* article reported that Google and Yahoo ..."

For a newspaper article:

"On February 22nd, 2006, *USA Today* reported that ..."

Or

"An article about the effects of global warming appeared in the February 22nd edition of *USA Today*. Todd Smith's report focused on the alarming rate of ..."

Or

"An article on global warming that appeared in the February 22nd issue of *USA Today* sounded the alarm ..."

For a web site: (Beware! Not everything presented in the form of a website is credible information. Note if your instructor has specified where your sources should originate, i.e., journals, periodicals, newspapers, etc. If you choose to select websites for your research you will need to evaluate the information.)

- you will need to supply the specific URL in the list of references. Do not recite a long URL in your speech. It is sufficient to report the sponsor/author of the site and the title of the web page (or section of the web site) where the information was obtained. It may also be beneficial to report when the site was last updated.

"According to information I found at www.ready.gov, the web site of the U.S. Department of Homeland Security, U.S. businesses and citizens ..."

Or

"According to information posted on the U.S. Department of Homeland Security's web site, …"

Or

"Helpful information about business continuity planning can be found on the U.S. Department of Homeland Security's web site, located at www.ready.gov …"

Or

"I consulted the web site maintained by the U.S. Department of Homeland Security to learn more about what businesses should do to plan for an emergency. In the section entitled 'Plan to stay in business,' several recommendations for maintaining continuity of business operations were offered. These suggestions included …"

For a journal article: .

"A 2004 study published in *Journal of Applied Social Psychology* reported that incidents of workplace aggression have increased …"

Or

"Research conducted by Dr. Bailey and Dr. Cross at Stanford University found that incidents of workplace aggression have increased over the past five years. Their 2004 study published in the *Journal of Applied Social Psychology* reported that …"

Or

"According to a 2004 study published in the *Journal of Applied Social Psychology*, …"

Or

"A 2004 study conducted by Bailey and Cross in the *Journal of Applied Social Psychology*, …"

Or

"In a 2004 study published in *Journal of Applied Social Psychology*, Bailey and Cross reported that …"

Or

"A 2004 study by Stanford University researchers found that incidents of workplace aggression …"

Or

"Bailey and Cross, experts in workplace aggression, authored a 2004 study that shows that incidents of aggression in the workplace are increasing. Their *Journal of Applied Social Psychology* article reports that …"

For a book:

"In her 2005 book, *Good Health at Any Age,* Dr. Gabriella Campos describes how we can maintain our health through healthy eating. She recommends ..."

Or

"Gabriella Campos, an expert in nutrition, describes what is needed to maintain a healthy diet in her 2005 book *Good Health at Any Age.* She contends that ..."

Or

"In her recent book, *Good Health at Any Age,* Dr. Gabriella Campos recommends ..."

Or

"In *Good Health at Any Age*, Dr. Gabriella Campos, an expert in nutrition, offers suggestions for ..."

For a television program:

"On February 21st our local PBS station aired a program called "The Insurgency." In this program ..."

Or

"According to "The Insurgency", a Frontline program aired by PBS on February 21st, ..."

Or

"Frontline, a PBS program, focused on the Iraq War in the television program entitled "The Insurgency." This show aired on February 21st and focused on the problems confronting ..."

For a personal interview:

"On February 20th I conducted a personal interview with Dr. Desiree Ortez, a psychology professor here at Eastern, to learn more about student responses to peer pressure. Dr. Ortez told me that ..."

Or

"I conducted an interview with Dr. Desiree Ortez, a psychology professor at Eastern Illinois University, and learned that peer pressure is a big problem for university students."

Or

"In an interview I conducted with Dr. Desiree Ortez, a psychology professor, I learned that ..."

Or

"I met with Dr. Desiree Ortez, a psychology professor here at Eastern, to learn more about … She told me that peer pressure is a major factor contributing to academic failure in college."

Or

"In a telephone interview I conducted with Dr. Forest Wiley, a gerontology professor at University of Illinois, I learned that the elderly are likely to feel …"

Or

"I e-mailed Dr. Forest Wiley, a gerontology professor at the University of Illinois, to get additional information on his research on the aging's use of the Internet. He told me …"

SUMMARY

Selecting and narrowing your topic and research and preparation are the most important steps toward developing a successful speech. Proper research skills come from being an information literate person. Information literate people know what they need information for, where to go to find it, and how to use it properly, as well as the ethical implications of information use. It is important to make use of all the research tools at your disposal, from librarians to the Internet, when seeking different types of sources and information for your speech. It is equally important to use a consistent and accepted citation style when referencing material you have gathered from other places.

KEY TERMS

accuracy

American Psychological Association (APA)

background information

bias

Chicago Manual of Style (CMS)

Communication/Mass Media Complete

Dewey Decimal Classification System

enkyklios paideia

evidentiary information

formal survey

ghostwriting

global plagiarism

incremental plagiarism

informal survey

information literacy

interviewing

JSTOR

Lexis-Nexis

Modern Language Association (MLA)

patchwork plagiarism

plagiarism

quadrivium

research question

tangential information

trivium

undercover interviewing

1. What are the three ways you can find a topic?

2. What are the five characteristics of the information literate researcher?

3. What are the three primary forms of information?

4. What are the three main places to find source material?

5. What are the three major citation styles?

1. Is it ever ethical to employ undercover interviewing?

THINK ABOUT IT

2. How do you determine whether you need to cite a piece of information?

3. Which reference style is better? Why?

_____

_____

_____

_____

ACTIVITIES FOR ACTION

1. Sit down with a group of friends, classmates, or colleagues and brainstorm topics for speeches. Each time a person introduces a statement about a topic they are interested in reframe it as a research question. By the end of this discussion you should have a list of potential speech topics that are written as research questions rather than topic statements.

2. Find a partner and go on a scavenger hunt for the following items: a magazine article; a newspaper article; a government document; a peer reviewed journal article in communication studies; a documentary film; a news page from microfiche records; a survey result; a blog entry; and an interview transcript. To complicate this activity, give yourself a topic that each item must relate to. For instance, find one of each item related to the topic of the "Beatles musical invasion."

3. Find a bibliography at the end of a journal article. If it is in APA format, translate it into MLA and CMS style; if it is in MLA style, change it to CMS and APA style; if it is in CMS style, reformat it into APA and MLA style.

ENDNOTES

1. Edward Alexander Parsons, *The Alexandrian Library* (Barking, Essex, England: Elsevier Publishing, 1952), 83-106.

2. Ibid.

3. Roy MacLeod, "Introduction: Alexandria in History and Myth," in *The Library of Alexandria: Centre of Learning in the Ancient World,* ed. Roy MacLeod (New York, NY: St. Martin's Press, 2000), 4-7.

4. Randy Pausch with Jeffrey Zaslow, *The Last Lecture* (New York, NY: Hyperion Books, 2008).

5. Erin Neff, "Gibbon's Speech Plagiarism: 15 Paragraphs Came from Copyrighted Talk by Alabama Woman," *Las Vegas Review Journal,* March 4, 2005.

6. http://speeches.empireclub.org/61435/data?n=2 (accessed May 28, 2011).

Delivery

- Discusses the elements of verbal delivery and ways to effectively use it when giving a speech
- Focuses on the various nuances of nonverbal styles and discusses the symbiotic relationship between nonverbal and verbal delivery
- Differentiates between the four main ways a speech is delivered

Practically SPEAKING

In the 1986 movie, *Ferris Bueller's Day Off*, the economics teacher, played by Ben Stein, goes on a tirade about the economy when his students do not respond to questions. Using a lethargic delivery, Stein woefully makes his potentially vibrant points seem irrelevant, boring, and hard to focus upon. Stein uses the term "anyone?" 14 times during the entire scene.[1] While he is speaking the students in the class predictably fall asleep, put their heads down on desks, and stare off into the distance, daydreaming. Stein's portrayal of the dreadfully boring teacher emphasizes the importance of vocal and physical delivery when addressing an audience.

The combination of word repetition, vocal emphasis, and proper posture and gestures can add force and meaning to a speaker's words, but when delivered in a monotone voice with no energy, the rhetorical effect is minimal. In addition to no vocal variety, Stein's posture is lethargic, making him appear as bored as his students. He lacks presence, despite having content.

Verbal delivery works in tandem with nonverbal delivery. The verbal content of Stein's speech in this scene is clear, but the repeated begging for "anyone" to answer does nothing to get the audience's attention. His leaning posture and pleading facial expressions underscore his poor verbal delivery and only worsen matters. As illustrated by Stein, verbal and nonverbal delivery can display the speaker's attitude toward themselves and the audience.

Too much focus on delivery, however, can also produce problems. A powerful delivery can detract from content if the audience members focus more on delivery than content. Good delivery comes from practice and balances a desire to gain and maintain attention with the need to keep the audience focused on the message. Audiences do not notice good delivery, rather they remember the content conveyed without saying much about how the speaker conveyed it.

A speaker may have great ideas, a new way to do something, or a way to improve life on campus, but if the speaker mumbles, does not project his voice, fails to make eye contact, and does not present himself in a pleasing physical manner, the ideas will likely be lost upon the audience. All of us have seen, or delivered, a speech in an awkward manner. This makes not only the speaker feel uncomfortable, but can also cause anxiety and even mental pain in the audience, and that makes it doubtful that the audience will believe the information or take an action the speaker desires.

This chapter will cover the basics of good speech delivery, both verbal and nonverbal, and how the two work together. It will also provide some commonsense ways to improve delivery and discuss the four distinct ways a speaker can deliver a speech to an audience.

Verbal Elements of Delivery

The most obvious aspect of public speaking is verbal delivery. Without a voice you cannot speak. That said, just because you have a voice does not mean verbal delivery is easy for you. In fact, mastering verbal delivery takes lots of practice even when you understand the fundamentals of verbal delivery. Those fundamentals include pronunciation and articulation. Both of those characteristics contribute to the development and use of different dialects and slang. In this part of the chapter we will cover each of those four aspects of verbal delivery and how they play a part in public speaking.

Pronunciation and Articulation

Having a strong vocabulary depends upon two things: knowing the words, and being able to pronounce them. If you only know the words and cannot speak them properly then all you can do is listen to someone speak, inhibiting your ability to respond. If, on the other hand, you can also pronounce the words correctly, then you can become conversant in a particular language.

Proper word *pronunciation*, the accepted standard of how a word sounds, is very important to a speaker. It is one thing in casual conversation to mispronounce words, but quite another in a formal public speaking situation. Mispronouncing words sends a message of lack of preparation and creates the possible impression that the speaker is illiterate or not very bright. See Table 5.1 for a list of commonly mispronounced words.

pronunciation
the accepted standard of how a word sounds when spoken

We mispronounce words for a variety of reasons. Sometimes we learn how to say a word from hearing others say it first, except they may wrongly pronounce the word to begin with. Other times we try to speak too quickly, resulting in slips of the tongue on more complex words. Whatever the reason, speakers need to correctly pronounce words. Mispronunciation damages a speaker's credibility, the heart of a speaker's ethos. It might not be quite as big a deal in conversation or even in the classroom, but in the business world it can mean getting a job or making a sale—or not.

Table 5.1

Most Commonly Mispronounced Words	
The website yourdictionary.com lists 100 of the more commonly mispronounced words on its website.[2] Do you make any of these errors? The left column notes how these incorrectly pronounced words would be spelled.	
Common Mispronunciation	**Correct Pronunciation**
anartic	Antarctic
aks	ask
calvary	cavalry
fedral	federal
hiarchy	hierarchy
irregardless	regardless
jewlry	jewelry
libel	liable
libary	library
nucular	nuclear
perogative	prerogative

articulation
....
physically producing the sound needed to convey the word

Closely related to pronunciation is *articulation*, or physically producing the sound needed to convey the word. In many cases we commit articulation errors by picking up bad habits from others through modeling; in other cases we are just plain lazy. Some of the more common articulation errors occur when speakers intermingle and blend two words together. For example, "I don't know" becomes "I dunno," "give me" is reduced to "gimme," or "would have" transforms into "woulda." There are more egregious articulation errors, such as running three words together like when "I bet you" becomes "Ibetcha." A speaker may get away with sloppy pronunciation and articulation in casual situations, but professional settings often demand correct speech.

Dialects and Slang

People from different regions of the United States sound different when they speak, yet they speak the same language and communicate with general success. Anyone who travels to Boston will hear people articulate their "a's" as "ah's," and anyone who goes to states below the Mason-Dixon line will find people saying "y'all" rather than "you all." The latter of these two examples is often referred to as southern drawl due to the slower speech pattern.

dialect
....
aspects of articulation, grammar, vocabulary, and pronunciation that differ from Standard English

So, what are these differences and how do they occur? They are referred to as *dialect*, or aspects of articulation, grammar, vocabulary, and pronunciation that differ from Standard English. The term "dialect" comes from the Ancient Greek term *dialektos,* meaning a tongue, or the language of a particular group of people that makes them distinct.

A dialect is a sort of subgroup of a language, and it can result in some miscommunication between a speaker and an audience when an audience is either unaware of or cannot decipher a speaker's dialect. As Sarah Trenholm notes: "Problems occur when one dialect is defined as the standard and given greater status than other dialects."[3] The important thing to remember is that dialects are regionally accepted errors of articulation and/or pronunciation, and one is not any better or more accurate than another.

Those who speak a particular dialect sometimes develop additions to the general standard vocabulary. In the case of Standard English, certain regions develop words and phrases that are understood by those who reside there, but not by those who do not. Over time these words are appropriated by the general population and become part of mainstream culture. When this happens the terms become *slang*, or words derived from dialects that most people understand but do not use in professional writing or speaking.

slang
......
words derived from dialects that most people understand but do not use in professional writing or speaking

Cultures usually develop their own forms of slang. Watch an old gangster movie and you will hear actors using terms such as "heater," "roscoe," "piece," or "rod" when referring to a weapon used to "bump off," "ice," or "whack" an enemy. If caught, the shooters might find themselves in "the big house." Each of these terms grew from a small part of society and infiltrated mainstream culture. The terms represented the language used by a subsection of Americans, and eventually they were immortalized in the movies and through other cultural experiences. At that point, the words no longer belonged to a particular group, but rather they became part of the general population.

Take the case of the word "ain't," which until recent versions of the Webster's Dictionary was not considered a word, but rather a slang pronunciation of the term "isn't." The use of the word "ain't" can even be seen in some landmark speeches in American history, such as the one delivered by Sojourner Truth at the Women's Convention in 1851 (see the nearby box).

Slang also is not cemented in society; that is to say, some terms may die over time. Think about the gangster example from the previous paragraph. Do you hear about people being sent to "the big house" for "bumping off someone" at the same level you might have 50 or 60 years ago? The answer is no, and the reason is that the usability of the terms as slang is dying out. Now you might hear that someone is "in the can" for "popping a cap" in someone. This phrasing, too, may leave common vernacular if it hasn't already!

Slang, although common, has no place in a professional setting or speech. For quite some time "that sucks" has been used to show displeasure, but carefully listen to how that sounds. Professionalism or intellect does not come to mind when we hear people use this phrase. The context surrounding a speech invites the use of Standard English, not slang.

Nonverbal Elements of Delivery

In addition to verbal delivery, or the words you use, nonverbal delivery also aids in the transmission of messages to an audience and can, in fact, play a much larger role in the success of a speech. Nonverbal delivery can be broken down into two

Ain't I a Woman?
by Sojourner Truth

Delivered in 1851 at the Women's Convention in Akron, Ohio

Born Isabella Baumfree, Sojourner Truth was raised in slavery. She worked the fields as men did and suffered many physical abuses, including beatings at the hands of more than one slave master.[4] Truth eventually became a free woman and well-known minister. One memorable speech she delivered in this role was entitled "Ain't I a Woman."

The speech was short, especially by the standards of the day, clocking in at only 3,356 words, but nonetheless compelling. She made use of repetition in her address, specifically a phrase that included grammatical slang. The inclusion and repetition of that slang phrase enhanced the delivery of the speech. Take a look at the following excerpt:

"And ain't I a woman? Look at me! Look at my arm! I have ploughed and planted, and gathered into barns, and no man could head me! And ain't I a woman? I could work as much and eat as much as a man - when I could get it - and bear the lash as well! And ain't I a woman? I have borne thirteen children, and seen most all sold off to slavery, and when I cried out with my mother's grief, none but Jesus heard me! And ain't I a woman?"[5]

In this speech Truth brought issues such as race and gender to the forefront of her audience's minds. Given that it took place in 1851, these issues would remain important for the American public for years to come. When one considers the lack of rights that all women had at this time and then considers her race, Sojourner Truth's speech was certainly remarkable.

distinct areas: nonverbal elements related to voice, and nonverbal characteristics of the body. These aspects of your delivery serve several purposes when it comes to speaking, and a successful presentation incorporates good nonverbal delivery with strong verbal delivery. In this part of the chapter we will discuss the two types of nonverbal delivery and the functions of nonverbal delivery for public speakers.

Vocalics

When people think of the nonverbal aspects of speech they focus on the body, but actually most nonverbal behaviors emanate from the voice. When we focus on how loud a person is, whether their voice is dull or nasally, and how fast or slow they speak, then we are looking at nonverbal actions. Think about it this way: are any of these things associated with pronunciation, articulation, or vocabulary? No, so therefore they are not categorized as elements of verbal delivery. We call these things a *vocalic*, or anything that contributes to the creation or maintenance of sound in a person's voice.

One vocalic is the volume of a person's voice. Volume refers to how loud or soft a person's voice is when they speak, and controlling it is trickier than you may realize. Volume can be augmented or reduced based on environmental factors, such as the acoustics of a wall. The distance between the speaker and the audience and whether a microphone is available for use can also influence volume. If a voice is too loud then the audience may leave; if it is too soft they may not receive the speaker's message.

Each of us, at one time or another, has been an audience member when someone was speaking too softly and we had to strain to hear what the speaker was saying. At its best this is a distraction, but it may also be considered either lazy or rude. It can show shyness, anxiety, a lack of preparation, being unsure, or a speaker's lack of interest in being there. In all of these cases, if an audience cannot hear a speaker then the credibility of that speaker is damaged.

That does not mean that the speaker should shout at the audience. Rather, the speaker should use sufficient volume so that the person farthest from him can hear with ease. The size of the room can often influence your decision on how loud you must speak. If you are in a large room, especially one not having a microphone, it might be necessary to simply ask if everyone can comfortably hear you. If not, perhaps you speak louder or move closer to the audience to make sure everyone can hear you.

Volume alone does not constitute vocalics. Another element is *tone*, or the syllabic emphasis on a sound that expresses emotion or meaning. Think about our example from the beginning of the chapter. The tone of Ben Stein's character illustrates how speech that has no tonal inflection or variety can quickly lose an audience by conveying a lack of interest in the subject, audience, and occasion. Monotone deliveries can also quickly bore the audience and distract them from the purpose and goals of the speech itself. If you are excited about your speech, topic, and opportunity to speak to the audience it will be conveyed in your tone and make the speech all the more interesting to listen to for the audience.

Tone also expresses different emotions when you adjust it for specific words. Sarcasm is often conveyed through the use of a different tone of voice when making a statement that otherwise might mean something else. Think about the inflection in someone's voice when they respond to the question, "How are you doing today?" If they respond "fine" it could mean they are doing ok, but it can also intimate that they are not ok if the word is given a sharper, more cutting edge. This is when we might hear someone say that they "heard" some emotion in the person's voice. Tone is a nonverbal vocalic that expresses emotion.

Another aspect of vocalics is the rate at which you speak. The rate, or pace, of your speech can be the result of a variety of things. The average rate of speech in the United States is 150 words per minute.[6] This rate may vary by region. For example, people often observe that individuals from the Northeast speak much faster than those from the rest of the country, so culture can play a role in speech rate. It is also quite normal for a nervous speaker to speak more rapidly than someone who is comfortable.

Just as failing to speak loudly enough can communicate many negatives to the audience, speaking too rapidly can also communicate nervousness, a desire to just get the speech over with, and the perception that you are speaking directly off of notes. If you are worried about your rate of speech there are a few things you can do. You might want to audiotape yourself in a normal speaking situation or practicing your speech. If you have a concern that you might get caught up in the moment and begin to speak rapidly, you might want to put visual cues in your notes, such as a hand-drawn slow or stop sign on your speaking outline to remind you not to speak too fast.

One final element of vocalics is pausing. Pauses are normal, necessary, and, in many circumstances, useful tools. Professors use this tactic quite often to quell students talking among themselves in class. Pausing can be effectively used, as when you stop after making a point you want the audience to consider. They also can be effective for allowing the audience to catch up, and you yourself to catch a breath. They can even be used to recognize and subdue an unruly or rude audience. Consider this scenario: Some students are chatting among themselves during class, and the professor pauses and looks at the students until they stop. They stop because the students feel that the whole class's attention is on their conversation, resulting in them ending the rude behavior.

Pauses can be a powerful tool for any speaker, as they can help emphasize something of importance. After providing a compelling statistic, or story, a pause of a few seconds will alert the audience that something dramatic was just said, or is about to be stated. As with all other vocal qualities, the pause must seem natural and timing is crucial. Using pauses effectively is a skill you learn with practice, and they can be a distraction if you are not careful. Awkward pauses make the speaker look unprepared, unsure, or nervous.

vocalized pauses

utterances that are not words and have no place in a speech, but are done instead of pausing the delivery of the speech

Some speakers feel pressure to speak all the time, and thus they do not pause. Instead they fill the perceived void with a noise like "er," "um," "ah," and "uh" when they speak. These utterances have a variety of names, but generally they are called *vocalized pauses*. Even polished speakers can fall prey to this speaking irregularity. We have all seen speakers stammer and overuse these annoying pauses and inflections, and we realize how much they hurt the delivery of the speech. Kept at a bare minimum they may not be much of a problem, but as a speaker you should strive to limit their interfering with your speech's delivery.

Kinesics

kinesics

nonverbal behaviors related to movement

Your voice, although an important element, is not the only nonverbal aspect of your delivery. Your body also conveys information about credibility and emotions to the audience through facial expressions, gestures, posture, appearance, and eye contact, otherwise known as *kinesics*. These nonverbal behaviors are often the hardest to control, but when you learn to do so they can significantly impact your speech.

The face is often the first thing people notice about you in any situation, and speaking is no different. Your face expresses emotions and sends messages to the audience in a way that can either aid or damage your ability to get your message across to an audience. If you try to say something you do not believe in, your facial expressions will often give you away, but when you do believe what you are saying then it can illustrate your sincerity to the audience in a way no amount of evidence or list of credentials ever could. How you handle your facial expressions is important, but not nearly as challenging as determining what to do with other parts of your body.

One of the things speakers often struggle with when giving a presentation is what to do with their hands. Hands can be effective tools for a speaker, but they also can become unwanted distractions if not treated properly. Hands are the primary source of a *gesture*, or physical movements used to convey a message. Skilled speakers use their hands to complement their messages, pointing to people mentioned in a speech when possible, making forceful motions to emphasize a point, or even smiling when telling a joke.

gesture

a physical movement used to convey a message

posture

the position of your body

In addition to gestures, your posture is also important when trying to convey a message to an audience. *Posture* refers to the position of your body, and when it comes to public speaking it means more than simply facing the audience. If you lean over the podium or slouch behind it, your posture conveys a negative impression to the audience, just as it does when you stand rigidly and do not move. The key to good posture in delivery is being comfortable, yet confident. See the examples of good and bad posture in Figure 5.1.

Figure 5.1
Examples of Bad Posture (top) and Good Posture (bottom)

Having a comfortable and confident posture is related to the effective use of gestures. To maintain the ability to gesture effectively in a speech you should not keep your hands in your pockets, folded in front of you, or even held behind your back. These positions all negatively impact your posture by making you appear uncomfortable. Good posture is relaxed and allows you to make use of your hands when needed.

The next aspect of nonverbal communication we will discuss is appearance. Some professors require students to "dress up" when speaking, some do not. Even if you are not expected to wear more formal clothing you should always dress neatly, with your hair in place, and never wear a hat or cap. If you do not respect your own appearance your audience will not respect you and you will never be able to get your message across to them.

Appearance also can boost your self-confidence and help you feel successful even before you say a word. Consider how you feel when you have on your best clothes. We all feel more competent and confident in what we do. When you dress professionally for a presentation it often results in better actual and perceived performance. Appearance is especially important for speakers who address an audience that is unfamiliar with them, because the first impression the audience makes of the speaker is based on the speaker's appearance. See Table 5.2 for appearance tips.

Table 5.2

Appearance Tips
• Dress neatly   • Do not wear headgear   • Comb or brush your hair   • Overdress rather than underdress

The last category of nonverbal action we will discuss is eye contact, perhaps the most feared nonverbal action undertaken by speakers. Novice speakers often get nervous when they realize they need to look at the audience during their presentation. This is understandable, but eye contact conveys confidence and interest in the audience, making it an indispensable aspect of any speech. One way to minimize the pressure created by eye contact is to look at a speech as a series of conversations. Instead of a speech consisting of you talking to a group of, for example, 25 people, view it as 25 individual one-on-one conversations. We typically are not afraid of individual conversations, and so we make eye contact with the other participant. Taking the same perspective on larger speaking engagements might help. In any event, eye contact, gestures, and posture all play a role in the delivery of a message to an audience.

Functions of Nonverbal Communication in Speech

As individuals we send more nonverbal messages than verbal ones, and when we deliver speeches these nonverbal messages are under even greater scrutiny by an audience than they are in everyday interactions. As such, it is important for speakers to understand the various purposes their gestures, posture, and eye contact can serve with regard to their presentation. In this section we will look at the five positive ways nonverbal messages can influence perceptions of your speech, and the one negative role they could play in your delivery if you are not careful.

One way nonverbal actions can influence your message is by allowing you to reiterate your verbal message without saying it. When physical actions restate verbal messages in this manner, then nonverbal behaviors *repeat* their verbal counterparts. You can make use of this function by pointing to people in the audience as you reference them, or using your fingers to count along when listing certain items or points.

Nonverbal messages can also amplify, or *accent,* your desired message. For example, when you wish to emphasize a point you can pound on the podium at the end of stating the point. When you get excited about something you are saying you can raise a fist in a mock sign of triumph. Not only do these behaviors support your message, but they increase its power and the likelihood the audience will understand your point.

Nonverbal actions are most effective, however, when they *complement* the verbal message. This occurs when the nonverbal message is the same as the verbal message. A perfect model of this is when a speaker laughs at a joke he inserts into his speech. By laughing, he displays the action associated with the verbal content of the joke.

© Christopher Halloran/Shutterstock.com

Facial expressions and body movement can also *substitute* for verbal content on occasion. A person who smiles after being introduced to speak does not necessarily need to state her enjoyment at being there as her smile conveys that message. When a speaker asks a question to which she (and no one else for that matter) knows the answer to, she may follow with a simple shrug of the shoulder instead of saying, "I don't know." These nonverbal actions substitute for verbal messages and can be effective ways to keep an audience's attention.

One other positive function nonverbal messages perform is to *regulate* an interaction. During normal conversations nonverbal actions such as pauses and hand gestures can cue responses and comments from the other person. During speeches they serve much the same purpose, allowing an audience to know when they can ask questions, when they should clap, and when they should cheer. Speakers most often employ regulating nonverbal cues to indicate an end to the speech, or to help guide question and answer sessions.

On the downside, nonverbal cues that *conflict* can negatively influence your ability to get your message across. These occur when your message says one thing, but your body sends the opposite message. This underscores the importance for you as a student to select a topic you are interested in and care about when preparing a speech for class. If you choose a topic you do not care about, your body and vocal variety will betray you. It is extremely difficult to hide your true feelings about a topic or speech because of the prevalence of nonverbal communication in any speech.

repeat
when physical actions restate verbal messages

accent
nonverbal behaviors that augment a verbal message

complement
when the action demonstrates the message contained in the verbal content

Former President George W. Bush uses nonverbal communication to make a point during a speech

substitute
physical actions that take the place of verbal messages

regulate
nonverbal actions that help govern the course of a speech or interaction

conflict
nonverbal cues that convey a message that contradicts the verbal statements of the speaker

MODES OF DELIVERY

Speech delivery encompasses more than verbal and nonverbal skills; it also refers to what style speakers use to deliver their messages to their audiences. Different contexts allow speakers the opportunity to bring different amounts of notes and preparation with them. There are four primary modes of speech delivery available, and in this part we will define and discuss each of them.

Memorized Speeches

As you can recall from the chapter on classical Roman rhetoric at the beginning of the book, Cicero considered memory one of the five canons of rhetoric because during his time people considered memorizing a speech a characteristic of quality speech-making. Another famous Greek, Demosthenes, felt that the three most important parts of public speaking were "delivery, delivery, and delivery." Nowadays, a *memorized speech*, the likes of which Cicero and Demosthenes delivered, are rare thanks in large part to Teleprompters and the accepted practice of using notes during a speech. Nevertheless, students often believe instructors will force them to memorize their speeches before they deliver them, something that is often not the case.

memorized speech
when a speaker commits an entire speech to memory and delivers with no notes in front of him/her

Memorized speeches depend upon an intimate relationship between the speaker and the text. In addition to delivering the speech, the speakers must also author the speech well in advance. They must practice the speech, not just so they remember the exact phrasing, but also so they can pinpoint when to change their volume and tone and when to make gestures to help emphasize points.

Memorized speeches are typically only possible when there is significant advance notice for a presentation. The speakers then use that time to develop and practice the speech as much as possible so they can commit the words and timing of nonverbal actions to memory. These are, hands down, the most time-consuming speeches to deliver, and they also come with certain drawbacks.

One such pitfall of a memorized speech involves the speaker's inability to adjust her message to audience feedback. When delivering a memorized speech there is no margin for changing the wording based on a disinterested (or interested) audience. For example, if you deliver a memorized speech designed to persuade an audience to vote for a specific candidate and you notice at one point the audience expresses dissatisfaction with one of your arguments, as the speaker you cannot adjust or defend the point you made any further than what you memorized, thus inhibiting your ability to adapt to the occasion. Conversely, if the audience appears to really respond to one of your arguments, you also cannot adjust to capitalize on that excitement. In effect, with a memorized speech your speech is *it*.

A second, and potentially more dangerous, risk associated with memorized speeches relates to freezing up. You may extensively prepare and practice the speech beforehand, but when you get in front of the audience you might forget something, causing you to pause too long and lose your place. Such a mistake can cost you dearly as you have no notes to fall back on. The only way to salvage this

SPOTLIGHTING THEORISTS: DEMOSTHENES

Demosthenes (384–322 B.C.)

Considered one of the greatest of the Attic orators in Ancient Greece, Demosthenes reportedly gave his first speech in court arguing to receive what was left of his inheritance. He became a speechwriter and lawyer in Athens, and eventually became one of the leading voices in opposition to Philip II of Macedon and his son Alexander the Great. Demosthenes, like Socrates and Cicero, eventually died in the service of his principles. He took his own life rather than be arrested by Alexander's supporters. Many of his contemporaries lauded him and his contributions to oratory.

Praise for Demosthenes came from many corners of the classical world. Cicero, the father of the five canons of rhetoric, proclaimed Demosthenes the "perfect orator"[7] and Quintilian stated Demosthenes was "by far the most excellent"[8] of the Greek orators. Like Cicero, Demosthenes believed that speakers should be educated on what they talk about and therefore often declined to speak on subjects he had not studied before. Additionally, Demosthenes valued delivery (gestures) above rhetorical flourish and style, believing that these elements of a speech contributed more to its success.

To that end, stories tell of Demosthenes practicing his own speeches in unique fashion. One story tells that he practiced his speech in front of a roaring waterfall in order to work on projecting his voice. Another speaks of how he would practice his presentations with pebbles in his mouth to concentrate on improving his pronunciation and articulation of words. For Demosthenes, delivery truly represented the most important aspect of any speech.

---

type of brain freeze is to continue speaking at the next part of the speech you can recall. This will at least enable you to get back in some form of rhythm.

Thankfully, for beginning students memorized speeches are not typically expected as it takes extraordinary amounts of experience with public speaking to become comfortable with this type of delivery. On the opposite end of the spectrum, however, lie speeches most students want to deliver: ones where the entire speech is right in front of you when you present.

Manuscript Speeches

Whereas most students fear the possibility of memorized speeches, they welcome the chance at delivering a *manuscript speech.* Manuscript speeches are commonplace today, although they may not seem to be so. Politicians frequently deliver them. When the president gives an address before Congress he speaks directly off of a Teleprompter; when he speaks from the Rose Garden he does so

manuscript speech
when a speaker has an entire speech written out word-for-word in front of him/her as s/he speaks

with the script right in front of him; and, when the president of your university or college speaks at a convocation or graduation he or she usually reads from a manuscript. Just because it is acceptable for a variety of occasions, however, does not mean it is the only, or even best, form of delivery.

Speaking off of a manuscript carries with it many positives for a speaker, particularly a newcomer to public address. You do not have to fear the freeze as you might with a memorized presentation. Your speech will come off as organized, or at least as organized as you made the manuscript. The opportunity to jump off the manuscript is possible, but it is constrained by the need to stay focused on your message. Finally, manuscript style speaking allows you to note where you need to make gestures and employ different nonverbal actions at moments during your speech. No wonder first-time speakers prefer the manuscript style!

Despite the enormous benefits afforded by manuscript style addresses, the form is not a panacea. Making adjustments to audience feedback, though possible, is extraordinarily difficult without experience. Additionally, there is a temptation to stare directly at the manuscript, reading to the audience, making you appear distant and disinterested in the audience—not to mention unable to gauge their reaction to what you say. Manuscript speeches invite speakers to focus on their script, and not the audience or their own gestures and reactions, making it hard to successfully incorporate effective and positive nonverbal communication into the presentation.

The main reason beginning speakers relish manuscript speaking is that it eliminates the freeze factor; however, it can also create a much less energetic speech and ultimately distance the speaker from the audience. There is a middle ground, however, between manuscript and memorized speeches and we will discuss that style next.

Extemporaneous Speeches

extemporaneous speech

a speech delivered with notes but not the entire speech in front of the speaker

Since instructors do not normally expect memorized speeches, and yet typically do not allow students to deliver manuscript speeches, how then are most student speeches delivered? The answer is that most student speeches are an *extemporaneous speech*, or a speech delivered with notes but not the entire speech in front of the speaker. Extemporaneous speaking requires practice, much like memorized speeches, but also allows for speakers to have organized references in front of them in case they lose their place during the presentation. These speeches, much like the other two speeches discussed above, have positive and negative qualities of which every speaker needs to be aware.

The primary benefit of using notes instead of a full manuscript or memorized style of delivery is that you will have a more natural and fluid delivery. You can adapt to audience feedback and expound on or eliminate examples and points based upon the audience's reaction to what and how you are saying something. Your vocal inflections and physical gestures are not planned and therefore do not risk coming across as rigid and robotic, as in the other styles of delivery. When you stress an inflection of a word or syllable, or gesture in support of a particular statement, it comes from your emotions, not your guide, providing your audience with a perception of authenticity.

A secondary benefit of extemporaneous speaking is improved eye contact. This also helps improve natural delivery. With only notes in front of you it becomes possible to provide more eye contact to the audience, increasing your connection and identification with them, thus making you appear more believable. As we discussed earlier, eye contact is an essential part of any successful speech, and extemporaneous speaking allows you to make eye contact with the audience while also being able to check your notes if you lose your place.

As you can probably imagine, extemporaneous delivery depends upon two things: adequate practice and a strong organized set of notes. To deliver a believable address with only notes you must spend a significant amount of time practicing the speech. First, you practice with a full text draft, but over time you reduce it to a speaking outline where only direct quotations appear in full text form. This speaking outline comes from paring down a full sentence outline, and still retains the same structural format of the original, only with far fewer words and phrases. The process of drafting, practicing, and then constructing a speaking outline for use during the actual presentation takes a lot of time, but the payoff when you speak more than accounts for that investment.

The most significant obstacles to a successful extemporaneous speech involve creating an effective speaking outline and keeping your notes organized. Some people who deliver speeches off of notes use bullet lists or even note cards in their speech. Bullet lists are dangerous because they are not structured, and thus you can easily lose your place when staring back and forth at the list. Note cards can be problematic, especially if they are not numbered for their order of occurrence, because you might drop them or put them in an incorrect order, causing you to lose your place or get flustered when delivering the speech. These problems, however, can be minimized and even eliminated through extensive practice and preparation for the presentation. There are, however, some speeches that allow for little to no preparation.

Impromptu Speeches

At one time or another in your life you will need to speak without any preparation, research, or notes. This unplanned, unprepared presentation is called an *impromptu speech*, and it can be as short as a minute or as long as 10, depending on the topic, speaker, and situation. This may also be the most nerve-racking type of speech. Even the most experienced orator will feel a bit jittery when called on to speak about something without any preparation.

impromptu speech
a presentation done with little or no preparation

When called upon to deliver impromptu remarks it is best to first collect your thoughts and quickly develop a mental outline of what you wish to say. Just because these speeches have no preparation time does not mean they should not be organized or logical. Two aspects are always handy when asked to deliver such remarks: the situation and the audience. Connecting your comments to both provides an easy way to focus your remarks.

Secretary of State Hillary Clinton delivers an impromptu speech at a press conference in Chappaqua, NY

©Marianne Campolongo/Shutterstock.com

One of the most common places where you may deliver impromptu remarks is during a celebratory event honoring someone or something. No one will warn you that you might speak, you will not have prepared for the moment, and you might be surprised at the opportunity, but remember to identify with the audience and the event. It may also behoove you to reference the fact that you had no idea you might be speaking, thus acknowledging to the audience the impromptu nature of the address. These are high stress speeches, but also often very short. Audiences also typically have lower expectations for impromptu speeches than they do for a planned presentation.

SUMMARY

Delivery is a complicated and important element of any speech, and it is also the one part of public speaking that engenders the most fear in people. Delivery is divided into three parts, each with equal importance. The first is verbal delivery, which focuses on correctly speaking the language. The second part of delivery involves nonverbal actions, from vocal variety to physical gestures and posture. Finally, the style of presenting the material allows for memorizing a script, reading off a manuscript, blending the two to read off of notes, or delivering unplanned remarks. We must remember that presenting the speech is just as important (and complex) as planning it.

KEY TERMS

accent	memorized speech
articulation	posture
complement	pronunciation
conflict	regulate
dialect	repeat
extemporaneous speech	slang
gesture	substitute
impromptu speech	tone
kinesics	vocalic
manuscript speech	vocalized pauses

REVIEW QUESTIONS

1. What are the two fundamentals of verbal delivery?

   _____

   _____

2. What is the difference between dialects and slang?

   _____

   _____

3. What are the two major nonverbal elements of delivery?

   _____

   _____

4. What are the five functions of nonverbal communication in speech?

   _____

   _____

5. What are the four types of speech delivery?

   _____

   _____

THINK ABOUT IT

1. How would you define great delivery?

   _____

   _____

   _____

   _____

2. Which of the nonverbal characteristics of delivery is most important?

   _____

   _____

   _____

   _____

3. How do you determine the proper relationship between nonverbal and verbal delivery?

   _____

   _____

   _____

   _____

ACTIVITIES FOR ACTION

1. Write down two sentences of average length about any particular topic; the content does not matter for this exercise. Then, take a sheet of paper and cut it into six pieces. On each sheet of paper write one of the following emotions: angry, happy, sad, confused, excited, depressed. Then, on the back of each sheet write a different emotion than the one on the front. Ask a friend to pick a sheet of paper, then give them the sentences you wrote and ask them to say those sentences using the emotion on the top of the paper they selected. Finally, ask them to convey the emotion on the other side of the paper without speaking. See if you or others in the audience can accurately identify the emotions.

2. Try saying the following tongue twisters as many times as you can in a row without any errors in pronunciation or articulation: "Sally sells sea shells by the seashore;" "How can a clam cram in a clean cream can?" "The thirty three thieves thought that they thrilled the throne Thursday." "Picky people pick Peter Pan peanut butter." And, if you really want a challenge: "Out in the pasture the nature watcher watches the catcher, while the catcher watches the pitcher who pitches the balls. Whether the temperature's up or whether the temperature's down, the nature watcher, the catcher, and the pitcher are always around. The pitcher pitches, the catcher catches, and

the watcher watches. So whether the temperature rises or the temperature falls the nature watcher just watches the catcher who's watching the pitcher who's watching the balls."

3. We all know the challenge presented by vocalized pauses and the importance of limiting their occurrence. To practice speaking without using a vocalized pause have a friend time you speaking on any given topic as long as you can until you use a vocalized pause. The larger the audience the better for this exercise, as everyone starts listening for the vocalized pauses. The person who goes the longest wins.

ENDNOTES

1. *Ferris Bueller's Day Off*, written and directed by John Hughes (Paramount Pictures, 1986).

2. http://www.yourdictionary.com/library/mispron.html (accessed June 10, 2008).

3. Sarah Trenholm, *Thinking Through Communication: An Introduction to the Study of Human Communication* (Boston, MA: Pearson Publishing, 2005).

4. http://www.lkwdpl.org/wihohio/trut-soj.htm.

5. http://www.feminist.com/resources/artspeech/genwom/sojour.htm.

6. http://www.ncvs.org/ncvs/tutorials/voiceprod/tutorial/quality.html (accessed June 9, 2008).

7. G. L. Hendrickson, trans., *Cicero: In Twenty Eight Volumes. Brutus, with an English Translation* (Harvard University Press, 1988), 41.

8. James J. Murphy, trans., *Quintilian: On the Teaching of Speaking and Writing* (Southern Illinois University Press, 1987), 136.

Presentation Aids

6

- Covers the various forms of presentation aids available today
- Discusses the concept of visual communication in general and, more specifically, how it applies to public speaking today
- Explores the complicated nature of presentation aids and how to maximize their ability to enhance your speech

Practically SPEAKING

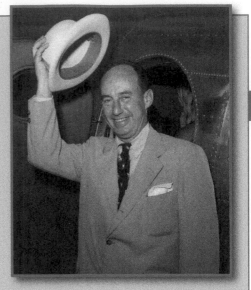

In 1952 Adlai Stevenson won the Democratic Party's nomination for president only to run against Republican former General Dwight David Eisenhower, who had led the Allied Command in Europe in World War II. Eisenhower, immensely popular, won the election. Not one to give up easily, Stevenson again won his party's nomination in the 1956 Presidential election, but again lost to General Eisenhower. After the election, when asked if he had any wisdom to offer to other politicians, Stevenson replied: "Yes, never run against a war hero."[1]

Four years after his second defeat the public elected John F. Kennedy president, and the new chief executive appointed Stevenson ambassador to the United Nations. In the autumn of 1962 events of the Cold War between the United States and the Soviet Union put the two nations' already strained relationship in a tenuous position. In October 1962, American U2 spy planes flying over Cuba photographed the construction of Soviet missile silos capable of delivering nuclear warheads to U.S. soil. President Kennedy demanded that the USSR immediately cease construction and disassemble the structures. The Soviets denied their existence and continued to build the weapon sites. President Kennedy then ordered a naval quarantine of Cuba to prevent any more Soviet cargo reaching the island. He also ordered Ambassador Stevenson to confront Soviet Ambassador Valerian Zorin in front of the United Nations and present photographic proof of the offensive weapons.[2]

Ambassador Stevenson employed visual proof. Up until Stevenson's visit to the UN the United States and the Soviet Union were in a war of words. However, when Ambassador Stevenson provided visual the proof he added further evidence supporting the United States's claims, making them almost impossible to deny. Had these pictures not existed, what we now refer to as the Cuban Missile Crisis might have ended quite differently.

Presentation aids, also referred to as visual aids, can greatly assist speakers in getting their points across to audiences. Some speeches, depending upon the topic and/or speech purpose, naturally lend themselves to visual reinforcement, but not all speeches require presentation aids. As the speaker you need to carefully consider what your message is and what you want your audience to get from the speech. If presentation aids help you accomplish your goals, then use them; if not, leave them out.

In this chapter we will first discuss the various forms of presentation aids available for use in presentations. We will then explore the concept of visual communication in general and, specifically, how it applies to the construction of effective presentation aids. Finally, we will provide some suggestions for how to maximize the ability of presentation aids to enhance your speech.

Presentation Aids

In this section we will cover traditional *presentation aids*, or visual devices used to assist a speaker in communicating ideas to the audience, such as models, graphs, charts, overheads, and objects. Next, we will discuss technological aids, such as videos and audio recordings, and Microsoft's PowerPoint. This section will end by discussing ways to combine both traditional and technological aids in a presentation.

presentation aids
visual devices used to assist a speaker in communicating ideas to the audience

Traditional Aids

Traditional aids, or aids that do not apply electronic means to communicate ideas to the audience, have been employed by speakers for quite some time. They are usually basic but can still enhance a speaker's points and assist the audience in understanding and following a speech. For example, for decades teachers and college instructors have employed overhead projectors and transparencies to allow audiences to see diagrams, models, or even outlines of presentations. Doctors use life-sized skeletons to demonstrate parts of the human body to medical students and patients.

traditional aids
aids that do not apply electronic means to communicate ideas to the audience

Those skeletons are an example of a *model*, a to-scale device that depicts an actual object. To-scale models can be replicas of objects that are the same size as the original or proportionally larger or smaller than the original. Suppose a biology student, Michelle, is speaking on human cell structure. Michelle will obviously need a model thousands, if not millions, of times larger than an actual cell for her audience to realistically picture what she is talking about. On the other hand, Brittany, a pre-med major, is presenting a speech about the workings of the human heart. She may use a same-size model to illustrate how the heart works if the audience is small enough. Finally, suppose Seth, an aeronautics major, is planning to speak on how the physics process of lift allows an airplane to defy gravity. He will need to use a scaled down model of a plane to demonstrate how lift occurs because an actual plane would be too large to use.

model
a to-scale device that depicts an actual object

Models, though, are not the only types of presentation aids you might use in a speech. If you plan on using statistical data to support your points you might want to use a *graph*, a presentation device that indicates relationships found in numerical data. Audiences like statistics, since people value numbers and feel

graph
a presentation device that indicates relationships found in numerical data

that they can interpret numeric data easier than other forms of evidence. Think of how your academic life is explained by statistics; everything is numerically determined, from your GPA, to the number of course hours in a semester, to rising tuition and fees, to the cost of textbooks. You interpret and understand this data rather easily. Graphs make more complicated numeric data simpler to interpret by illustrating it to audiences in a visual manner.

Suppose Jodie, a Computer Science major, decides she wants to study how much time college students spend using various media. Jodie creates a self-report survey and distributes it to students in large lecture classes, asking them the percentage of time they spend using various media. Jodie's results are as follows: The students report spending 25% of their time watching TV/gaming; 20% on the Internet or using a computer; 30% on a cell phone talking/texting; and 25% on music. Jodie decides to make a bar graph for her research presentation (see Figure 6.1).

Figure 6.1
Sample Bar Graph

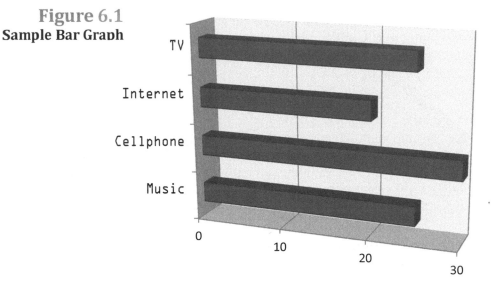

With this graph she can both verbally and visually explain to the audience how much time students spend with various media. In a speech, the graph, in addition to her verbal explanation, will make it easier for the audience to understand her point.

The bar graph used by Jodie is only one type of graph available to you. Another graph you could use to depict data is a pie graph. A pie graph works best when trying to illustrate how portions of a whole are allocated. For example, you attend a presentation by a retirement investment firm and a representative explains how you can diversify your investments in the firm's program. He shows you a graph like the one shown in Figure 6.2.

Figure 6.2
Sample Pie Graph

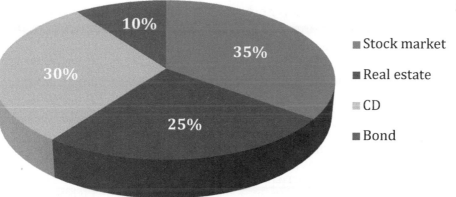

- ■ Stock market
- ■ Real estate
- ≡ CD
- ■ Bond

In this pie graph you can see that 35% of your investments are in the stock market, 25% in real estate, 30% in CDs, and 10% in bonds. The division of your money makes better sense when laid out in this visual manner.

Sometimes you need presentation aids to present lists of items to an audience. Under these circumstances the most effective presentation aid would be a *chart*, which is a visual device that helps you list and summarize blocks of information.

chart
a visual device that helps you summarize and/or list blocks of information

If you are delivering a speech about the relative economic strength of the United States to your economics class, you may wish to visually depict where the United States falls on the list of per capita wealth for nations around the world. To do this you could create a chart listing the richest countries, from highest to lowest (see Table 6.1).

Table 6.1

Sample Chart	
Country	Per capita
1. Luxembourg	$55,100
2. Norway	$37,800
3. United States	$37,800
4. San Marino	$34,600
5. Switzerland	$32,700
6. Denmark	$31,100
7. Iceland	$30,900
8. Austria	$30,000
9. Canada	$29,800
10. Ireland	$29,600[3]

This chart makes it easy for you to explain where the United States fits in comparison to other countries in a way the audience can understand and is more likely to remember.

transparencies

clear sheets containing information illuminated by a projector

Depending on the topic and what presentation equipment is available you may need to use overhead *transparencies*, which are clear sheets containing information illuminated by a projector. Some people consider this medium archaic. Though certainly not flashy, in some circumstances transparencies may be your only option. For example, even though classrooms around the country are being fitted with technology, there are still quite a few that do not have computers and digital projector equipment. In these rooms, using a transparency projector may be the best way to visually present material to the audience. Transparencies allow you to show, among other things, charts and graphs to your audience. Additionally, transparencies allow presenters to interact with material as they can draw and write on the transparency while speaking.

object

a tangible item used in conjunction with a speech

Some speeches are made richer by the use of an *object*, which is a tangible item that supports and/or explains your speech topic. In a speech where you explain how to properly swing a golf club you can talk at length about the mechanics involved, but the best way to get your point across to an audience is to demonstrate the process to them. In this case you would need a golf club (and plenty of space!). You could stand in front of the audience and slowly go through each step using the golf club to illustrate certain aspects of the swing to the audience. Here, an object helps get your points across to the audience in a more effective way than simple description.

Pictures are yet another type of presentation aid that is available. Suppose you

are presenting a speech on the French Quarter in New Orleans. Pictures, if large enough to be seen, of locations such as St. Louis Cathedral, Bourbon Street, the French Market, and Cafe du Monde will help provide more concrete images for your audience of the places you are talking about. If your goal is to persuade the audience to donate time, money, or food to a homeless shelter, images of those who would be helped by those donations might increase the persuasive appeal of the speech. Pictures, as the saying goes, are sometimes worth a thousand words.

Photos of Bourbon Street (top) and the New Orleans skyline (bottom)

Traditional aids are not outdated; rather, they remain some of the most useful presentation aids available to you. Models, graphs, charts, transparencies, objects, and pictures all can assist you in your speech by simplifying complex information for your audience. Even with the advent of more advanced aids these traditional forms of assistance can still be effectively incorporated into your speech.

Technological Aids

Technological advances have increased the number of available presentation aids for a speech. In this section we will discuss the distinctive qualities of these electronic presentation aids, beginning with video. In addition to video, audio recordings can also assist you when trying to get a point across to an audience. After covering video and audio we will discuss the program most people today erroneously believe is the only presentation aid available: PowerPoint. Finally, we will explore combining traditional and technological presentation aids in the same speech, an approach made possible thanks to technology.

Some speech topics are enhanced with the use of video. Videos can be movie clips, news stories, or cuts from homemade recordings. The key is that the clips are relevant to the speech topic and that they help explain or demonstrate a key point in the speech. Video also should be carefully planned and cued in advance so as not to take up too much of the speech's time or be overly distracting or possibly irrelevant. Earlier we talked about using a golf club as an object to assist you in demonstrating how to properly swing the club. Suppose you do not own a club or cannot demonstrate the swing due to an injury. You could find a film depiction of the most complicated step in the swing to visually illustrate the necessary movements to the audience. In this instance video becomes a very good aid for presenting complicated information to an audience. However, if you simply show a clip of a golfer from television and let it play for a long time with no explanation, then the video clip will do more harm than good to your speech.

If you just want the audience to hear something, an audio recording might be all you need. If you choose to speak to your audience about the hidden messages in old Beatles albums when played backward, you could find audio examples to play for the audience. Following the playing of those clips, you then could explain what was said and how the sounds got there. This exposure to the audio recording itself is far more effective than simply describing the curious messages. It also will enhance your ethos in much the same way the pictures did for Adlai Stevenson at the beginning of the chapter.

PowerPoint, Microsoft's presentation software, is a third technological aid that has become popular both for professors and students in the classroom. Professors can put their lecture outlines on the software and let it guide them and the class through the lecture. Some professors email or upload lecture notes and distribute them for their students in advance of class. PowerPoint, however, is most effective when it is used in conjunction with verbal messages.

To maximize the effectiveness of PowerPoint presentations you need to minimize a slide's ability to distract the audience. There should be just enough on each slide to enable the audience to keep up with the speaker, and rarely, if ever, should full sentences be crammed on a slide. When long sentences appear the audience tends to read the slide and ignore the speaker, defeating the purpose of presentation aids. Slides should be readable for everyone in the room listening to the speech, so fonts and colors must be adjusted accordingly. PowerPoint is one of the most effective programs for designing presentation aids that incorporate both traditional and technological aids. See the boxes that follow for an example of how to properly develop and use a PowerPoint presentation.

DEVELOPING A POWERPOINT PRESENTATION

Earlier in this chapter we noted the popularity of Microsoft's PowerPoint in presentations. In this section we will demonstrate the visual theories and design principles in a practical application.

Suppose Hillary, an economics major, has decided to present an informative speech on the cost of college for students living on campus who use the school's dining plan. She does national research and then compares it to the results of a survey and interviews she has conducted. She finds students at her university have paid roughly the same amount as those in similar situations at other institutions.

She feels that since she has lists of items and statistics that the best way to present the info will be to carefully prepare a PowerPoint presentation. Hillary wants a slide that is a brief overview of her speech. She creates a slide for that purpose with a picture of a student union she found online. She picks a background color for her slides that matches her school's colors and chooses a font that is not distracting and is easy to read.

Cost of College at State U.

Speech overview

- Average cost of college nationally per year
- State U. average cost per year
- Data is for students living on campus

Hillary then creates a slide for information within the body of her speech. She wants it to be simple and easy to understand, so she places a chart on the slide. The chart depicts several expenses and their associated costs:

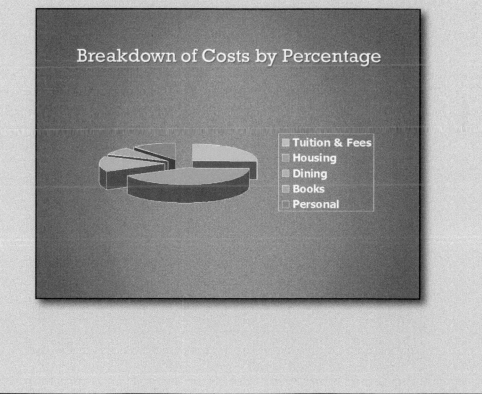

Annual Costs at State U.

- Tuition and fees: $3,900
- Residential housing: $6,300
- Dining plan: $2,220
- Books and supplies: $1,090
- Personal expenses: $1,750

Hillary then creates a pie graph to reveal the percentage portions of each item on a chart.

Breakdown of Costs by Percentage

- Tuition & Fees
- Housing
- Dining
- Books
- Personal

After creating that slide Hillary decides the form and depth are distracting and harder to understand than a more traditional approach, so she creates the following slide to explain the data:

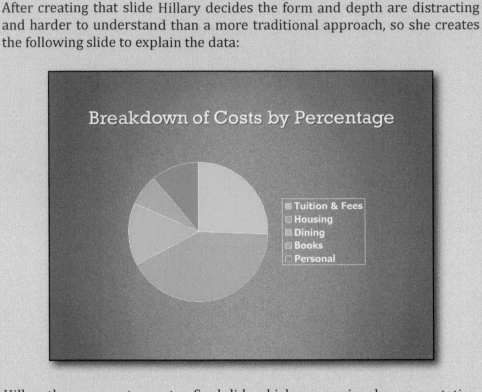

Hillary then goes on to create a final slide which summarizes her presentation. She feels comfortable that the four slides professionally and easily accomplish what she wants. In this example, Hillary has used proper form, depth, and color to create slides that provide enough information to make the message easier for the audience to understand, while not distracting from the speech's purpose.

PowerPoint is an extremely powerful tool; however, the software should be used with caution as the many capabilities it contains can be distracting. If you are taking a public speaking class then it is likely that your professor will give you some guidance on the use of presentation aids. Keep in mind that standards and expectations often differ among instructors. As such, any questions should be directed to the instructor teaching this course.

PowerPoint has custom templates, designs, fonts, and other features you can use to enhance your presentation. Unless otherwise instructed, use these features at a minimum. Using this software, you can choose to show the entire slide or sections of the slide either line by line or object by object. This may be advisable when making certain points. The software also allows you to use animation and to zoom, swivel on appearance, fly in, fade, and perform other actions (see Table 6.2). This can be a distraction, or even an annoyance, to audience members. Unless you are in a class that stresses creativity and artful display, approach these tools cautiously and, again, consult with your instructor.

When using PowerPoint, the use of a presentation clicker is advisable. Otherwise, this software can hinder your delivery by requiring you to stay by the computer's keyboard to transition between slides. A presentation clicker assists you with this and allows you to move around. In some locations, the computer may not be situated where you can center yourself before the audience, and the presentation clicker remedies this as well, as most clickers will accurately function several yards away. Plus, most clickers allow you to terminate the view if you so choose.

Finally, Microsoft's PowerPoint has an easy-to-use help function that can be accessed by pressing F1 on your keyboard. Typing in a topic typically leads to very usable information.

As technology has increasingly become a part of academics, students and professors now have the capability to deliver dynamic performances with a *multimedia presentation*, which combines and integrates video, audio, pictures, and notes into one medium. Not all topics are conducive to this presentation format, but when used effectively multimedia presentations can assist you in the delivery of difficult and complex material. Demonstrating knowledge of how to put together a multimedia presentation also enhances a speaker's ethos. You can use PowerPoint to craft multimedia presentation aids.

multimedia presentation
a presentation aid that combines and integrates video, audio, pictures, and notes into one medium

As noted above, you can use PowerPoint to incorporate animation into your slides. On the surface, this is a terrific new option when developing a presentation, but as with any presentation aid, you must be judicious in choosing when and what type of animation to use. Too much animation can distract the audience and make them pay attention to the slides and not you and your message. It is also important to be consistent in your use of animation. For example, if you wish to animate the title of each slide by making it "whoosh" onto the screen as you change slides, do so for *every* slide change, not just one. You can also use the animation function to illuminate a key part of a picture which can be very useful.

In the PowerPoint program there is a tab for animation options on each slide. There are 12 different options you can select from, each providing a unique movement for the text or image you place on the slide. See Table 6.2 for a description of each of the various animation options available in PowerPoint. Visual creativity through the use of animation can help make your presentation more dynamic if you implement it properly and practice with the animation tools you plan to use. Now, let's take a moment and discuss how you might actually use PowerPoint to get certain key concepts across to your audience in a dynamic fashion.

Table 6.2	PowerPoint Visual Effects
Appear	The text immediately appears
Fade	The text gradually appears in view
Fly in	The text quickly moves up into place from the bottom of the page
Float in	The text gradually moves into place
Split	The text begins to appear quickly from both sides of the word/phrase
Wipe	The text appears from the bottom of the word/phrase up to the top
Shape	The image appears to take form slowly on the slide
Wheel	The image appears slowly in a clockwise motion
Random bars	The image appears as if formed by the addition of various bars on top of each other
Grow and turn	The image moves from a distance to its place by turning on its side
Zoom	The image moves quickly from a distance into its place without turning
Swivel	The image turns three times before settling in its proper place

Suppose you want to deliver a speech about the Center for Strategic International Studies (CSIS)[4] and its "Coming Seven Revolutions."[5] CSIS claims the seven coming revolutions are: population, resource management, technology, information flows, conflict, economic integration, and governance. You could use PowerPoint to integrate all the following: animated graphs that denote the rapid rise of the world population and grow accordingly while you speak; pictures to show pollution; video to show a clip from an interview with *The New York Times* columnist and author Thomas Friedman on economics; and a chart of the number of pirate attacks per year off the coast of Somalia. PowerPoint allows you to incorporate both traditional and technological presentation aids into the same presentation. To accomplish this type of presentation, however, requires quite a bit of familiarity with Microsoft's PowerPoint, so if you are new to the program be sure to give yourself plenty of time to develop your PowerPoint presentation and to practice your speech delivery.

In addition to familiarity with the software program, you also should be knowledgeable about the theories underpinning visual communication. In the next section we take some time to elaborate on the theories related to visual cues and design principles. These two concepts are of paramount importance when creating a presentation aid. Following that discussion, we provide some concrete suggestions and guidelines for effectively incorporating visual communication concepts into the development of successful presentation aids.

VISUAL COMMUNICATION CONCEPTS

Thanks in part to television and the Internet, people increasingly are becoming visual creatures. We depend upon our eyes, oftentimes in deference to our other senses, to tell us about the world around us. Unfortunately, we all see things differently even if we seemingly see the same thing because we focus upon different stimuli. When we see something several things happen. First, we select a visual stimulus; next, we organize that stimulus in our brain so it makes sense to us, thus giving it meaning.[6] This process is how each of us develops our own *frame of reference,* or our own singular perspective of the world around us.[7]

Visual Theory and Practice

Due to the differences in our frames of reference you cannot assume that since you have presented visual evidence to an audience they will see it the same way you do. For that reason you must understand how to craft presentation aids in a way that takes the myriad perspectives in an audience into consideration. In this section of the chapter we will discuss the elements of visual depictions that can encourage particular meanings from audiences. We also will examine the principles of design associated with presentation aids to help you create effective images that will complement your speech.

Visual Cues

Think about the things that often catch your eye. Colorful images are far more appealing than those that appear dull or even in black and white. An image's shape, or the shapes within a picture, also determine how attractive we consider something. Additionally, the details of the image might make us pay more attention. Finally, "active" images are more likely to gain our attention and maintain our interest. In this section we will discuss each of these visual cues, and how they might contribute to the development of an effective presentation aid.

The *color pattern,* or collection of hues in your presentation aids, should be pleasing to the audience and not distract them from your speech. There are six colors in the color spectrum: red, orange, yellow, green, blue, and indigo.[8] When you construct your aids, ensure that the colors you select for your visuals work together. For instance, when using PowerPoint do not use a yellow background with white lettering, as your audience will not be able to read your notes. But simply making out the words is not enough. When you use black lettering on a white background the audience will see what the words are, but such a color scheme does not illustrate creativity on your part. You also should test the colors you think work together, because sometimes they may appear effective on your monitor, but on a large projection screen they may bleed together and become hard for an audience to decipher.

frame of reference
our own singular perspective of the world around us

color pattern
collection of hues in your presentation aids

form

how an item appears in terms of its representation, size, and texture

Colors are not the only visual cue you should consider when creating your presentation aids. If you plan to use models or objects consider their *form*, which is how they appear in terms of representation, size, and texture. Obviously, the item needs to be large enough, but it also has to resemble what it represents. For example, if you are discussing the plans for a new building in the center of town, you need to make sure the model you put together for a presentation aid is an accurate depiction of what the real building will look like. Grabbing any old model of a building will not do, as it will provide the audience with a visual that does not accurately depict your verbal explanation.

depth

the graphic nature of an item; involves both level of detail and the amount of background provided for the image

Your presentation aid also needs to take *depth*, or the graphic nature of an item, into consideration. Depth refers to both the level of detail you provide a visual image and the amount of background provided for the image. Take the model of the building we just talked about; you may want to be able to open and close the model to show the inside of the building and how it is designed. To do that you need to provide detail to each room in the model, giving it significant depth. Perhaps you also wish to show pictures of the proposed site of the building so the audience can get a clearer idea of how it might fit with its surroundings. Those pictures would provide greater background than a simple empty lot; they should be taken from a distance far enough away to show the buildings that would surround the new structure.

movement

appearance of or actual activity depicted with an image

One final visual cue to take into account is the level of action in the images you use. *Movement*, or the appearance of actual activity depicted with an image, can be effective if properly employed, but it can also be distracting if not crafted with care. Two ways in which movement can be distracting in PowerPoint presentations are through the use of the function that allows for words to "swim" on and off of slides and the creation of graphics such as exploding fireworks. Such movement may seem exciting, but in actuality it detracts from the overall message; audiences focus on the fireworks and moving words, instead of what you are saying. An example of a more effective use of movement is the use of pictures that illustrate people doing things instead of head shots or portraits.

Careful planning with visual cues can result in an effective presentation aid that successfully complements your speech. Color, form, depth, and movement are all important aspects of a presentation aid and, if you pay them proper attention, they can enhance your speech without being distracting. Visual cues represent only half the visual communication concepts relevant to developing effective presentation aids, however, as design principles must also be considered.

Design Principles

Design principles generally, but not exclusively, concern media such as PowerPoint. These principles should guide you in developing a presentation aid that works together with your speech to effectively communicate your message. They concern where and when to implement the presentation aids, how to create aids that do not distract the audience from the speaker, and how to make sure all elements of the presentation aids complement each other and the speech.

When preparing presentation aids, you need to think about how the different elements of your presentation aid work together. To do this you must consider where to place items and how to arrange them so the audience sees something that makes sense and is appealing to the eye. This is often referred to as the design principle of *balance*, or the position of elements within the image. There are two types of balance. The first is *axial balance*, which is formal and strives for equal distribution of the elements of a visual so they do not appear tilted on one side of the image (see Figure 6.3). The second form of balance is *asymmetrical balance*, which emphasizes imbalance, thus creating an impression of stress, energy, and excitement (see Figure 6.4).[9] Oftentimes your topic dictates which type of balance you select for your presentation aid images.

> **balance**
> the positioning of elements within the image

Figure 6.3
Axial Balance

Figure 6.4
Asymmetrical Balance

> **axial balance**
> formal balance that strives for equal distribution of the elements of a visual so they do not appear tilted on one side of the image

Suppose you wanted to deliver a speech on rap music. It is unlikely you would employ a strictly formal style because rap music feeds off of energy and excitement. Instead, you would create images using asymmetrical balance to create the impression of such energy for your audience. On the other hand, if you delivered a speech on how to change the oil in your car, the formal style would be more appropriate because chaos and excitement are not something you want to engender in your audience with such a topic.

> **asymmetrical balance**
> emphasizes imbalance thus creating an impression of stress, energy, and excitement

A second design principle to consider when developing presentation aids involves making images and wording work together effectively. You should integrate images and words so that what you want conveyed is in the foreground of the presentation aid, keeping the background simple. This idea is called *contrast*, or how objects and letters stick out from the background. You never want the audience to have to strain to interpret presentation aids; they should be easy to understand. As we mentioned above regarding color patterns, you should ensure that your colors go together well and do not clash or bleed as this will negatively impact the contrast. Additionally, if you are using a photograph or a video, make sure the background helps the image stand out by using a color like black to fill it in. This use of contrast helps direct the audience to focus on the video or photo, rather than the background.

> **contrast**
> how objects and letters stick out from the background

In addition to balance and contrast, presentation aids also need harmony. *Harmony* occurs when all parts and aspects of the presentation aid complement one another within the aid's framework. The color and image choices you select should work with and reflect the tone of the speech you deliver. For example, if you deliver a speech trying to persuade people to donate to breast cancer research, you may use pink wording on a blue or black background. Additionally, you might place a pink ribbon in the upper corner of each slide. These color and image schemes work in tandem with the message and augment the theme of your appeal. On the other hand, if you were to use black letters on a white background,

> **harmony**
> when all parts and aspects of the presentation aid complement one another within the aid's framework

The iCloud Formal Announcement by Steve Jobs

Delivered June 6, 2011, at the Worldwide Development Conference, San Francisco, CA

Apple has been known for its technology for many years. From innovative desktop computers and easy-to-use laptops, to revolutionary developments like iPhones, iTunes, and iPads, the company is known for its technological wizardry. Steve Jobs, the well-known co-founder and chief executive officer of the corporation, was battling medical conditions when he appeared at the Worldwide Development Conference in June 2011 to announce Apple's latest product: the iCloud.

iCloud is an online storage device and a way to synchronize all Apple devices to enable the user to have common applications and programs on each device.[14] Such a complicated device required Jobs to use presentation aids to help his audience understand just what the iCloud could do. Appearing on a large stage, Jobs frequently moved around, talking as he walked, with a presentation clicker in his right hand. Behind him was a large dark blue wall with the images of Apple devices. As Jobs talked about the iCloud, he would change images, but the constant picture was of a cloud above each of the Apple devices he showed the audience.[15] Jobs showed the symbols for the three major features of electronic devices: mail, contacts, and calendars. He then used animation to switch between the symbols while showing data being synchronized automatically.[16]

The presentation was dynamic, informative, and made understandable through the use of creative presentation aids. It lasted only seven and a half minutes, but due to the presentation aids, the audience was fully informed of the power of Apple's newest technology.

or green on red, it would send a less forceful message and would not work with your appeal as well as the pink color scheme.

Proper choices for images also enhance the harmony of a visual aid. When the images represent the things you speak about it helps reinforce the message you send to the audience. For example, in June 2011 when Apple founder Steve Jobs announced the rollout of the iCloud, the company's latest product, he used images of a cloud covering all other Apple products to represent the iCloud itself, as well as the fact the product was meant to cover and integrate all of Apple's electronic platforms. Although it seems like an obvious choice, the use of a cloud image helped create harmony between the visual aid Jobs used, the topic of his speech, and the definition of what the product was meant to do.

Each of these three design principles can work to help you create artful and pleasing aids for your speech. After you decide which presentation aid fits your speech best, you can begin to construct it with a knowledge of how visual cues and design principles work. This will enable you to craft a creative and effective presentation aid that advances your speech. In the next part we will synthesize the chapter and provide some general guidelines for how to construct your presentation aids.

DEVELOPING AND USING PRESENTATION AIDS

Theories drive application in a variety of fields, and visual communication and the development of presentation aids is no different. So far we have discussed the different types of presentation aids you can use during a speech and the theoretical ideas that should guide your creation of such presentation aids. In this part of the chapter we will first provide some tips and guidelines for constructing your presentation aids based on the relationship between aid types and visual communication concepts. We will then detail some tips and guidelines for how to effectively use your presentation aids during your speech.

Guidelines for Presentation Aid Development

When putting your speech together it is advisable to think about and develop your aids as you prepare and structure the presentation. The power of presentation aids is that they can assist you in helping the audience to understand complicated and complex material. To maximize the effectiveness of your presentation aids, it is important to remember three rules when developing your aids in advance of your presentation: Parsimony, Practicality, and Practice.

First, presentation aids should make complex information simpler and easier to understand for the audience. To do this the presentation aid cannot be convoluted, extended, or extravagant; instead it should be parsimonious, or simple. A parsimonious image gets the point across to the audience without belaboring it or simply repeating the complexity of the concept in a different medium. As a rule of thumb, keep in mind *Occam's Razor*: "one should not increase, beyond what is necessary, the number of entities required to explain anything."[10] Put another way, all things being equal, the simplest explanation is the best explanation. Sir William of Occam was referring to verbal explanations, but the idea that the simplest is best applies to visual images just as well because when you use extraneous and unnecessary presentation aids you not only confuse your audience, but you also hurt your speaking credibility.

Occam's Razor
one should not increase, beyond what is necessary, the number of entities required to explain anything

You also should avoid creating distracting visuals. Complicated, extravagant presentation aids detract from the speech and cause the audience to focus on the aid and not the speech. As a general rule, paragraphs and full sentences are not advisable for placement on slides, as they keep the audience focused on something other than the speaker and the message. Pictures not directly related to the speech topic also keep audiences wondering about their purpose as a visual instead of keeping track of the speaker's argument.

practicality
the proper places within the speech (the where, when, and how) you can and should make use of presentation aids

Where parsimony calls for presentation aids to be simple, yet effective, and not distracting, *practicality* refers to the proper places within your speech—the where, when and how—you can and should make use of presentation aids. For instance, if you are speaking about the "Big Dig" transportation project that took place in Boston during the 1990s and early 21st century, then you might show pictures of the situation before the project began, then the blueprint of the plan the city enacted, and finally what the completion of the project looked like. These pictures could correspond with particular points of your speech and help the audience visualize what you are describing. As such, they would become practical. However, pictures of cars, buses, or even a large map of the area may not help you further your goals despite being tangentially relevant to the topic. When selecting your presentation aids, be practical about determining what the audience needs to see.

Finally, it is imperative that you practice your speech while using your presentation aids. This will enable you to become not only familiar but also comfortable with them. Work on making the references to presentation aids a seamless part of the speech until the motions and actions are natural to you. By seeming natural to you, they will also appear that way to your audience, and your presentation will be more effective.

In terms of practice, you should arrive at the speech location well in advance of the presentation if at all possible. This way you can make sure your presentation aids will work in the room in which you will speak. In many classrooms the computer and monitor are off to one side, not near the center of the room. Are you comfortable walking back and forth to change slides or pictures? If you are using PowerPoint or another computer assisted aid, be sure to have a backup plan in case something doesn't go as planned. If you saved your presentation to a disk, email it to yourself as well in case the computer cannot read the disk. Also, get to class early so you can save your presentation to the desktop before the class starts, thus making it easier to load it when it is time to give your speech.

Using presentation aids within a speech is more involved than simply creating an aid, showing up, and giving the speech. The presentation aid is a part of your speech, and so you should develop it in tandem with your speech. Keep the aids simple, choose the necessary moments in the speech to employ presentation aids, and practice using them with your speech. After you have practiced and feel comfortable with the whole speech, it is time to actually make the presentation.

Using Presentation Aids During the Speech

Many times speakers incorrectly use presentation aids and damage their speech delivery. Some of this misuse stems from an individual not practicing his speech with the presentation aid in advance of the presentation. There are, however, other reasons for misuse. This section will provide you with some commonsense tips to help ensure you properly use your presentation aids during your presentation.

First, during your presentation you will need to reference your aids. For example, if you discuss statistics then you will likely use a table or graph of those statistics as a presentation aid. You will need to reference the trends it depicts so the audience sees the relationship. If you discuss the arrangement of the Gateway Arch in St.

SPOTLIGHTING THEORISTS: WILLIAM OF OCCAM

William of Occam (b. circa 1285–d. circa 1349)

William of Occam was born around 1285 in the community of Ockham in Surrey, England. As a young man he joined the Franciscan Order of the Catholic Church and studied theology at Oxford University. During his course of study his theological views aggravated many of his instructors, preventing him from graduation. Pope John XXII eventually summoned him to the Papal Court in Avignon, France, in 1324 to discuss his controversial views on apostolic poverty.[11]

A former Oxford chancellor, Jogn Luterell, presented charges against William, but he was never condemned as he fled Avignon before the ruling could be announced. While living in a self-imposed exile in what we now call Germany, William of Occam wrote scathing criticisms against the papacy. He also wrote on the principle of parsimony, which became known as Occam's Razor. It stresses that we should keep things as simple as possible.[12]

William studied Aquinas and Aristotle and published many treatises on a wide range of subjects. His personal belief was that more is not necessarily better. In fact, he believed in using the least amount possible to achieve desired ends. He did not think that science needed multiple theories and hypotheses when one could explain what needed to be known. His ideas have continued to be valued by scientists, economists, and even politicians to this day. The best example of its recent application in political and popular culture is the popularity of the phrase "Keep it simple, stupid," or as James Carville famously opined in the 1992 presidential election, "It's the economy, stupid." William of Occam eventually died in exile around the year 1349.[13]

Louis you may need to point to particular features of the structure so the audience sees what you are talking about. Do not assume your audience will see things as you do and assume that presentation aids speak for themselves; they do not.

Many novice speakers also look at and talk to their presentation aid. Keep your eyes on the audience, not the aid, because when you look at the aid you lose your connection with the audience and you project your voice away from them, making it hard for them to hear you. Instead, refer to the aid and occasionally glance at it, but remember that the audience should be your primary focus. When referencing the aid you should also be clear about what is relevant in the aid itself; in other words, tell people what they should pay attention to. This can be done in several different ways:

- <u>This is a picture of</u> the site where engineers planned to build the Panama Canal.
- <u>Notice</u> the swamp-like area around the camps where the workers lived.

- This is a bar graph representing the number of students in each major; the height of each bar illustrates the number students in the major last year.

- The legend indicates that the area covered in yellow represents the land purchased in the Louisiana Purchase.

Another common mistake is the use of handouts as presentation aids. Handouts are not presentation aids and often work to distract an audience from the speaker. If you do use handouts, you will need enough copies for each audience member, and you should not distribute them until after you have finished speaking. Audience members are curious and if you provide them with a handout they will focus upon that and not upon you, thus leading them to miss the point of the presentation.

Finally, it is imperative that your listeners be able to clearly and easily see the presentation aid. Your presentation aid, whether it is a model or a PowerPoint slide, must be large enough for all to see. To ensure your entire audience can see the presentation aid you should go to the place where you will be speaking and see the size of the room. You also should try and get as much information on the estimated audience size as possible. That is easy in your class but when delivering an address at a business meeting, audience-size will be more difficult to measure. Finally, you should remember the principles of color and contrast to make sure the presentation aid is readable.

Presentation aids can be a great asset to you if used properly. For a summary of presentation aids "do's" and "don'ts", see Table 6.3.

Table 6.3

Presentation Aids Checklist	
Do	**Don't**
Carefully prepare	Use if not needed
Practice	Talk to the aid
Make large enough for all to see	Focus on the aid
Make sure the technology works	Assume email will work
Have a backup plan	Assume technology is working
Make aids visually pleasing	Use slides as an outline
Keep it simple and relevant	Use as giant notecards

SUMMARY

Presentation aids can greatly enhance your speech. Keep in mind that there are many different kinds of aids, ranging from traditional to technological forms. Presentation aids must be pleasing, easy to understand, and relevant to your speech topic. You will need to practice them until you are fluid and comfortable with them as a part of your speech. Developing effective presentation aids takes time and effort, but the payoff can be immense when you deliver a presentation about something complicated to an audience and they walk away with an understanding of what you spoke about.

asymmetrical balance	harmony
axial balance	model
balance	movement
chart	multimedia presentation
color pattern	object
contrast	Occam's Razor
depth	practicality
form	presentation aids
frame of reference	traditional aids
graph	transparencies

REVIEW QUESTIONS

1. What are the two main types of presentation aids?

    _____

    _____

2. What are the six types of traditional presentation aids covered in the chapter?

    _____

    _____

3. What are the four types of visual cues?

    _____

    _____

4. What are the three design principles covered in the chapter?

    _____

    _____

5. What are the three rules to keep in mind when developing presentation aids?

    _____

    _____

THINK ABOUT IT

1. When would a presentation aid possibly be a detriment to your speech?

_____

_____

_____

_____

2. How could you show emotion in a presentation aid?

_____

_____

_____

_____

3. How might a presentation aid be unethical?

_____

_____

_____

_____

ACTIVITIES FOR ACTION

1. Take a look at some paintings and pictures and put them in two piles: those you like, and those you don't. Write a brief statement regarding why you either like or do not like the images. Then go through and determine if those you like and those you don't employ the same types of design principles.

2. Take a look at the text of a speech pre-1920 and make a list of ways in which the speech could have been improved using presentation aids. When the list is complete, choose one of the presentation ideas you came up with and create it. Then deliver the speech (without changing the text) using the visual aid. See if it actually does improve audience retention of the content of the speech.

ENDNOTES

1. "Stevenson, Adlai Ewing," http://etcweb.princeton.edu/CampusWWW/Companion/stevenson_adlai.html (accessed October 18, 2008).

2. "Foreign Affairs, Cuban Missile Crisis, August 29-October 28, 1962," http://www.u-s-history.com/pages/h1736.html (accessed October 18, 2008).

3. "Internet World Stat," http://www.internetworldstat.com/richest-countries-world. htm (accessed October 19, 2008).

4. Center for Strategic International Studies, www.csis.org (accessed October 19, 2008).

5. The Coming Seven Revolutions, www.7revs.org.

6. David Moore and Francis Dwyer, *Visual Literacy: A Spectrum of Visual Learning* (Englewood Cliffs, NJ.: Education Technology Publications, 1994).

7. Ibid., 35.

8. Jeremy Vest, William Crowson, and Shannon Pocbran, *Web Design: An In-depth Guide to the Art and Techniques of Web Design* (Clifton Park, NY: Thomson, Delmar Learning, 2005).

9. Asa Berger, *Seeing Is Believing: An Introduction to Visual Communication* (Mountain View, CA: Mayfield, Publishing Company), 56-57.

10. Principia Cybernetica Web, "Occam's Razor," http://pespmc1.vub.ac.be/occamraz. html (accessed October 25, 2008).

11. "Biography," http://wotug.ukc.ac.uk/parallel/www/occam/occam-bio.html (last accessed October 25, 2008).

12. Ibid (accessed October 25, 2008).

13. The Internet Encyclopedia of Philosophy, "William of Ockham, c.– 1280 – c. 1349," http://www.iep.utm.edu/o/ockham.htm (accessed October 25, 2008).

14. Steve Jobs at Worldwide Technology Conference: http://news.cnet.com/8301-13579_3-20068773-37/jobs-announces-apples-icloud-storage-service/ (accessed June 21, 2011).

15. Steve Jobs at Worldwide Technology Conference: http://news.cnet.com/1606-2_3-50105998.html (accessed June 21, 2011).

16. Ibid.

Analyzing Audience

CHAPTER OVERVIEW

- Discusses how audiences can be broken down and analyzed before a speech
- Explains how audience analysis can be employed in developing points and using language within a speech
- Outlines how to effectively analyze a speech during its delivery

The 2008 presidential primaries represented the first time in over a half century when neither a president nor vice president sought their party's nomination for president. The campaigns for both the Democratic and Republican contenders were bitterly divisive, and each candidate needed to find a way to appeal to groups that normally would not support them. For instance, Republican Senator John McCain needed to quell criticism over what some party members saw as his questionable conservative record.[1]

In 2007 the Conservative Political Action Committee (CPAC) invited all the major candidates to speak at the conference and McCain was the only one not to attend.[2] As a result, he was crushed in the straw poll by his competitors and many conservatives refused to support him.[3] As the year progressed, McCain took further criticism from the right for his immigration policies, his refusal to vote for the Bush tax cuts a few years prior, and his maverick nature. The criticism became so severe for McCain in 2007 that his campaign almost went bankrupt.[4]

The Arizona senator's fortunes changed, however, in 2008 when voting began, and by the time he reached the podium at CPAC he was the likely Republican nominee for president. He had won significant election victories the previous week, and just a few hours before McCain's speech his chief rival, Mitt Romney, announced the suspension of his campaign. McCain could now attempt to unite the party behind him. Unfortunately for the senator, however, the audience still viewed him with skepticism at best, hostility at worst.

McCain needed to tailor his speech to the scene he faced. He knew he faced conservatives, but what kind? What was their age? Where did they come from? What was their economic status? Would race play a part in their perceptions of him? Were they ready to believe in his candidacy? What political principles did they espouse? The answers to these and other questions influenced the word choices within his speech and the evidence he chose to use to deflect their potential criticisms. But even knowing these things in advance, McCain still needed to be attuned to his audience while delivering the speech. All of these assessments are part of audience analysis, an essential skill for any speaker.

This chapter will discuss the various elements of audience analysis that can help you craft and deliver a successful speech tailored to your listeners. It begins with a discussion about the types of audience analysis available to you before you give a speech. It then discusses how that information, once collected, can be used to inform your decisions on phrasing and organization within the speech. Finally, it explains how audience analysis does not stop when the speech starts, but rather continues during the speech. Finally, it provides tips and suggestions on how to gauge the effectiveness of your message while delivering a speech.

METHODS OF AUDIENCE ANALYSIS

The old axiom, "Information is power" underscores the importance of audience analysis when speaking. Knowing about your audience allows you to make better choices regarding the examples, language, and organizational patterns you might use in a speech, thereby increasing your power as a speaker. Gathering information about your audience, however, is unlike gathering research materials for your speech, which you should remember reading about in Chapter 3. As a matter of fact, some of the audience characteristics you uncover may very well inform your decisions about where to research and what research to cite within your speech. This section explains three different ways of analyzing your audience, but all of them may not be available every time you speak. Like most other skills presented in this book, treat them like tools in a toolkit. When they are available and make sense to use, use them.

Demographics

One of the most common ways of analyzing an audience involves collecting *demographic data*. Many of us recognize demographic data when we see it, and oftentimes we conduct rudimentary demographic analyses ourselves. Take, for example, the first day of class. You enter the room and look around at your fellow students, examining the makeup of the class. You note roughly how many women and men there are, and perhaps the number of minorities. You often subconsciously use this information when selecting your seat in the room.

demographic data
information on selected population charac-teristics used by the government, market researchers, and speech writers

We also encounter demographic data when we watch the news. Political election campaigns, like the one we discussed at the opening of this chapter, have developed into machines driven by demographics. Politicians seek to win the youth vote, the African American vote, the senior vote, or the middle class vote. Candidates often deliver speeches or use examples and statistics that appeal to that subsection of the population. Research groups and news organizations often report on polls that measure support for a candidate within a particular demographic group, especially immediately following an election. An *exit poll* helps politicians understand their appeal to different parts of the population so as to better refine their message for the next election.

exit poll
questions asked fol-lowing an election that measure election results in terms of de-mographic categories

Market researchers also make use of demographic data when evaluating television shows. Different television programs appeal to different demographic groups, and that information allows studios to find specific advertisers for those shows that have products that appeal to the specific demographic groups that watch the show. For example, CBS debuted a show called *Jericho* in 2007 that received enthusiastic support from some fans but that did not translate into strong ratings with the coveted 18–49 demographic, resulting in its eventual cancelation. So angry were the fans that they mounted a campaign to save their show by mailing thousands of peanuts to CBS management. CBS finally gave in and restored the show for a short seven-episode season in 2008, but the ratings were not much better so the network canceled it again. *Jericho* is an example of a show that did not appeal to a demographic targeted by the network, and so the show lacked power to persuade advertisers to buy air time, leading to its cancelation. Just as with television shows, when speakers are unable to appeal to their audience they lose their *efficacy* and are less likely to be successful at sending their message to their listeners.

efficacy
the ability to produce a desired result

Demographic categories measure a variety of different aspects of a population. They detail observable and identifiable characteristics through survey techniques. Every time you place a checkmark next to your race or provide your age on a document you are contributing to demographic information databases. Think about your college applications: You checked these off and sent them back to the universities of your choice. The universities then used this information to examine the appeal of their college to certain targeted populations. Demographic information is powerful, and for that reason the use of it for anything other than description is prohibited by law.

In the United States most demographic categories are protected by law from discrimination. Race, age, sexual orientation, and religious affiliation represent specific groups shielded from discrimination. So, on the aforementioned college application, you could not be rejected from a school for checking the box next to, say, "African American." Demographic information, however, can be used to help construct appeals to select groups in a variety of ways.

One such way it can be used is through more complicated parceling of the population. Demographic questions and results can often be cross-sectioned to examine more than just one group, such as "Hispanics." That group can be categorized to explore responses from "Hispanics, ages 18–26," or even "Hispanic Catholics, ages 18–26 in Miami, Florida." Imagine the variety of uses for such information when designing messages to appeal to that group. The applications are nearly endless and the potential success of the message reaching the segment of the audience it is designed to reach increases as well.

A few moments ago we mentioned several different demographic categories. Most of us recognize these categories and can learn from a simple question. When examining demographic information on age, oftentimes the category is broken up into 8–10 year segments. For example, the young adult category is often broken down into those people who are 18–26, and middle age is usually seen as 40–50. The elderly are often typecast as the over-65 crowd. Appeals that work with one group might not work with another.

SPOTLIGHTING THEORISTS: GEORGE GALLUP & JOHN ZOGBY

Anyone who even remotely follows politics and public opinion in the United States today has heard the names "Gallup" or "Zogby." The Gallup Organization and Zogby International are two of the most well-known polling corporations in the world.

George Horace Gallup (1901–1984)

George Gallup grew up in a farming family in Iowa in the early 20th century and attended the University of Iowa, where he eventually received a Ph.D. in Political Science. Initially, Gallup pursued a career as a college teacher and researcher, but after stops at the University of Iowa, Drake University, and Northwestern, he left academia altogether for a position with the Young & Rubicam advertising agency. He spent 16 years with Y&R conducting public opinion surveys before leaving to found the American Institute of Public Opinion in 1935.

In 1936 his neophyte organization gained national attention by accurately predicting the presidential election with only 5,000 respondents. This was in contrast to a larger poll conducted by *Literary Digest* that got the results wrong. Gallup, however, was not always right himself as was famously the case in 1948.

In 1948 Gallup ended polling three weeks before the presidential election between incumbent Harry Truman and challenger Thomas Dewey. As a result, he forecast Dewey as the winner in a landslide. Early in the morning the day after America went to the polls Truman was announced the winner, casting a pall over Gallup's polling efforts. Never again did Gallup order polling to end before Election Day.

In 1958 Gallup consolidated all his polling operations into what we know today as The Gallup Organization. Despite his death from a heart attack in Switzerland in 1984, the organization has continued to be a success and is seen as one of the most reputable sources of public opinion data in the world.

John Zogby (1948–)

John Zogby is the founder of Zogby International, a competitor to the Gallup Organization in the polling field. Zogby, a native New Yorker, was born in upstate New York and attended LeMoyne College and Syracuse University. He has taught history and political science at SUNY-Utica and the Arthur Levitt Public Affairs Center at Hamilton College. He received an honorary doctorate degree from both SUNY and the Graduate School of Union University. Zogby also serves as a Senior Advisor at the John F. Kennedy School of Government at Harvard University and is Senior Fellow at the Catholic University of America's Life Cycle Institute. In addition to his academic credentials, Zogby also is a member of the board of directors for the Advertising Research Foundation.

In 1984 he founded Zogby International, which conducts polls around the world. Although newer on the scene than Gallup, his group quickly gained notoriety in 1992 when he published a poll that showed popular former New York Governor Mario Cuomo would lose in a general election in New York to then President George H. W. Bush. This poll receives some credit for Cuomo's departure from that race. In 1996 his poll came within a tenth of a point of accurately predicting the real result of the presidential election. In 2000, he correctly predicted the cliffhanger presidential election when many had predicted an easy Bush victory.

Zogby has also been on the cutting edge of polling practices. He makes it standard practice to weight his political polls using party identification, something unheard of in the decades dominated by Gallup polls. He also has begun developing an interactive online polling device using a significantly larger representative sample than is typically available to pollsters.

Another category often used is race, although potential answers are often limited. A form usually has slots for white/Caucasian, African American, Hispanic, and Asian/Pacific Islander, with anything else relegated to the label of "other." Sometimes, depending on what the researcher analyzing these demographics is looking for, these categories are broken down a bit further. Regardless, this information can help when picking out examples for use in a speech that resonates with a particular racial group.

Take the case of Mary Church Terrell, a nineteenth century social activist who spoke out against gender and racial discrimination. Terrell often had to balance her speeches with examples that appealed to both women and African Americans at a time when the experiences of both had some commonalities, but also some

SPEAKING of CIVIC ENGAGEMENT

What It Means to Be Colored in the Capital of the U.S.
by Mary Church Terrell

Delivered October 10, 1906, to the United Women's Club, Washington, D.C.

In 1906 the United Women's Club invited African American advocate and teacher Mary Church Terrell to speak, and she delivered scathing commentary on racial equality in Washington, D.C.[5] Terrell noted in her opening that the nation's capital had been labeled the "colored Man's Paradise" but declared such a title must have been bestowed out of irony, because "it would be difficult to find a worse misnomer for Washington."[6] Terrell also argued that conditions for African Americans had worsened in the 15 years of her residence there, and that although many other minorities could find lodging, unless a black person had acquaintances they likely could not find a bed. She noted that if she resisted current standards that she would be "cast into jail and forced to pay a fine for violating the Virginia laws."[7] Such issues reflected the direct experiences of African Americans of her day, but her speech was not simply about race—after all it was delivered at the Women's Club!

Ms. Terrell vividly described the limitations on the possibility of education, specifically that black school children received a lower quality education than that of white children. Within her speech she also referenced many more examples of injustice and discrimination, all designed to connect the causes of women and African Americans, as the causes of these two groups were priorities in her life.

In the closing paragraph of her speech, Ms. Terrell made a statement of a stern tone: "It is impossible for any white person in the United States, no matter how sympathetic and broad, to realize what life would mean to him if his incentive to effort were suddenly snatched away."[8] Mary Church Terrell lived to see the successes of the women's suffrage movement and the significant victory of *Brown v. Board of Education*, dying shortly thereafter at the age of 90. In recognition of the power of her voice on civil rights issues, the United States Post Office honored her with a stamp in 2009.

significant differences. Terrell needed to pay attention to the racial demographic of her audiences each time she gave a speech to make sure she used the best possible examples.

Religion is also often used as a demographic category, and depending on what the purpose of the information is, it can be broken down in a variety of different ways. Religion is most commonly explored by denomination, or the specific religious faith a person practices. This refers to labels such as Catholic, Protestant, Muslim, Buddhist, Jewish, and the like. On the other hand, religion also can be explored by asking people how often they attend church services. Do they go once a week? Once a month? On holidays? Not at all? Just like racial demographics, this information can help you determine how strongly to make a point, as well as craft strategies for identifying with audience members through examples or quotations with which the audience might be familiar.

Education level and socioeconomic status are two other demographic categories that might be measured in advance of a speech. In the 2008 primary campaign we discussed at the beginning of the chapter, Senator John McCain, a Republican candidate for president, received a significant amount of support from those who felt that national security was a major issue. On the other hand, former Massachusetts Governor Mitt Romney was seen as pro-business and economically conservative and was supported by those who favored those topics. The demographic characteristics of these audiences played a part in the candidates' ability to construct messages that appealed to these groups.

©Gage Skidmore/Creative Commons

Former Massachusetts Governor Mitt Romney

Group membership also fits the description of a demographic category and can help a speaker when trying to tailor a message to a particular audience. Group membership refers to any affiliation not already discussed, like membership in the National Rifle Association, or Mothers Against Drunk Driving. Clearly these memberships contribute to a person's identity and the groups themselves obviously contain a large number of individuals with common characteristics. Group membership can tell speakers a lot about their audience, thus helping them make sound decisions about what to include in a speech.

Table 7.1

Possible Demographic Categories	
• Age	• Race
• Gender	• Sexual orientation
• Income level	• Religion
• Education	• Zip code
• Political party affiliation	• Vocation

One final demographic category worth noting is sexual orientation. Much like the other categories we have discussed, sexual orientation can also help speakers better understand their audience and construct messages more likely to appeal to them. Sexual orientation refers to whether a person is attracted to the same sex, the opposite sex, or both. Savvy speakers try to infer characteristics about their audience based upon this demographic category and tailor their speeches accordingly. It is an important demographic to measure in many cases; however, as is the case when referring to any of the demographic data mentioned above, it suffers from one major drawback: generalization.

Demographics are descriptive statistics, but in today's day and age they sometimes cause people to make erroneous generalizations about their audience based on the breakdown the statistics reveal about their audience. Often, people assume that a demographic category functions in unison, and that there are little differences among members within a category. For instance, suppose someone uses a demographic that says 54% of the students support eliminating the football program to say that "students support eliminating the football program." The statement used to describe the data is not entirely accurate because it makes a blanket statement about the student body that denies the fact that many students do not want to cut football from the athletic department. Care must be taken to accurately represent demographic results when citing them in a speech. Likewise, paying attention to the demographics of an audience before delivering a speech can help a speaker tailor his message to the audience.

Demographics also do not measure what motivates a person or population. Oftentimes, researchers make false assumptions about motives based on demographic data. As ethical and astute speakers, we must be careful not to make this mistake. For a list of several possible demographic categories, see Table 7.1.

Psychographics

psychographics
data that measures attitudes, beliefs, behaviors, and motivations

Psychographics help provide information not available through demographic data. This type of data can tell a researcher about the beliefs, behaviors, and motivations of an individual, and one group of scholars at Stanford University even developed a program that breaks down this information even further. Psychographic information can provide even more useful information when constructing a speech because it gives a speaker insight into why a specific population acts the way they do. When you understand that, you can design your message even more specifically toward an audience, increasing the likelihood your speech will achieve the results you want it to.

One significant area measured by psychographics is beliefs. This is different than measuring, say, religion, which is a demographic category. Beliefs encompass more fluid categories of information than denominations of faith. They examine such things as attitudes toward issues or ideas. Beliefs are often as static a part of a person as their demographic characteristics, making them just as important to someone attempting to appeal to them. Measuring psychographic data is a more complicated process than determining the demographics of a group, and therefore it requires more advance time to gather and analyze.

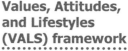

A psychographic inquiry can be fueled by demographic data to make it more useful. For example, a speaker is about to give a speech on eliminating the death penalty to representatives for the United States Catholic Bishops Association and wants to know what they believe on issues related to that topic. The speaker designs a survey to gather that information, including questions like "Are you

GOOD   **BAD**

| Extremely | Quite | Slightly | Neither | Slightly | Quite | Extremely |

Figure 7.1
Example of a Likert Scale

opposed to the death penalty?" and "How strongly do you believe in the sanctity of life?" The first of those questions is an affirmative/negative question with only two possible answers. The latter is a *Likert scale* question that may have several potential answers ranging from "not strongly at all," "very little," "no opinion," "somewhat strongly," or "very strongly." Averaging out the audience responses to these questions helps give the speaker a better idea as to how to structure and approach his speech on the death penalty. See Figure 7.1.

Likert scale
a way of measuring how strong a person's beliefs, attitudes, and values are. They usually consist of 3-7 possible answers

In addition to beliefs, psychographics also measure the motivations of an individual or group. What drives them to make the decisions they make, or act the way they do? Are they motivated by success? Fear? Money? Achievement? Psychographic questions can be designed to gather information on these characteristics. Oftentimes, the questions describe specific hypothetical scenarios and people are asked to answer based upon the answer given. They can be offered choices as well within these scenarios to better inform their decisions and better illustrate to the researcher why they made the choice that they did. Again, like beliefs, inquiries seeking to determine this type of data are more often than not driven by demographic data. Understanding what motivates your audience can assist you when developing the appeals you make within a speech. Properly motivating your audience will only improve the efficacy of your speech.

Beliefs and motivations both influence the behaviors of people and groups, and those behaviors are a third focus of psychographics. Behaviors are the actions an individual or group takes, often as a result of their beliefs and motivations. Behaviors can be idiosyncratic, or unique, or they can occur consistently, illustrating a trend of that population. Knowing the trends of a group or individual can help speakers predict the effect the words they use will have on an audience, making behaviors an important psychographic statistic when choosing what words to use within a speech.

We hope it is apparent that demographic and psychographic statistics have a tremendous amount of application in the marketing industry, in addition to their uses for speechwriters. In fact, one of the primary tools for categorizing individuals and groups according to psychographic information was developed for market researchers by the Stanford Research Institute. The *Values, Attitudes, and Lifestyles (VALS) framework* uses psychographic data to place people into one of eight categories, each indicating the beliefs and motivations of that class of people while predicting what type of market behaviors can be expected from

Values, Attitudes, and Lifestyles (VALS) framework
a tool used for categorizing individuals and groups according to their psychographic traits

medium
....
the channel through which the message travels (Note: Medium is singular for the plural term media)

innovators
....
people involved in change, who have high self-esteem and plenty of personal resources

thinkers
....
mature, responsible, well-educated professionals who are motivated by ideals

believers
....
people motivated by ideals, but who do not have a significant amount of resources

achievers
....
people who are motivated by success, politically conservative, and work oriented; they value the familiar

strivers
....
people who are low in resources, but motivated by achievement

them.[9] This information is then used to target consumer messages. VALS can also be adapted for use in the speech development process because the only thing that is different is the *medium* through which the message is communicated: for market strategists it is transmitted through commercials, but for public speakers it is transferred through a much longer speech.

Innovators are the first subgroup in the VALS framework. These people are often involved in activities that stimulate change. They have high self-esteem and a significant amount of personal resources. They like the finer things in life, primarily because they can afford them and change easily from what they already have. As you can guess, they are very concerned with image. An audience that consists of innovators is therefore likely to be most receptive to messages that stress improving the quality of life and express good taste.

The second subgroup of the VALS framework consists of *thinkers*. Like innovators, this group of people has lots of personal resources, but unlike the previous group, they are not primarily concerned with image. They make rational decisions and are often well-informed on world events. They are concerned with change, but not change to make themselves or their work appear better; rather, they value change that actually makes things better. Speakers addressing thinkers should take care to structure their arguments carefully and logically, and be sure to demonstrate an appreciation for social improvement.

People who are motivated by ideals but do not have lots of resources are called *believers* in the VALS system. These middle-class individuals are conservative consumers who prefer familiarity and consistency in their lives. Believers' lives revolve around ideals that emanate from entrenched systems and organizations like churches, nations, and community groups. That being the case, appeals that stress connections to these groups and the values they represent resonate with believers.

The VALS framework also includes *achievers*, who are similar in some ways to believers. Like believers, achievers are middle-class economically, but instead of being motivated by ideals, achievers are motivated by success. That motivation comes from their focus on work, and they value things that let others know they have succeeded. Achievers are also conservative and respect the rules and status quo, just as believers do. Achievers want to be pushed, and speakers should be attuned to that characteristic if they know this is the audience to which they are appealing.

A fifth category of people in the VALS framework are called *strivers*. Strivers are essentially achievers without the financial resources. They are motivated by achievement, and are even more "about the bling" than their achiever counterparts. This group goes so far as to try and emulate those they admire in as many ways as their resources permit them to. They are, for all intents and purposes, striving to be something they are not. Due to the similarities they share with achievers, it makes sense that appeals to this group mostly mirror those directed toward achievers.

Experiencers, the sixth group in the VALS framework, are motivated by image and have the capability to express and improve it. They are a high-resource group and are typically younger than the other groups. They tend to stay physically active and spend a great amount of time on social activities, illustrating their image-conscious nature. They also make many purchases, especially on new products and services, so they can maintain their appearance as trendy and popular individuals. New, creative ideas appeal to them, and they are also the most susceptible of all the groups to the logical fallacy, bandwagon, which we will discuss later in Chapter 13.

experiencers
people motivated by image who have the capability to express and improve it

More economically challenged individuals who value self-sufficiency are referred to as *makers* in the VALS matrix. Makers have few resources and focus on familiar things like family, work, and physical activities. They have little time to spend on staying up to speed on current events so they do not care much for the broader world. Due to their emphasis on being self-sufficient, makers value things that are practical and functional. They are a fairly logical group who are more apt to listen to something if it can be demonstrated as purposeful and applicable in their daily lives.

makers
a low resource group that values self-sufficiency and the familiar

The eighth and final VALS framework category is *survivors*. Survivors have neither the resources nor the desire to improve their own image or be motivated by ideals. They are motivated more by need. Survivors try and do just that: survive. They are the least likely of any VALS group to be persuaded by anything other than the practical benefit something might have in their lives.

survivors
the lowest income bracket and the oldest median age of any VALS category

Table 7.2

VALS Framework		
VALS Descriptor	**Characteristics**	**Behavior or Appeal**
Innovators	High self-esteem, image conscious	Wine-tasting events High fashion
Thinkers	Personal resources, logical, not about image, change that improves things	Work to improve blighted neighborhoods
Believers	Conservative, like familiarity, consistency	Active in church and/or respected civic groups
Achievers	Success-driven with resources	Status symbols as proof of success
Strivers	Success-driven, few resources	Desire status of Achievers
Experiencers	Many resources, stress on image	Trendy clothes and technology, health clubs, active night spots
Makers	Self-sufficient, practical	Not trendy, not into image or status
Survivors	Few resources, motivated by need, thrifty	Spend money on essentials, not trendy

As you can see, the VALS framework illustrates both the complexity and usefulness of psychographic information about an audience. Try to think of the context in which you might encounter members of each group, but just like demographics, try to avoid believing that all these different categories function as one monolithic whole. Use this information strategically to get your points across and increase your ability to identify with an audience, but remember this knowledge does not automatically result in success. For a summary of the VALS framework, see Table 7.2.

Other Ways to Gather Audience Information

open-ended questions
••••••••••••
items on a survey that allow room for the person taking the survey to answer in his/her own words

fixed-response questions
••••••••••••
items on a survey that allow only for pre-scribed answers

Thus far we have explored two significant forms of data, demographics and psychographics, which can be ascertained through the use of survey instruments. Surveys can contain *open-ended questions* or *fixed-response questions*. Surveys are quite useful if you have the time, but a lot goes into their creation, distribution, collection, and analysis. Not only must you provide time for yourself to create the proper questions, but you also must allow your audience time to answer. Following that, you must again allow for time to analyze the results you find and then use that information to inform your speech. Because of their time-consuming and somewhat cumbersome nature, surveys are often difficult to employ before giving a speech. Instead, we try to find out desired information through a variety of other methods.

If we cannot conduct a survey ourselves, the first place to look to find the demographic statistics we need is on the web. If an organization is hosting the speaking event you often can find information on its membership through either its homepage or simply by calling it directly and asking for the statistics. The older the organization, the more likely you will find more detailed information on its membership.

Another technique for discovering information about your potential audience is through interviewing. If potential members of the audience are available and willing to speak with you in advance of the presentation, arrange appointments with them to gather specific information you need to help you develop your speech. Interviews primarily consist of open-ended questions because demographic questions are simply not suited for conversation, and the answers to some of them (like race and gender) are readily identifiable without asking the person. An added advantage to the interviewing strategy is that throughout the course of the interview you will develop a relationship with one of your audience members, thus increasing your comfort level when you actually deliver the address. Interviews are much more personal than a survey and, if used correctly and creatively, they can be very beneficial to the speaker.

If there is no organization to poll and if individuals who might attend your talk are not easily found and approached in advance of the speech, then the next step to gathering audience information is through on-site analysis. It is possible to conduct interviews at the site of the speech. However, that information can only help with small brief changes to the wording and structure of your speech. "Working the room," as some refer to it, does, however, increase your identification with the audience by letting them see you walk among them before the presentation. Many people try to work the room when at dinner parties or other social events, but speakers also can employ this technique before their speech to get a feel for the audience's disposition toward them and the occasion.

So far we have discussed methods of gathering specific types of audience information, but discovering the information is only half the battle to successfully appealing to your audience or even just capturing their attention. In the next part of this chapter we explore how you can wield this information when developing your speech, and we discuss various tips for doing so with regard to verbal and organizational strategies.

AUDIENCE ANALYSIS AND SPEECH DEVELOPMENT

When you know the makeup of your audience it becomes much easier to construct appeals to them. Speaking in terms the audience knows, using examples designed to resonate with them, and referencing statistics they are more likely to care about becomes easier when you know who they are, what they care about, what they believe in, and what motivates them. After all, why use a BMW as an example of a car to buy when talking to an audience of low-income people? It makes no sense. Understanding your audience can help you create a more effective speech.

This section talks about two ways to make use of audience analysis information. The first is through verbal appeals, or the specific construction of what to say so you can better identify with your audience. The second strategy is through how to say it, or the organizational structure of your speech. Both the content and structure of any speech can be modified and magnified based upon information from an audience analysis.

Content Strategies

There are three main ways of making use of your knowledge about an audience to augment your ability to successfully appeal to them. The first involves using the data as part of a strategy for identifying with the audience, or making you seem as though you are one of them. Secondly, audience analysis information allows you to incorporate knowledge of the audience into your speech. Finally, it allows you to choose more appropriate examples, statistics, or testimonials for the speech. Each of these builds upon the other to help you establish a strong rapport with your audience.

Identifying with your audience is possibly the most important result of conducting audience analyses. The information you find can help you understand who your audience is, and when you know that, you can find things you have in common with them. Once you determine what you have in common you can immediately stress those common bonds in your introduction, thus making yourself appear similar to the audience. Such an approach enhances your ethos, or credibility, with the audience and strengthens your ability to appeal to them.

For example, Anya is a 21-year-old college senior at New York University with a major in criminal justice. She plans to go to law school so she can eventually work in the district attorney's office in Los Angeles, where she grew up. When she was younger she observed the Rodney King riots of 1992 and watched as increasing gang activity tore apart her community, so she decided to pursue a career that would enable her to prevent those things from happening again. Now, as valedictorian of her senior class, she is addressing commencement on her campus.

She is at a ceremony celebrating graduating from school on the other side of the country from her native home, so how can she identify with her audience immediately? There are several ways.

First, like her audience, she is graduating and thus roughly the same age as many of them. Second, she knows that many of those in the audience live in New York City which, like Los Angeles, has also suffered from gang activity and occasional social unrest in the past two decades. This information can help her develop a speech that both celebrates the joy of graduation while also calling on her audience to help improve society. This can be done quickly in the speech by telling an abbreviated version of her story and linking it to New York. She could, perhaps, cite examples from the class's days at the school where fellow students may have been victims of crimes, or just mention they have all watched the news about crime in the city for the last four years. By making such references in her speech, Anya becomes more credible to the audience when calling on them to be more socially conscious. Audience analysis helps you find ways to connect with your audience in a very real way.

Think of the information you glean from audience analysis as contributing to the relationship between you and your audience. Picture a triangle where you are one corner of the triangle, the audience is another corner, and the message is the third corner (see Figure 7.2). You need to find a way to connect with the audience, and the best way to do that is through the message. The audience also wants to find a way to connect with you, and that also occurs through the message. The stronger your message appeals to the commonalities

Figure 7.2
Connecting with the Audience

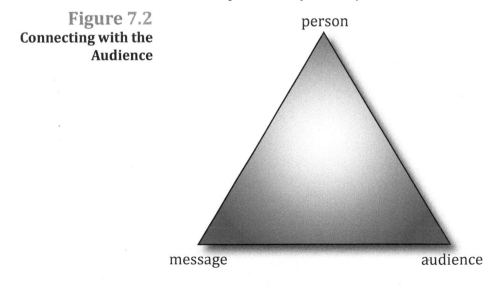

person

message   audience

between you and your audience, the stronger your connection will be with the audience.

There is another way to identify with your audience through the use of words, but it can only happen after you establish common ground with your listeners. "We" language allows you to speak as if you are a member of the audience's group, and once you establish a connection between yourself and your listeners, this type of language should be used often. Instead of saying "I," say "we." Instead of saying "me," say "us." This approach enhances your connection to the audience, but if you use it too early, without creating common ground, it will actually diminish your credibility. People need to know *how* you are one of them before you declare that you are one of them.

A second way to use audience analysis information to enhance your connection with the audience is through incorporating what you know about your listeners into the speech. Obviously, this takes a bit of preparation and only the most advanced public speakers can successfully do this in an impromptu manner, but it is nonetheless another tool for you. University and college presidents often identify and reference outstanding graduates and alumni in their commencement speeches. They use these graduate references to help show that they are familiar

Former Secretary of State Colin Powell gives a commencement speech

©Dean Evangelista / Shutterstock.com

with their entire student body and also to identify with the students to whom they are speaking. In addition to citing specific students as representatives for the whole class, they may provide demographic data on the graduating class as well, such as the average age, the oldest and youngest graduates, the percentage of graduating students from particular ethnic and racial groups, and other such information. These types of references enhance the image that the president of a university is connected to, and familiar with, his or her students.

Another way to incorporate information about your audience into the speech is through descriptive statements. At many graduation ceremonies the college president will describe the demographic characteristics of the graduating class. This illustrates knowledge about the group to whom they are speaking and demonstrates that they cared enough about the group to "do their homework." Citing statistics alone probably will not do much, but creatively incorporating this information into a speech can go a long way to establishing a bond with your audience.

The third and final strategy for using audience analysis information to enhance the content of your speech involves the selection of stories, statistics, and examples that will resonate with your audience. When you know who your audience is it becomes easier to reference things that are familiar to them. The more you appear to know about them, the more you appear to be one of them. For example, if you are giving a speech in support of a presidential candidate and you know 80% of your audience is over the age of 65, then perhaps you could open your speech with a story about your own grandparents and what they feel is important about the upcoming election. The reference to your grandparents creates a common bond between you and the majority of your audience, potentially making them more receptive to your message. If you plan on speaking about the dangers of drunk driving or drug use to your class, then citing statistics about that age group and those activities increases the power of your message. Even Aristotle would recommend you select the appropriate inartistic proofs to enhance your ability to connect with the audience.

Information about your audience helps you make informed choices about the content of your speech. It ultimately helps you find ways to identify with your audience members through incorporating that information into your speech through the use of specific examples, statistics, and stories that are more likely to appeal to your listeners. Content, however, is not the only area where this information can help improve your speech.

Organizational Strategies

Knowledge of the audience can influence the way you organize your speech, specifically how you arrange your main points and when (or even if) you reference members of the audience. The organization of points in a speech is one of the most important parts of the developmental process, and information about your audience can help you choose the best arrangement for your information. Traditionally, there are two ways to organize points in a speech, but knowledge about your audience can help you determine which one will work best for your speech.

One way to arrange main points for maximum effect involves placing your strongest point first. Each point that follows then builds off the foundation of the first main item. This allows you to draw your audience in immediately with a strong start and then build your case from there. In some ways this method serves as a "backup" attention-getter. This organizational pattern typically works best when an audience is not already prone to believing or agreeing with you or the topic of your speech. A strong first point then helps draw them in and realize that you have a valid argument that is worth listening to. So, when you determine there is initial dissonance between you, your audience, and/or your topic through audience analysis before the speech, consider arranging the points so that the strongest comes first.

Quintilian expounded on this approach to arrangement even more. He taught his students to make their strongest point first and to treat the strongest points of the speech individually and in depth. In other words, spend time on the strongest arguments and connect with the audience, while taking the weaker elements of your speech and lumping them together so as to appear stronger. In fact, he advised students to ditch the weakest parts of the argument if they need not be used—something you can determine both before and during a speech. For instance, if you notice your strongest cases are having a large impact on the audience, you may decide adding in the weaker cases might not be needed. This approach to crafting and delivering points makes as much sense today as it did when Quintilian lived.

The other traditional way of organizing a speech places the strongest point at the end of the body of the speech. This pattern puts less powerful points at the beginning and builds toward the most important main point in a *crescendo* pattern. Such an organizational approach could enhance the pathos of an appeal by building excitement, interest, and emotional attachment to the argument made by the speaker. This approach typically works best when you know the audience already agrees with, or is prone to agree with, the subject of the speech. It is even better when the speaker can create a strong sense of identification with the audience.

crescendo
an organizational pattern where the strongest point is placed at the end and is built up to by smaller main points

One other organizational strategy that benefits from knowledge about the audience is knowing who, how, and when to reference members of the audience within your speech. Carefully planned references, and even the occasional impromptu nod from the speaker, can promote the appeal of your speech. If certain points within a speech will be magnified by relating them directly to the audience, or to a characteristic of the audience, then it makes sense to do so. Only when you are aware of those characteristics through survey information, or know members of the audience by working the room and interviewing, can you make proper use of this technique.

Creating your speech is not simply the process of putting words on paper; it also involves using audience analysis to choose the proper words. When time allows, analyzing the audience before a speech is an invaluable tool for any speaker. There is one approach to audience analysis, however, that does not involve extensive advance preparation and is, in fact, available to every speaker.

ANALYZING THE AUDIENCE DURING THE SPEECH

Every speaker can watch, learn from, and adapt to an audience during a speech. There are also several tactics speakers can employ to maximize their ability to connect with and influence an audience based upon that constant feedback. This section details two ways a speaker can analyze the audience while speaking and offers some suggestions as to how to adapt during a speech based upon that information.

Observing the Audience

Speakers play the role of both message deliverer and message receiver during a presentation, and so in some ways they are also an audience. The vast majority of the time speakers do not act as an audience to verbal cues from those to whom they are speaking, but rather they receive nonverbal messages from the audience while they speak. They can then use that nonverbal feedback to change certain things about their delivery and measure whether or not those changes are effective.

One key nonverbal activity speakers should be attuned to is eye contact. Not only should speakers themselves make significant eye contact with their audience, they also should monitor the amount of eye contact they receive from the audience. If the audience is looking away, at a wall, or reading, then chances are they are not paying attention and adjustments to the presentation need to be considered to recapture the audience's focus.

Audience members may also shift in their seats or move around during a speech. Sometimes this may be due to the discomfort of the chairs they are sitting in, but other times it may indicate boredom. If you are delivering a long presentation then such shifting is to be expected from time to time, but if your speech is short and they move around a lot it might indicate restlessness.

Two physical behaviors an audience may exhibit also might tell a speaker something about the reception of his or her message and whether adjustments should be considered. The first is if audience members continually check their watches or a clock in the room. This more often than not tells a speaker she has been talking a little too long and has lost the audience's attention. The other behavior audiences may exhibit is note-taking. If the audience is taking notes then they are most likely paying attention to your message and no adjustments may be necessary. But, take note of whether they can keep up with your pace and allow them time to write by pausing or at times slowing down the delivery.

Polling the Audience

Another useful way to gain information about an audience during a speech is through impromptu polling. When you poll an audience during your speech the results are neither scientific nor generalizable, but they do provide immediate information for you and your audience. The most common occurrence of audience polling during a speech is during the introduction, when many people start with a question for the audience. Speakers ask the audience to raise their hands if they agree/disagree with a statement, or if they ever did or experienced something relevant to the speech.

Polling in this manner also can help you learn about whether or not the audience comprehends the information which you provide them. Oftentimes, stopping the speech to ask the audience if they understand or if they need something repeated can be a useful tool. It allows the audience to consider the information they have been given, determine if they need clarification, and play an active part in the speech. In short, it encourages cognitive activity and participation on the part of the audience. However, be wary of engaging your audience in a conversation as you do not want to lose control of the situation.

Polling during a speech does not need to be public; that is, it can be done anonymously. If you plan to conduct an anonymous poll during the speech and use the results at a later time, be prepared to do so. This will require either a paper ballot or, if the room is equipped with technology, electronic devices to calculate responses for you. Many classrooms are moving in this direction, and yours may be one of them. These *classroom response systems*, or clickers, are

classroom response systems
∙∙∙∙∙∙∙∙∙∙∙∙∙∙∙∙∙∙∙∙∙∙
devices that allow students to answer questions posed during a lecture and provide tabulated results of the poll for everyone in the room in a timely manner

two-part devices. The first part is a clicker that audience members (students in this case) use to answer questions posed through PowerPoint presentations. The second component is the software that allows for tabulation of the poll results so the presenter can gather immediate feedback on audience comprehension, agreement, or even enjoyment regarding the speech or portions of the speech.

As you can see, audience analysis can and should be conducted during a speech as well as before. Just as preparatory audience analysis allows you to design speeches for maximum impact, audience analyses during a speech also allow you to make adjustments in an effort to maintain audience attention and even increase your ability to identify as one of them. We now turn our attention to methods of adapting to audience feedback during a presentation.

Example of a handheld classroom response keypad

Strategies for Adapting to Feedback During Delivery

Audience analysis during your speech can help you determine how to proceed when giving the speech. Those adaptations can occur immediately or later during the speech, but it is important to be aware of what you can do to increase the impact of your speech based on the audience's reaction to it. There are also two things you can do from the very beginning to increase the likelihood that the audience will pay attention and not get distracted or bored during your speech.

The first thing you can do in reaction to the audience's behavior at the beginning of the speech is make sure you effectively use the space you are speaking in. If there are many more chairs than audience members, and if those members are sparsely populating the room, ask them to move to the front in the same general area near you. This does two things for you. First, it decreases their ability to not pay attention because they are so close to the speaker. Second, and more importantly, it creates a more intimate setting where the speaker appears closer to the audience in proximity and personality.

The second action a speaker can employ either at the outset of the speech or at some point during the address involves eliminating a barrier between speaker and audience. Podiums are very useful items, but sometimes they act as an obstacle between a speaker and an audience. To increase the intimacy of the speaking environment, and to demonstrate your comfort among the audience (thus increasing your ability to appear as one of them), either move out from behind the podium and walk amongst the audience, or remove the podium entirely. These actions can make an audience feel more at ease with the speaker, thus making them more receptive to the message.

Other adaptation strategies work better during the speech. If, for instance, you notice that people look confused or seem to be lost, stop and ask them if they understand, or if they need something repeated and/or clarified. Revisit points through the use of impromptu internal summaries of the information if the audience appears not to understand a connection you make within the speech.

Sometimes people can seem bored or disinterested in a speech, and in this case it becomes important to vary your actions as the speaker. Remember, people's attention spans are not very long and so you need to change things up every once in awhile to "restart" their attention span. This can involve changes in the rate or tone of your speech, a noticeable change in the volume of your voice, going off on a short but interesting tangent, or moving from behind the podium. These surprising changes in your presentation behaviors will work to counteract negative audience behaviors you may notice. Adapting to the audience based on how they react to you as speaker is an important element of a successful speech.

SUMMARY

This chapter explained the importance of audience analysis before and during a speech. We also discussed the different types of information you can and should try to find about your audience and provided several methods of gathering that data. We then detailed some suggestions about how to make the best use of audience analysis information when developing your speech. Finally, we learned about what to look for in your audience during a speech and how to adapt to their reactions. Remember, there can be no speech without an audience and no effective speech without understanding who the audience is, where they come from, and what they care about.

KEY TERMS

achievers	Likert scale
believers	makers
classroom response systems	medium
crescendo	open-ended questions
demographic data	psychographics
efficacy	strivers
exit poll	survivors
experiencers	thinkers
fixed-response questions	Values, Attitudes, and Lifestyles (VALS) framework
innovators	

REVIEW QUESTIONS

1. What do demographic data consist of?

_____

_____

2. What do psychographic questions measure?

_____

_____

3. The VALS program categorizes people according to what two significant characteristics?

_____

_____

4. What are some useful methods for researching demographic and psychographic data?

_____

_____

5. What audience characteristics would lead you to consider placing the most important main point first? Last?

_____

_____

6. What are some ways of measuring audience responses during a speech?

_____

_____

7. What adjustments can you make at the outset of a speech to help you identify with an audience and increase their attention?

_____

_____

8. What were some of the challenges Mary Church Terrell faced when speaking?

_____

_____

1. Is there a difference between audience analysis and stereotyping? If so, what is it?

_____

_____

_____

_____

2. Are there any ethical considerations for audience analysis?

_____

_____

_____

_____

3. Do we rely on survey information too much when developing speeches in today's society?

_____

_____

_____

_____

4. How could an unethical speaker use audience analysis to his advantage?

_____

_____

_____

_____

5. Is it possible for a speaker to overuse audience analysis?

_____

_____

_____

_____

ACTIVITIES FOR ACTION

1. Once you have a speech topic in mind and you know where you will deliver your speech, devise a list of questions regarding demographic and behavioral/attitudinal beliefs. Format these into a survey for your audience to take in advance. Use a Likert scale for attitudinal questions, and phrase them as statements rather than questions.

2. Go to a website for a popular dating service, such as www.match.com or www.eharmony.com, and look at a handful of profiles. Take a look at the questions they ask and the options from which people can select their answers. Determine if these are demographic or attitudinal questions.

3. Watch a few films where characters deliver speeches, such as *The Contender, City Hall, Remember the Titans,* or *Mr. Smith Goes to Washington.* Listen to the speeches in these films and identify how these speeches are designed to reach the audiences in the film. Do they employ inclusive language such as "we" or "us"? Do they use a crescendo pattern to conclude the speech? What is done to make the speeches effective? This also can be done with contemporary speeches, but films are fun and effective to look at in this manner.

ENDNOTES

1. Michael Grunwald, James Carney, and Michael Scherer, "A Right Fight," *Time* (February 18, 2008), 37.

2. June Kronholz, "Will McCain Make Nice to the Right?" *The Wall Street Journal* (February 6, 2008), eastern edition, sec. A.

3. Ivy J. Sellers, "CPAC 2007 Hosts Record Crowd of Enthusiastic Conservatives," *Human Events*, March 19, 2007, http://findarticles.com/p/articles/mi_qa3827/is_200703/ai_n18755647 (accessed May 23, 2008).

4. Robert Novak, "Fred Thompson's Progress," *Human Events.com,* July 21, 2007, http://www.humanevents.com/article.php?id=21616 (accessed May 23, 2008).

5. Mary Church Terrell, "What It Means to Be Colored in the Capital of the U. S.," www.americanrhetoric.com. http://www.biography.com/articles/Mary-Church-Terrell-9504299 (accessed June 11, 2011).

6. Ibid.

7. Ibid.

8. Ibid.

9. SRI Consulting Business Intelligence, http://www.sric-bi.com/VALS/types.shtml (accessed May 23, 2008). For the transcript of this speech, see: http://www.whitehouse.gov/news/releases/2001/09/20010920-8.html (accessed May 23, 2008).

Language

CHAPTER OVERVIEW

- Defines meaning and details the characteristics of language
- Relays some basic forms of language that help construct messages
- Provides guidelines for determining the most effective language choices when constructing a speech

Practically SPEAKING

In the United States, as in many democracies, there is a fundamental right to free speech for every citizen, but even that right is not absolute. For instance, we cannot yell "fire!" in a crowded theatre because that speech may result in the creation of a harmful situation. For the longest time, curse words could not be uttered on prime time television, although now that is hardly the case. Language is controversial because it is powerful. It can move people to action, convey a sense of identity for the speaker, or conjure one for the audience. Because language is powerful, even the right to free speech is curtailed. One famous legal case that underscores the power of language and illustrates society's desire to control it in some way involved the late comedian George Carlin.

Around 2:00 p.m. on a Tuesday afternoon in 1973, WBAI (FM), a radio station in New York City, aired a 12-minute segment from a monologue delivered by Carlin. The monologue, entitled "Filthy Words," was initially recorded before a live audience in California and concerned the words a person could not say on public airwaves. Carlin listed the seven words that fit that category and then discussed them in detail. Right before the station broadcast the words, it warned its audience that the monologue included language that might offend some listeners. Unfortunately for the radio station, not everyone heard the warning. One man complained to the Federal Communications Commission (FCC), and that government agency quickly responded.[1]

The FCC ruled that Carlin's satirical presentation was indecent because it depicted sexual acts and bodily functions, calling his presentation "obnoxious" and stating it reduced humanity to its "bodily functions." It further pointed out that the radio station was at fault because it aired the satire at a time when children would hear it.[2] The case eventually found its way to the U.S. Supreme Court. It ruled that the FCC did not censor the station because it did not edit it in advance or prohibit the broadcast from airing. For the Court, reviewing content after airing is not an issue of censorship.[3]

The Supreme Court's opinion, written by Justice John Paul Stevens, discussed why Carlin's monologue was not subject to the protection of the First Amendment. He wrote that Carlin's monologue was offensive and lacked literary, political, or scientific value and was not related to the marketplace of ideas. Additionally, Stevens claimed that time of day, content of communication, and the medium used are all important considerations when defining obscene and indecent language.[4]

In the case of Pacifica and Carlin, language proved to be inappropriate for some audiences. The words, in effect, endangered the standards and practices of society. Carlin attempted to point out what he saw as the silliness of language choices, but in so doing illustrated the reverence and power we accord language. In this chapter we will explain how you may tap into that power and enhance your speech. First we will discuss the basic building blocks of meaning to illustrate the source of language's power. We will then examine several different types of language strategies that can help you enhance the appeal and effectiveness of your message. Finally, we will offer some concrete guidelines for choosing these words when putting together a speech.

MEANING AND SYMBOLS

Meaning, as we have pointed out in earlier chapters, can be expressed both verbally and nonverbally. In both instances we exchange meaning through symbols, and in that respect symbols are the building blocks of how we understand the world. Language is a common way in which we communicate meaning to others, and the symbolic base of language is letters. Letters are, for all intents and purposes, symbols that when connected to form words mean something. Words also are symbols that represent objects, thoughts, values, feelings, and ideas, and they are the foundation of communication. When we share an understanding of what symbols mean we are able to connect with each other in meaningful ways about the world around us. In this section of the chapter we will explore the four characteristics of any language.

Language Characteristics

All languages share three characteristics, regardless of their cultural, ethnic, or regional origins. The first characteristic of a language is that it is *arbitrary*, or that the symbols used to represent things are not intrinsically connected to those things. Since meaning is arbitrary it can change over time as different groups ascribe different definitions and purposes for words. The word "hot," for instance, formerly only meant raised temperature but now also refers to the attractiveness of something ("she/he is so hot") or the success of an action ("he's a hot hitter right now"). We also develop new words every year to the point where the English language has expanded exponentially over the past few hundred years. Words and phrases like "affirmative action," "mother board," and "airline" did not exist until the last century. The arbitrary nature of language illustrates its flexibility, as language changes according to our need to explain the world around us.

arbitrary
symbols used to represent things that are not intrinsically connected to those things

Because language can change and is dependent upon constant use to sustain itself, some languages can disappear. When a language is no longer used by a group we call it a dead language, but this does not mean we do not know how to use it or that we cannot read it. For example, Aramaic is considered to be a dead language and yet there are still people who know how to use it and read it—it just isn't a language you will overhear while waiting in line at the DMV! Some scholars focus their efforts on preserving and understanding language and how it reflects a particular culture. One of the more renowned researchers in this area was Mary

Haas, who worked on American Indian languages and did important work on the Thai language before World War II. In essence, Haas and other scholars like her focus on trying to understand the arbitrary qualities of language.

The fact that language is arbitrary also can be a bit shocking. Why do we call a cat a "cat"? It could very well have been labeled "schmoog," but it was not. There was no reason behind the selection of the symbol "cat" to represent that furry little creature. It just happened and people implicitly agreed to that meaning for the symbol "cat." It was a completely arbitrary creation of a symbol to represent something in our world so we could communicate about it.

ambiguous
language that does not have precise, concrete meanings

Another component of language is that it is *ambiguous*, or that it does not have precise, concrete meanings. Cultures imbue words with a variety of meanings, but even within that culture each word has an agreed upon range of potential interpretations. For instance, the term "cool" can refer to temperature or the appeal of someone or something. Even holidays like Thanksgiving vary in meaning from country to country based upon the specific circumstances surrounding that holiday. As a speaker it is always important for you to understand the potential interpretations words can have and use them in the proper context with your audience so that your message is as clear as possible. It is through the ambiguous nature of language that many misunderstandings develop, unless the meaning of the word is made clear.

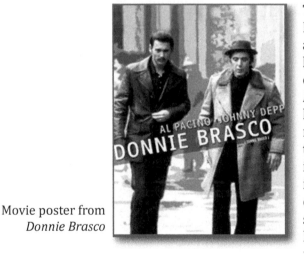

Movie poster from
Donnie Brasco

Take, for example, the phrase "friend of mine." For many people this phrase defines a level of association between you and another person; however, different people have different definitions of exactly what a friend is. In the movie *Donnie Brasco*,[5] Al Pacino's character introduces someone he recently met, played by Johnny Depp, to the mobsters for whom he works. On the way over to the introduction he clearly spells out that when he introduces him to his bosses as "friend of mine" it means he is connected but not officially a part of the organization. He further explains that if he said "friend of ours" then Depp's character would have been accorded more respect because it would mean he was a full member of the mob. This example illustrates how ambiguous language can be, and how important it is to make sure the audience knows the meaning of the words and phrases you use.

abstract
words are not concrete or tangible items; they are only representations

The third component of language is that it is *abstract*. Abstract means that words are not concrete or tangible items; you cannot touch them or feel them as they simply represent something else. Language is removed from the actual objective phenomena it represents, thus making it an abstract construct. Words can vary in their abstractness, according to the degree to which they accurately represent the real thing. The tool for identifying and measuring the degree to which our language is abstract is called the ladder of abstraction, a concept developed by Alfred Korzybski and S. I. Hayakawa in the 1960s.[6]

8

SPOTLIGHTING THEORISTS: MARY HAAS

Mary Haas (1910–1996)

During the 1930s the most renowned linguist of the era, Edward Sapir of Yale, trained a small number of graduate students. One of those students, Mary Haas, went on to become a renowned linguistic researcher and teacher in her own right.[7] Her dissertation concerned the Tunica Indians, a tribe once located in present day Louisiana, and she earned her Ph.D. in 1935. She also did linguistic work on several other Southeastern American Native American languages, including the Choctaw, Alabama, and Creek.

Prior to World War II she worked with the Thai language assisting in the preparation of

training materials to be used by the Armed Services. In 1942–1943 she taught Thai at the University of Michigan. In 1943 Haas began teaching Thai in the Army Specialized Training Program at Berkeley. After the war she became a permanent member of the Berkeley faculty.[8]

Haas was a faculty member at that university until 1977 and during that time she directed the Survey of California Indian Languages. She is credited with leading students in doing valuable work on languages that have nearly become extinct.[9] Mary Haas died in 1996 at the age of 86.[10] The scholarly journal *Anthropological Linguistics* published a memorial in its 1997 Winter issue.[11]

The ladder of abstraction depicts the most abstract term at the top of the ladder, and the closest to the objective phenomenon at the bottom. So, in Figure 8.1, at the top of the ladder you see "animal." On the level below that, representing a term slightly less removed from the object, is the term "human being." Since there are several billion human beings on the planet we move to the next level and see "musician." Again, even though this term narrows our original term significantly, it is still abstract. The next rung uses the term "rock musician," improving the connection between the term and described object. Finally, on the bottom rung of the ladder of abstraction we see "Bruce Springsteen," a very specific use of language that is as close to representing the object as possible through words.

Figure 8.1
Ladder of Abstraction

The ladder of abstraction also is illustrative of the fourth quality of any language. Scholar Kenneth Burke first noted that language, like human beings, is *hierarchical* in nature. That is, it places values of more and less on everything. Think about how we talk about advancing in the workplace. We move up from the mailroom. We don't make lateral moves. When we go to a hotel we want to stay

hierarchical
language that is structured according to more or less, higher or lower

in the penthouse on the top floor. Language, much like our social lives, reflects a hierarchy where one thing is more important, or valued more, than another.

Language is arbitrary, ambiguous, abstract, and hierarchical but it is also very useful. Language uses symbols to represent the world around us and serves as the foundation for our ability to connect with each other. Whereas in this section of the chapter we explained the characteristics of language, in the next section we will discuss general forms of language we use in everyday encounters. Understanding what language does for us and how it does so is essential for determining which terms and phrases we should incorporate into our speeches in order to maximize their effectiveness.

FORMS AND USES OF LANGUAGE

Language can be used in many different ways to send a message to an audience. Sometimes single-word strategies are the best way to convey meaning to an audience. In other instances clusters of words form a coherent impression of something for people as well. In the United States and many other places around the globe, we are free to employ either, both, or neither of these approaches thanks to freedom of speech. In this part of the chapter we will first discuss some single-word strategies you may find useful in developing your speech. We then detail a few word-cluster strategies that also might be beneficial in constructing your speech. Third, we will explain a few creative ways to structure language within a speech. Finally, we cover the ethical issues related to word choice and freedom of speech.

Single-Word Approaches

single-word approach
....
meaning is derived from individual words used in a strategic way

In this part of the chapter we will cover three types of single-word approaches to making language meaningful in a speech: metaphor, simile, and ideograph. A *single-word approach* does not necessarily mean that only one word is required for meaning to be transferred, but rather that meaning is derived from specific individual words used in a strategic way. We are all probably quite familiar in some way with the first two of these strategies and also probably can recognize words that fit into the third category although we may not recognize the name of that type.

metaphor
....
comparisons that show how two things are alike in an important way, despite being quite different in most ways

The first single-word approach is a broad category that contains a variety of distinct subsets. *Metaphor* is the broad term used to define comparisons that show how two things are alike in an important way, despite being quite different in most ways. We often use metaphors to add color, flavor, and vividness to our everyday experiences. Take the following phrase as an example: "I will now shed some light on the issue." Obviously, there is no actual light, but a lack of understanding is compared to darkness, and the speaker's intention to provide knowledge is compared to illuminating that darkness through providing light. Another example is describing a person who is adept at gardening as having a "green thumb." Again, the person's thumb is not actually green, but the color reminds people of grass and plants, thus making the connection and comparison between the activity and the person who enjoys it. There are a variety of different forms and types of metaphors, but rather than go into any great detail explaining the forms and types we have provided you with the list shown in Table 8.1.

Table 8.1

Types of Metaphors		
Type	**Description**	**Example**
Dead metaphor	Meaning lost in time	"Son of a gun"
Submerged metaphor	One part is implied	"He legged out a base hit"
Mixed metaphor	No logical connection between the metaphors	"His machine gun mouth was going like a house afire"
Synecdoche	One element represents the whole	"She drives some really cool wheels"
Metonym	A word that says something but refers to a related matter	"I want to buy this. Do you take plastic?"
Extended metaphor	One main subject which applies to other metaphors	"I think that the world is one large main stage and politicians and military leaders are actors"
Absolute metaphor	There is no connection between the topic and the metaphor	"Light up another smoke and put a nail in your coffin"
Complex metaphor	When a metaphor is the root to another metaphor	"We need some light on the subject"

A second single-word approach is often confused with metaphor but, in fact, holds one major distinction that separates it in theory and practice. A *simile*, like a metaphor, is a comparison between two objects, but whereas metaphors make both objects appear as if they are equal, similes allow each object in the comparison to retain their unique differences. When you use the word "like" or "as" in comparing two objects you are using a simile because the two objects in the comparison are similar but not equal. Here is an example of a simile: "The quarterback threaded that pass like a needle." The needle and the trajectory of the pass keep their distinctive qualities, but the comparison gives the object a reference to which some aspect, such as difficulty, can be ascribed. Another example: "She is strong as an ox." In this example the two objects in the comparison retain their distinctiveness while sharing a specific characteristic.

simile
a comparison between two objects that allows each object in the comparison to retain its unique differences

Similes sometimes need further explanation so their intended meaning can be properly conveyed. Consider this statement: "Her face was like an autumn sunrise." The intention is to convey a comparison regarding beauty; however, more detail of this simile provides greater and more specific meaning for the object. Just like metaphors, similes are very useful tools for enhancing the vivid nature of a speech and allowing an audience to visualize a concept or object within your speech.

ideograph
....
an ill-defined, politically powerful term or phrase that can push people to action

A third single-word approach to conveying meaning was identified by scholar Michael Calvin McGee in 1980. An *ideograph* is essentially an ill-defined, politically powerful term or phrase that can push people to action. As shown in Table 8.2, examples of ideographs include terms such as "freedom," "terror," "rule of law," "equality," and "liberty," just to name a few.[12] Each of these has significant cultural resonance in the United States and has served as a justification for a variety of different arguments. As recently as 2001 and 2003 President George W. Bush used the terms "freedom" and "terror" to call for military action against Afghanistan and Iraq, respectively. They also have been used to justify actions such as warrantless wiretapping and indefinite imprisonment at Guantanamo Bay. "Equality" was used during the civil rights era to push for desegregation and has recently appeared again to justify changes in the tax code. Ideographs are very powerful because the meaning of the term or phrase is culturally provided. You can use such terms within your speech to augment the emotional dimensions of an appeal for action.

Table 8.2

Examples of Ideographs	
• Freedom	• Terror
• Rule of law	• Equality
• Liberty	• Justice

Each single-word approach to conveying meaning discussed in this section holds specific power thanks to the arbitrary, ambiguous, and abstract nature of language. You can use them to effectively enhance your speeches by creating a more vivid and concrete presentation. The more vivid the descriptions you use and the more concrete the detail you provide, the more the speech will appeal to an audience. Single-word approaches, however, are not the only strategy available to you when making language choices within your speech.

Word-Cluster Approaches

word-cluster approach
....
meaning is conveyed through more complex structures such as stories

Meaning is not simply found to be potent in simple words and phrases. In many instances meaning is transmitted through more complex approaches that use language to construct meaning for an event, person, or culture. For the sake of simplicity we will call this a *word-cluster approach* because, unlike the single-word approach, meaning is not contained in individual words used in a strategic way; rather, meaning is conveyed through more complex structures such as stories. In this section we will explore two different word-cluster approaches to conveying meaning: rhetorical history and myth. Either of these tools can be used by you to present information or make an argument in a vivid, creative, and interesting manner.

The first word-cluster approach we will examine involves how we understand and communicate about our past. Think about your past, the country's past, and even world history. Everything you know about these things is only part of their story, but these parts of our past are often used to justify actions in the present. These *arguments from the past* appropriate parts of history to justify present or future actions. Arguments from the past employ stories and explanations to convey meaning. Those stories are interpretations of events and provide the power for arguments from the past.

arguments from the past
appropriating historical events, facts, or people to justify present or future actions or explain events in the here-and-now

Take the events of September 11, 2001, for example, when terrorists attacked the World Trade Center and Pentagon. Immediately following these events people compared the attack to the Japanese sneak attack on Pearl Harbor that precipitated World War II. That comparison imbued 9/11 with certain qualities inherent in Pearl Harbor, thus allowing 9/11 to also become a justification for war against the Taliban in Afghanistan in the same way Pearl Harbor allowed war to be declared against Japan. In this case a past event is used to provide significance to a present situation so future policy can be enacted.

Language, as we have noted, is imprecise and only somewhat represents an objective reality. History is always incomplete because we were not there and our understanding is based on the reflections and documents that have survived the past. These provide an imprecise understanding of the past because they are incomplete and because they rely on words—which are ambiguous themselves—to tell the story.

A second word-cluster approach is even more abstract than incomplete stories about our past because it does not need to rely on even some actual facts. A *myth* is a rhetorical construction that tries to explain natural events or cultural phenomena and is used to identify with a group and justify actions or beliefs. Myths also carry similar power to arguments from the past. Speakers often use myths to identify with an audience that shares the values the myth contains, but myths also can be used as justification to preserve a seemingly sacred event, object, or institution, as well.

myth
a rhetorical construction that tries to explain natural events or cultural phenomena and is used to identify with a group and justify actions or beliefs

One of the central myths of any culture is the founding, or origin, myth. Early Mesopotamians portrayed their founding in the story Gilgamesh, while the Romans looked to the story we now call the Aeneid for the myth of their inception. The Aenied allowed Romans to connect their past to the legends of Troy and also served to glorify and legitimize Roman values and practices. Founding myths are useful because when a speaker tells a version of the myth it allows him to connect with an audience by identifying with their past and the values expressed within the story. The meaning of myths is not inherent in one word or phrase; rather, myths represent a more elaborate and complex use of language.

Myths and arguments from the past are both stories, and as such they need to follow some semblance of a sequence. Psychologist Walter Fisher proposed a reason that explains why such stories are effective at making arguments and explaining the world around us. His *narrative paradigm* argues that humans are storytelling beings by nature and evaluate all stories according to two

narrative paradigm
humans are storytelling beings by nature

narrative coherence
⋯⋯⋯⋯⋯⋯
the degree to which a story makes sense in the world in which we live

narrative fidelity
⋯⋯⋯⋯⋯⋯
the degree to which a story matches our own beliefs and experiences

elements. First is that the story has *narrative coherence*, or that it makes sense in the world. Myths and appropriations of past events need to make sense in our world for us to believe them when they are told to us. Second, stories must have *narrative fidelity* for us to find them acceptable. This means the story must not only make sense, but it must match our own beliefs and experiences. Stories such as arguments from the past and myths must, in essence, be believable and relate to our own worldview in order for them to be effective within a speech.

Simply knowing the characteristics of language and some of the ways in which it can be used to creatively and artfully convey meaning is not enough; in fact, it borders on the dangerous. It is also important that you understand the ethical dimensions of using language to convey meaning. In the next part of this chapter we will discuss some of the ethical issues that are only relevant in a society where you have freedom of speech.

SPEAKING of CIVIC ENGAGEMENT

"I Have a Dream" Speech
by Dr. Martin Luther King, Jr.

Delivered August 28, 1963, at the Lincoln Memorial in Washington, D.C.

"I Have a Dream" is one of the most, if not the most, referenced and used speech in public speaking classes and other liberal arts classes. It is worthy of such recognition not only because of its historical significance, but also due to its beautiful tone, structure, and use of metaphor, parallelism, and other language devices.

Dr. King used many metaphors in the speech. One in particular stands out.

"In a sense we've come to our nation's capital to cash a check."[13] This statement infers that a check needs to be cashed to fulfill an obligation. Dr. King extends the metaphor further to make his point: "It is obvious today that America has defaulted on this promissory note, insofar as her citizens of color are concerned. Instead of honoring this sacred obligation, America has given the Negro people a bad check, a check which has come back marked 'insufficient funds.'"

This masterful orator also used a form of repetition to emphasize his points:

"Now is the time to rise from the dark and desolate valley of segregation to the sunlit path of racial justice. Now is the time to lift our nation from the quicksands of racial injustice to the solid rock of brotherhood. Now is the time to make justice a reality for all of God's children."[14]

This speech will go down in the annals of great speeches for centuries to come. Reading the speech is one thing, but actually hearing it and even viewing it brings forth the full power of the day and the man who later lost his life due to his course to improve the lives of millions of people.

Structuring Language

The way you structure language within a speech can also help enhance both your ability to deliver meaning and the audience's ability to retain the meaning of your speech once it is over. In this section we will cover four specific strategies for creatively structuring language within your speeches (see Table 8.3). Strategic use of these structural patterns will greatly enhance your speech, but overuse or inappropriate use will damage your speech, so be judicious in choosing when to use any of these.

The simplest structural strategy can often be the most effective at helping audiences follow your speech as well as retain the main points from it. *Repetition* occurs in two forms, but both involve repeating the same words or phrases. The first form occurs by using the same pattern of words whenever you introduce a new point. The pattern is not immediately repeated because there is data and evidence between the repeated phrase, but audiences quickly determine the pattern, thus making it easier for them to identify when you introduce a new main point. The other version of repetition takes place when you want a specific claim, point, or piece of information to resonate with an audience. Here you simply repeat what you just said. For example: "American Idol was number one in the ratings last fall. Number one." The number is repeated, emphasizing to the audience that the number was important to know and remember.

repetition
repeating either the same phrasing pattern for main points, or a phrase you just stated, in order to maximize the audience's ability to receive the information

A second structural strategy also involves repeating something, but not words or phrases. *Alliteration* repeats the same consonant or vowel sound in subsequent words and audiences notice this form of speech because it is unique. Phrases like "peace, progress, and prosperity" or "direct, deliberate, and decisive" repeat the same consonant sound at the beginning of three words that follow each other, making it more pleasing to the ear. Additionally, the words build on and relate to one another, thus underscoring your description of an object.

alliteration
repeating the same consonant or vowel sound at the beginning of subsequent words

Repeating patterns of sounds or words is not the only structural way to enhance a speech. We can also use *parallelism*, similarly structuring related words, phrases, or clauses. By structuring different phrases and words in a similar fashion you can emphasize importance and create memorable wording that the audience is more likely to remember. One of the more famous examples of parallelism can be found in a speech by Martin Luther King. In fact, his use of parallelism is probably why you remember it. The "I Have a Dream Speech," as it is often referred to, is an example of this linguistic device because he uses the title phrase eight times in the speech in the same grammatical structure.

parallelism
similarly structuring related words, phrases, or clauses

The fourth and final structural strategy we will cover involves inverting language. *Antithesis* calls for you to take two ideas that sharply contrast with each other and juxtapose them in a parallel grammatical structure. A famous example of antithesis comes from John F. Kennedy's inaugural address: "Ask not what your country can do for you—ask what you can do for your country." On the one hand he decries socialism, and on the other he inspires individual effort. These are two ideas that compete with one another but work together to make a point in this statement. This is one of the more difficult structural strategies to employ, but the reward for the effort within the speech is high.

antithesis
two ideas that sharply contrast with each other and are juxtaposed in a parallel grammatical structure

Table 8.3

	Speech Structure Strategies	
Type	**Example**
Repetition	"The TV show *The Simpsons* has been running since 1989. 1989!"
Alliteration	"I want this report clear, concise, and concrete."
Parallelism	"My hobbies are hiking, boating, and fishing."
Antithesis	"To err is human, to forgive divine."

Ethics and Language

As we have discussed, language is a powerful tool that can help you accomplish the goals of any presentation. As the adage goes, though, with great power comes great responsibility, so you must be careful not to abuse language when constructing and delivering your speech. In this part of the chapter we will discuss two examples of language that cross the line from helpful to abusive.

profanity
coarse and irreverent language

The first way in which language can be used unethically should come as no surprise to anyone as we hear examples of it everyday. *Profanity*, or coarse and irreverent language, is all around us—in movies, on the street, within songs, and in many other places. Oftentimes we use this language because we let our emotions get the best of us, but that does not make it right. There was a reason that the words George Carlin labeled "the seven dirty words" were considered outside the norm and inappropriate. Those seven words are common, but in some areas and within some cultures other words that you may not believe to be profane may be considered profane, so it is important to know your audience when making language choices.

Many novice speakers believe that saying something profane at the beginning of a speech is a great way to get the audience's attention, but that is not an advisable course of action. Many audience members may see it as unethical, unprofessional, and damaging to your credibility. This runs the risk of aggravating and alienating your audience from the very beginning. Some topics may call upon you to use profane language, such as an informative speech about George Carlin's monologue, and in those instances it is important to let the audience know that some language you will use is necessary, but that they might find it offensive. When you issue advance warnings of this form of language it makes you appear much more considerate of the audience and shows your understanding of the appropriate use of language in a professional setting.

hate speech
rude and crude speech that attacks or demeans a particular social or ethnic group, many times with the intent of inciting action against that group

The second form of language that is considered unethical has become the source of legislation in some states. *Hate speech* is rude and crude speech that attacks or demeans a particular social or ethnic group, many times with the intent of inciting action against that group. Hate speech uses offensive and emotional language to incite hate in the audience and neither the language used nor the goal it is used to achieve are ethical. In the 1930s and 1940s Adolf Hitler used such language to move his country to war. He blamed the ills Germans faced on the Jewish community and began a program of systematic elimination of that group that we now refer to as the Holocaust. Kenneth Burke, the noted philosopher we mentioned earlier, published an essay in 1939 that pointed out the power rooted in Hitler's unethical language.[15]

Burke's analysis of Hitler's rhetoric provided the foundation for quite a bit of scholarship on similar language. Burke noted that Hitler's hate speech followed a particular structure whereby a social ill is found, a cause is identified, a defense of the good qualities of society is presented, and then action must be taken to rid society, or purify it, of the ill. One quality of this rhetoric is the *dehumanization* of a particular social group. In Hitler's speech, Jews were portrayed as less than human, thereby making it easier to purge them from society. In other instances enemies are compared to rats, insects, or even diseases to make the audience appear better than the hated group. Scholar Robert L. Ivie later took Burke's work and expanded it to illustrate that dehumanizing enemies in a battle makes it easier to motivate people to fight wars. Hate speech dehumanizes a particular group of people to make it easier for an audience to agree to action against them. For this reason it is often much more dangerous than profanity.

dehumanization

making people seem less than human in order to more easily motivate action against them

Guidelines for Using Language

So far we have covered the characteristics of language, some language strategies that can help you achieve your goals, and two very dangerous pitfalls of language use to avoid. We will conclude the chapter by providing five specific guidelines to help you determine the best possible language constructions to use within your speech.

1. **Use Language You Know and Are Comfortable with:** One of the common pressures speakers feel is the misplaced idea that they need to sound smart. Understand that you sound smart by presenting evidence in a logical, cogent fashion and making a clear argument, not by filling your speech with big words. In fact, if used too often, complex words can lose an audience and also hinder your efforts to identify with them. You need to sound conversational and natural, not formal and forced.

2. **Eliminate Wordiness:** Be economical in your choice of words. Just like every speech has a purpose, so too does every word. Be concise and clear rather than overly intricate and elaborate in your descriptions. Avoid using words that are unnecessary in helping you make your point. Excess words take attention away from the points within your speech and can confuse the audience.

3. **Know When to Use a Thesaurus and When Not to:** An essential tool for any speaker also becomes a threat to a speech's success if used improperly. A thesaurus can help you find synonyms for words you may find yourself using quite a bit in a speech. However, when using a thesaurus you must be sure that you know the synonym, are comfortable using it, and use it in the proper context. Varying how you say something is a great way to

Online Help

www.merriam-webster.com
www.dictionary.com

Kenneth Burke (1897–1993)

Born in Pittsburgh near the turn of the twentieth century, Kenneth Burke remains one of the most influential American philosophers of all time. Unlike many other twentieth century scholars, Burke never received a college degree. In fact, he dropped out of not one, but two, universities. He preferred to write on his own, rather than pursue a doctorate and career as a professor. He wrote multiple books and essays that influenced a variety of different disciplines.

Burke graduated from high school in Pittsburgh and then enrolled at The Ohio State University. Soon after attending he dropped out and chose to enroll at Columbia University. That experience also ended in his withdrawal from school. His lack of a college degree or formal higher education did not deter him from entrenching himself in academic life, however.

In 1939 he examined speeches by Adolf Hitler, then the chancellor of Germany. In this essay he eerily predicted the problems Hitler would cause in Germany simply by looking at how he managed to use speech to seize power. The essay entitled, "The Rhetoric of Hitler's Battle," proposed a process by which Hitler's speech explained away the troubles of the German people by scapegoating people of Jewish descent and purifying what it meant to be Aryan. This work helped future scholars work to identify the ways in which leaders talk about enemies and war, and even apologize for wrongdoings.

Burke also wrote original poetry, fiction, and a plethora of literary critiques that are still essential reading for students in many different fields. His early interests in music and poetry led to his later exploration of language and symbols as explanations of the structure of human action. He eventually theorized that all human action is drama.

Burke's dramatic pentad is still one of the most fascinating ways to understand the relationship between thought, speech, and action. He divided drama, or speech/action, into five component parts: the act, the agent, the agency, the scene, and the purpose.

A message always contains either an explicit or implicit subject performing an action. This subject is the agent, and what the speaker states the subject is doing is the act. For example, when your mother says "take out the garbage" you are the implied agent and taking out the garbage is the act. Agency is how the act is performed by the agent, and the scene is the context within which the act takes place. Looking at the example again, the agency is through manual labor and the scene is a dirty house. The purpose within the message is why the act is to be performed, and in the above example, the reason is to clean the dirty house.

APPLICATION OF KENNETH BURKE'S PENTAD

The following is an excerpt of a speech delivered by Oprah Winfrey on June 15, 2008, to the graduating class of Stanford University:

"The world has so many lessons to teach you. I consider the world, this Earth, to be like a school and our life the classrooms. And sometimes here in this Planet Earth school the lessons often come dressed up as detours or roadblocks, and sometimes as full-blown crises. And the secret I've learned to getting ahead is being open to the lessons, lessons from the grandest universe of all, that is, the universe itself. It's being able to walk through life eager and open to self-improvement and that which is going to best help you evolve, 'cause that's really why we're here, to evolve as human beings. To grow into being more of ourselves, always moving to the next level of understanding, the next level of compassion and growth."[16]

PENTADIC ELEMENT	APPLYING THE PENTAD
Agent	Graduates
Agency	Openness
Act	Learning
Scene	Life on earth
Purpose	To evolve into better people

According to Burke, all five components of the pentad work together within a message according to a ratio. The ratio helps an analyst understand which parts of the drama are most dominant and important to the message's success. In our "take out the garbage" example, the most important ratio is the scene/purpose ratio. This pentadic approach is emblematic of how complicated Burke understood language to be, and how he believed language related to thought and action.

Although he was influenced somewhat by Marxism, throughout his life Burke never strictly adhered to any ideology or dogma.

He also never held a permanent academic post anywhere, preferring to stay as fluid in his career as he did in his works. He passed away in 1993, having left an indelible mark on communication, philosophy, education, and literature.

So influential was Burke that many master's theses and doctoral dissertations employ and/or analyze Burke's criticism and theories. There also is a scholarly organization called the Kenneth Burke Society, and many different English, Philosophy, and Communication Academic Organizations have a Kenneth Burke Division dedicated to exploring or employing his work.

enhance the appeal of your speech and make it easier for the audience to pay attention, but using words just because they are different is a bad idea. Remember the first guideline: Use language you know and are comfortable with.

4. **Use Active, Rather than Passive, Voice Whenever Possible:** A simple way to inject excitement into your speech is to use active verbs. Active verbs depict movement. Passive voice, on the other hand, is boring and easily identified. Read through a draft of your speech and look for forms of the verb "to be," such as the following: "was," "being," "were," "is," and "are." These all indicate the passive voice. When you correct these constructions, look to craft sentences where there is a subject followed by the action it performs, followed by the object upon which it takes the action. Think about the following statements:

> Passive Voice: *"Harold and Kumar were driving to White Castle so they could buy a snack."*

> Active Voice: *"Harold and Kumar drove to White Castle to buy a snack."*

Which of these sounds more appealing? Which avoids the passive voice? As the example also illustrates, taking care to use active voice sentence constructions also eliminates wordiness.

5. **Use "I, Me, We" Language:** This guideline essentially asks that you take ownership of your ideas and statements. Be clear what is your language and what is attributed to someone else. Words like "we" and "our" also help you connect with your audience by making it appear as though you speak as a member of a collective group that includes the audience. This type of language helps you differentiate between your claims and the data that supports the claims, speak more forcefully without being rude, and enhance your relationship with the audience in a subtle but effective manner.

SUMMARY

Without language we would not be able to understand the world around us, let alone communicate with each other. It also is controversial, as we saw with the case of George Carlin and his monologue. Without language, life would be quite dull indeed. In this chapter we discovered that every language, from Cyrillic to Greek to English, has four common characteristics. We also explored some word strategies that creatively and effectively help convey messages. Finally, we provided some general guidelines for you when constructing and delivering your speech to an audience. The creative and efficient use of words can vastly improve any speech you might deliver.

KEY TERMS

abstract	myth
alliteration	narrative coherence
ambiguous	narrative fidelity
antithesis	narrative paradigm
arbitrary	parallelism
arguments from the past	profanity
dehumanization	repetition
hate speech	simile
hierarchical	single-word approach
ideograph	word-cluster approach
metaphor	

REVIEW QUESTIONS

1. What are the four characteristics of language?

   _____

   _____

2. What are the three single-word strategies for enhancing a speech discussed in this chapter?

   _____

   _____

3. What are the two word-cluster approaches for enhancing a speech discussed in this chapter?

   _____

   _____

4. What are the four structural strategies for using words to enhance your speech?

   _____

   _____

5. What are the three unethical uses of language discussed in this chapter?

   _____

   _____

6. What language tools did Dr. King use in his "I Have a Dream" speech?

_____

_____

1. Where did language originate?

_____

_____

_____

_____

2. Are there any other common characteristics of language in addition to the four mentioned in this chapter?

_____

_____

_____

_____

3. Are speech and language different? If so, where is the line between speech and action?

_____

_____

_____

_____

4. How do you see language evolving in the future?

_____

_____

_____

_____

1. Print out the text of Dr. Martin Luther King, Jr.'s "I Have a Dream Speech" discussed in this chapter. Go through and highlight as many metaphors as you can find, and then see if you can determine their type. Think about whether or not those specific word choices and metaphor types he employed made the speech as powerful as it was.

2. Sit down and watch (or read) the famous vaudeville skit, "Who's on First?" by Abbott and Costello. What characteristics of language discussed in this chapter contribute to the humor of this classic comedy sketch?

3. Print out a famous speech—it does not matter by whom—and count how many versions of the verb form "to be" appear in the text of the speech. The chances are, it will be quite a small number. These forms include "have," "has," "was," "were," "be," and "being," to name just a few of the more common forms it takes.

4. Take a look at the Bugs Bunny cartoons from World War II. Watch a few of them, and then look at the posters the government produced during that era as well. What animals are depicted and who do they represent? Are they metaphors? If so, which type? In terms of ethics, do they dehumanize the subject? If so, how?

ENDNOTES

1. Kent R. Middleton, William E. Lee, and Bill F. Chamberlin, *The Law of Public Communication* (Boston, MA: Allyn & Bacon, 2005), 405; T. Barton Carter, Marc A. Franklin, and Jay B. Wright, *The First Amendment and the Fourth Estate: The Law of Mass Media* (9th Ed.), (New York, NY: Foundation Press, 2005), 817.

2. Pacifica Foundation Station WBAI(FM), 56 F.C.C.2d 94, 32 P&F Rad. Reg. 2d 1331 (1975).

3. *Federal Communications Commission v. Pacifica Foundation*, 438 U.S. 726, 98 S. Ct. 3026, 57 L.Ed.2d 1073, 43 R.R.2d 493, 3 Med.L.Rptr. 2553.

4. Ibid.

5. *Donnie Brasco*, directed by Mike Newell (Culver City, CA: Tristar Pictures, 1997).

6. S. I. Hayakawa, *Language in Thought and Action*, 3rd Ed., (New York, NY: Harcourt, 1972).

7. Mary Haas: http://www.sealang.net/thai/haas-uc.htm (last accessed June 9, 2011).

8. Ibid.

9. www.britannica.com: http://www.britannica.com/EBchecked/topic/250703/Mary-R-Haas (accessed June 9, 2011).

10. Mary Haas: http://www.glottopedia.de/index.php/Mary_R._Haas (accessed June 9, 2011).

11. http://www.indiana.edu/~anthling/v39-4.html (accessed June 9, 2011).

12. Michael C. McGee, "The Ideograph: A Link Between Rhetoric and Ideology," *The Quarterly Journal of Speech* 66 (1980), 1-16.

13. "I Have a Dream," by Dr. Martin Luther King, Jr. www.americanrhetoric.com. http://www.americanrhetoric.com/speeches/mlkihaveadream.htm (accessed June 24, 2011).

14. "I Have a Dream," by Dr. Martin Luther King, Jr. www.americanrhetoric.com. http://www.americanrhetoric.com/speeches/mlkihaveadream.htm (accessed June 24, 2011).

15. Kenneth Burke, "The Rhetoric of Hitler's Battle," *The Philosophy of Literary Form*, 3rd Ed. (1941; Berkeley, CA: University of California Press, 1973), 191-220.

16. Oprah Winfrey, "Commencement Address at Stanford University," June, 15, 2008: http://www.americanrhetoric.com/speeches/oprahwinfreystanfordcommencement.htm (accessed November 24, 2009).

ose: To inform my audience about a concept

ose: To inform my audience about the concept of libertarianism

nent: Libertarianism is based upon the principles of individualism and nment power.

ntion Getter: Ask yourself what the role of government in a perfect world d be.

esis Statement/Introduce Topic: The political philosophy known as arianism believes that individuals should be responsible for a lot of their own , while the government should have a limited role.

redibility Statement: I am a registered libertarian, and have always been ated with the role of government in our daily lives, so I went and spent the w weeks researching this political philosophy.

review : Today, I would like to share with you what the central tenets of arianism are.

A. Libertarians believe that each individual should be able to do as he or

Outlining

CHAPTER OVERVIEW

- Explains the principles and guiding philosophy behind the practice of outlining
- Details the components of a full-sentence preparation outline
- Explains how to create a speaking outline from a full-sentence outline

Practically SPEAKING

One of the signature events in the history of the dreadful disease HIV/AIDS occurred, oddly enough, at the Republican National Convention in Houston, Texas, on August 20, 1992. HIV/AIDS had spread at an exponential rate from the late 1970s until this time, but the reaction from governments—in particular the Reagan and Bush administrations in the United States—was tepid at best. It is no coincidence that these presidents were Republican and therefore needed the support of members of the so-called religious right to receive their party's nomination. In order to do so, they could not be seen fighting on behalf of a disease that was, at the time, largely perceived as an affliction that affected drug users and homosexuals. This all changed thanks to a well-prepared, well-delivered, and poignant speech given by Mary Fisher, a heterosexual, blonde-haired, blue eyed daughter of a major Republican Party donor who had contracted the disease from her first husband, but before the birth of her children.

Fisher knew she was walking into a very difficult situation, but she used every contact she and her family had to speak at the convention. In fact, President George H. W. Bush supported her appearance at the convention, which ultimately paved the way for the speech to take place. The first three days of the convention were characterized by a conservative religious tone, where another speaker, Patrick Buchanan, specifically attacked homosexuals and other groups as destroyers of American culture. Other speakers also took a very anti-gay tone in their addresses at the convention. Fisher herself worried that the organizers of the convention would turn off her Teleprompter or even boo her off the stage.[1] It was such a nasty environment for someone like Fisher to try and speak that she took extra precautions when preparing and delivering the speech.

Fisher spent a great deal of time constructing her speech, incorporating vivid and beautiful language into her earnest appeal for a more humane approach to treating HIV/AIDS victims. She called the climate encouraged by people like Buchanan a "shroud of silence" for a disease that afflicted people from all walks of life, including herself. Most interestingly for this chapter's focus, however, Fisher carried a complete transcript of her speech with her in the event the rumors were true and the Teleprompter was turned off. Ultimately, this did not happen, but the amount of practice and the need to prepare materials to speak from should not be forgotten.

Fisher may have used a transcript, as many speakers do when they have access to a Teleprompter, but in order to get to that point the speech must first be organized and ordered through an outline. As acclaimed author Pearl S. Buck once noted, "order is the shape upon which beauty depends,"[2] and the beauty and power of Fisher's speech would not have been possible without a clear structure for the presentation. All speech contains an idea, a premise, but in order to convey the idea the points relating to it must be coherently organized. Outlining provides us with a mechanism for doing just that.

In this chapter we will explain both the theoretical and practical aspects of outlining. We will discuss the principles behind this organizational process and also the development of a full-sentence preparation outline. We then will explain how to turn a full-sentence outline into a shorter speaking outline that is far more effective at producing an extemporaneous speech. Finally, we will provide practical direction for how to craft a good outline.

OUTLINING PRINCIPLES

Outlines are one of the most crucial components of a properly organized speech, and they are not simple things. In fact, most speeches and situations you will encounter call for two outlines. First, you should develop a full-sentence preparation outline which essentially works as your speech draft. Then, after practicing with this outline until you are comfortable with it, you will reduce it to a much shorter speaking outline. This chapter first provides the principles that guide the creation of an effective outline. It then gives you directions and models for how to format a full-sentence outline. Finally, it explains why outlines are much more useful than drafts and illustrates how to change full-sentence outlines into speaking outlines so you are not reading off your materials during your speech. Keep in mind, though, no matter how good your outline, if you do not practice with it, your speech will not be as successful as it could have been.

Much like the other aspects of public speaking, the process of outlining is grounded in theory. Many people believe that simply establishing bullet points or jotting down some notes is enough to call something an outline, but that is not the case. Outlines, in fact, are formal structures that organize content, but it is important to remember that the elements of an outline are not a part of the content of a speech. There are three tenets of outlining theory that are important to keep in mind when crafting an outline for a speech. In this section we will discuss each of the three principles relevant to developing outlines for speeches, but first we will detail the symbolization technique, which is the foundation of an effective outline.

Outlines are formal constructs that help organize the elements of a speech through the use of consistent symbolization. The symbols refer to things like main points and subpoints within the three main parts of the speech. As such, those three parts—the introduction, body, and conclusion—are not indicated by symbols. The first level within each part of the speech consists of main points, and these main points are indicated by Roman numerals. The second level, consisting of those subpoints related to the main points on the first level, are indicated by capital letters. A third level might also become necessary if you have a sub-subpoint, or an item that relates to the subpoint designated by a capital letter. Items on this level are indicated by Arabic numerals. Here is a sketch of how the symbol system for an outline works:

Body (denotes the part of the speech)

    I. Main point

        A. Subpoint (related to main point above)

            1. Sub-subpoint (related to subpoint A above)

            2. Sub-subpoint (related to subpoint A above)

        B. Subpoint (related to main point above)

            1. Sub-subpoint (related to subpoint B above)

            2. Sub-subpoint (related to subpoint B above)

    II. Main point

In this sketch you can see how each symbol designates something else but is related to the level above it. The basics of symbolization also illustrate one of the principles of effective outlining.

subordination
the organization of a hierarchy of ideas where the most general appear first, followed by subsequently more specific ideas

The idea that what appears on one level is more general than the information appearing in levels under it is called subordination. *Subordination* is essentially the organization of a hierarchy of ideas where the most general appear first, followed by subsequently more specific ideas. In the example above you can clearly see how each of the subpoints relate to the main point and how each of the sub-subpoints are subordinate to specific subpoints. The subordination of ideas allows for a more clear articulation of logic, as well as a more thorough articulation of the relationship between statements. Subordination is also indicated by the fact that each time you move from main point to main point, or between parts of the speech, the symbols reset. For example, in the example above, the sub-subpoints for each different subpoint begin with the number (1), and are not numbered consecutively, which would indicate they were all related. The use of ranked symbols allows subordination to occur within an outline, and it also allows you to put into practice another principle of effective outlining coordination.

coordination
all information on the same level has the same significance

Using symbols to rank items in an outline allows for the coordination of ideas and concepts. *Coordination* refers to the notion that all information on the same level should have the same significance. So, looking at the outline above, all Roman numerals indicate main points, while all capital letters are subpoints. Even though these items will be different in content, their meaning and significance is the same as indicated by their appearance on the same level of an outline. Subordination and coordination are the first two principles of effective outlining, and now we will cover the final principle.

division
in order to divide a point you need to end up with two or more items

Consider that each time you provide subpoints related to a main point, or even main points to a specific purpose of a speech, you are dividing the information into its component parts. This is important because when you divide something you must have more than one piece after the division occurs. If you divide a dollar between two or three people, all three do not end up with one dollar, right? *Division* is the third principle of outlining, and it states that in order to divide a point you need to end up with two or more items. So, in terms of symbols within an outline, there can never be a Roman numeral "I" without there being at least a Roman numeral "II"; there can never be an "A" without at least a "B"; and there can never be a "1" without at least a "2."

Now that we have covered the three basic principles of outlining and detailed the symbolization system used within an outline, we can discuss more specifically the components of a full-sentence preparation outline and a shorter speaking outline.

PREPARATION OUTLINE COMPONENTS

After you have conducted research on your topic, identified the types of information you have found, and formulated your specific purpose and thesis statement (or argument), you are ready to begin constructing your speech. The natural temptation for anyone is to sit down and write a draft in essay format first; however, this is a dangerous proposition. Instead you should outline your speech structure using traditional formatting. The outline you create after gathering and organizing information for your speech is called a preparation outline. *Preparation outlines*, also commonly referred to as full-sentence outlines, are essentially detailed outlines that use full sentences next to symbols in an effort to help you organize the speech. They identify all the main components of an outline discussed in this textbook. They clearly separate the main parts of the speech, including the general purpose, specific purpose, thesis statement, introduction, body, and conclusion.

preparation outlines
detailed outlines that use full sentences next to symbols in an effort to help you organize the speech

In this section of the chapter we will discuss and illustrate how outlines work to organize the components of your speech. This information will be more specifically adapted to the different genres of speeches and discussed in more detail in the chapters dedicated to each type of speech later in the book.

General Purpose Statements

Before beginning the outline proper, you must first identify what you are trying to do with the speech. The *general purpose statement* is a brief statement representing what you intend to accomplish in the speech. There are three different types of general purpose statements: to inform, to persuade, and to celebrate.

general purpose statement
a brief statement representing what you aim to do with the speech; there are three types

The first general purpose is "to inform." When the chief aim of your speech is to provide an audience with information or, as we will discuss in greater detail later in the book, deliver an informative speech, then your general purpose is to inform. This general purpose serves as the chief goal of your speech. There are instances where you will be called upon to provide information and that information may result in a persuasive effect on the audience. The effect in this case, however, was not the chief aim of the speech; the goal of your speech was to inform.

A good example of this may be when a sales leader is asked by the company to give a report on sales revenue for a particular territory. If that information is provided and the company's leadership feels the territory has underperformed, they may then use it as a reason to hire a different sales representative in the hopes of increasing productivity. Such an effect was not the general purpose of the speech, however. The general purpose of the sales leader's speech was to inform, not persuade.

The second possible general purpose for a speech is "to persuade." When your goal is to move the audience to do something, believe something, or act in a particular way, then your general purpose is to persuade. Just as when your general purpose is to inform and you may have the side-effect of persuading the audience, when your general purpose is to persuade you will in all likelihood provide the audience with information. All good persuasion, as we will learn later, contains solid evidence and information. Your chief aim, however, is to move the audience to action, not provide them with data; providing information is the means to an end rather than the end itself when your goal is to persuade.

The final possible general purpose we will discuss is "to celebrate." This is typically the purpose of epideictic speeches, and we will discuss them later in the book in greater detail. That said, when you seek to celebrate a person or occasion with an audience then your main goal is to praise. In these situations you primarily seek to enhance or create an emotional connection between the audience and the subject of your speech, not inform them about the topic in question or move them to perform some sort of action. Think about the case of your grandparents' 50th wedding anniversary. In giving a toast at this momentous occasion you seek to praise the love between your grandparents and their dedication to each other. You may provide some stories or information in doing so, and as a byproduct of the speech the audience may be persuaded to love your grandparents even more, but the goal was neither of those things—it was simply to praise them.

Identifying the general purpose of your speech is essential to its success. The general purpose is the broad foundation of your speech and knowing the purpose of your speech can help you stay focused on your goals as a speaker when constructing the remainder of your presentation. That said, as broad as a general purpose is it naturally lacks specificity. In the next part of this chapter we will detail how to craft the specific purpose of your presentation, a task that is much easier to accomplish when you know your general purpose.

Specific Purpose Statements

After you determine your general purpose for the speech, you next need to determine the specific purpose statement. The *specific purpose statement* is a narrower version of the general purpose statement that identifies what you will talk about, what you will say about it, and what you hope the audience will gain from the speech. In this part of the chapter we will briefly discuss each of these three components of a strong specific purpose statement.

It is essential to understand that the specific purpose statement is not a "general purpose plus." Specific purpose statements should begin with the phrase "After my speech, the audience will," or "My specific purpose is to inform (or persuade) the audience," or something similar. This helps make the specific purpose statement a declarative sentence that identifies the specific goal you seek to accomplish through the speech. Rather than something you would directly say to your audience, the specific purpose statement is a guiding principle for organizing your speech. Everything you do in the speech should help fulfill the goal of the specific purpose.

Immediately following the aforementioned beginning phrases of a specific purpose statement, you need to insert a verb that best captures your intent with the speech. If you are delivering an informative speech, for example, you want your audience to "learn," "understand," or "be familiar with." If you are preparing a persuasive speech, however, you want your audience to "believe," "feel," or "do." Finally, if you are designing an epideictic speech you may want your audience to "remember," "recall," or "celebrate." These verbs help you focus on achieving a particular goal with the audience related to the type of speech you deliver. See Table 9.1.

Table 9.1

Action Verbs for Specific Purpose Statements	
Informative speech	"to learn," "to understand," "to make aware of"
Persuasive speech	"to believe," "to convince," "to agree with"
Epideictic speech	"to remember," "to commemorate," "to recall"

Once you insert the verb that best captures what you seek to achieve with the specific purpose, you need to identify both the speech topic and what you will say about it. This is where you include the specific topic on which you will be addressing the audience and mention the main points that will compose the body of the speech. Here is an example of a strong specific purpose statement for an informative speech:

> **Informative**: My specific purpose is to tell the audience what breast cancer is, what causes breast cancer, and what treatments are available for breast cancer.

Notice that after the opening clause of the specific purpose statement the verb "tell" appears, identifying what the speaker hopes the audience will do as a result of the speech. It is not persuasive, but rather informative and indicates simply that the audience will learn something they did not know before. Following the verb, the specific purpose statement also identifies what the topic is (breast cancer) and establishes exactly what information about the topic will be addressed in the speech. Thus, it narrows down the general purpose to a specific subject. Now, let's look at an example of a specific purpose statement for a persuasive speech:

> **Persuasive:** After my speech, the audience will know what Jimmy Choo shoes are, where they can be purchased, and why they should purchase them.

The specific purpose statement for the persuasive speech is quite similar to the one for the informative speech. In fact, the biggest difference—other than the topic—is found in the change of verbs. The declaration in this sentence is that the speaker desires the audience to feel like purchasing Jimmy Choo shoes after the speech. This is a specific action on the part of the audience sought by the speaker, thus making the specific purpose statement indicative of a persuasive speech. Finally, let's examine a specific purpose statement for an epideictic speech:

> **Epideictic:** After my speech, the audience will know that today is Labor Day, what Labor Day represents, and why it is important for us to celebrate.

Like the persuasive specific purpose statement and the informative specific purpose statement, the epideictic version also is distinguished by the verbs it uses. In addition to the verb "celebrate," note the use of the term "us" in the above statement. As we will discuss later in the book, one of the central tenets of epideictic speeches is their focus on shared communal values, hence the key term "us." Additionally, this statement makes the goal of the speech (to celebrate) quite obvious, thus placing it in the epideictic genre.

Developing a strong specific purpose statement provides you with a solid anchor as you develop your speech outline. It tells you what your goal is, what your topic is, and how you plan to address that topic. As you can see, the key difference between specific purpose statements for different types of speeches lies in the language choices. More importantly, however, specific purpose statements provide you with a rubric for the next component of your outline: the thesis statement.

Thesis Statements

thesis statement
the verbalized foundation of your entire speech in a single sentence which presents your topic, main points, and goal to the audience in an explicit and understandable way

Just as the specific purpose statement builds upon the general purpose statement, so too does the thesis statement flow from the specific purpose statement. Generally speaking, the *thesis statement* reformulates the specific purpose statement for an audience's ears. It is the verbalized foundation of your entire speech and presents your topic, main points, and goal to the audience in an explicit and understandable way.

It should be clear that no speech would contain a statement to the audience that begins with, "After my speech the audience will," and so the specific purpose needs to be changed into something more suitable for public consumption. Let's revisit each of the above examples of specific purpose statements and demonstrate how they can be reconfigured to serve as verbalized thesis statements. Let's look first at the informative specific purpose statement:

> **Informative Specific Purpose Statement**: My specific purpose is to tell the audience what breast cancer is, what causes breast cancer, and what treatments are available for breast cancer.

How can we turn this into something that sounds more like something you would say to a group of your classmates? Let's try the following:

> **Informative Thesis Statement:** Today, I will talk to you about what breast cancer is, what causes it, and what treatments are available.

Small changes to the language help make this something you would be more comfortable saying to the audience and also help you maintain your focus when developing your outline. How about the persuasive specific purpose statement?

Persuasive Specific Purpose Statement: After my speech, the audience will know what Jimmy Choo shoes are, where they can be purchased, and why they should purchase them.

Persuasive Thesis Statement/Argument: Today I want to argue that you should purchase Jimmy Choo shoes because of their unique qualities, cost, and availability.

Again, notice how the small language changes help to focus the speech for the audience in a way that seems like something you would say, rather than read or write. Finally, let's examine the epideictic specific purpose statement and how we might consider changing it into a thesis statement:

Epideictic Specific Purpose Statement: After my speech, the audience will know that today is Labor Day, what Labor Day represents, and why it is important for us to celebrate.

Epideictic Thesis Statement: Today is Labor Day, originally established by President Grover Cleveland to recognize the importance of the American labor force, but now an important holiday because it gives us all a reason to celebrate the end of summer!

This thesis statement is a bit more detailed than the specific purpose statement but is crafted in a way that sounds more likely to be spoken than written. It fits well within the beginning of a speech and clearly establishes the goal of the speech, the topic, and how that topic will be covered within the speech.

Now that we have detailed the foundational elements of an outline—the general purpose, specific purpose, and thesis statements—we can turn to the organization of the outline itself. Each speech today contains three basic elements: the introduction, body, and conclusion. As we will learn in future chapters, this format is slightly different from that taught by the Greeks and Romans; however, the core elements are the same. Keep in mind, we will return to these concepts later in the book when we discuss constructing specific types of speeches.

Introduction

Your introduction needs to accomplish five main goals, and your outline will help ensure that it does just that. First, your introduction needs to get the attention of the audience. Next, it needs to state your thesis or argument, which simultaneously introduces the topic of your speech and makes it relevant to your audience. Third, the introduction needs to establish your credibility on the topic. Then the introduction needs to preview the main body of the speech. Finally, the introduction needs to provide a transition to the body of your speech. Let's look at how an outline organizes information and helps you accomplish these goals.

Introduction

    I. Attention-getter

    II. Thesis statement [introduces topic]

    III. Credibility statement

    IV. Preview statement

[Transition to body]

It is important to note that if it takes more than one sentence to accomplish the attention getter, thesis statement, or credibility statement, then according to the outlining principles we discussed earlier, you will need to drop down and use capital letters to continue that segment of your speech. Doing so will allow you to subordinate your ideas and more clearly demonstrate an organized and logical speech.

transition
....
connective statements that signal you are finished with one point and moving on to another

When moving from the speech introduction to the body, you need to use a transition. *Transitions* are connective statements that signal you are finished with one point and are moving on to another. When moving from the introduction to the first main point in the body, transitions should connect the introduction to the first point in the body. In Table 9.2 you will see some examples of phrasing options for transitions from the introduction to the body of the speech:

Table 9.2

Example Transition from the Introduction to the Body
"With these ideas in mind, let's look at my first main point"
"Now that you know what I am going to cover, let's get started"
"Since I have told you what I am going to, I am going to dive right into the topic"

In an outline you will notice that the transition does not receive a symbol designation. This is because the outline must follow the principle of coordination, whereby each symbol designates items of the same level of significance. Transitions are not main points of an introduction or any part of the speech, for that matter. They also are not subpoints or subordinate ideas to other elements of the section of the speech. For that reason they are "set aside" in their own place in an outline. Next, we will discuss the speech body.

Body

The body of a speech follows the same principles that the introduction does, but it contains different elements. The body, for instance, does not contain attention-getters and credibility statements; rather, it includes main points and subpoints. That said, strong evidence within the body of your speech can enhance your ethos during the speech. Like introductions, the body does make use of transitions between main points. Additionally, the body of a speech makes use of internal previews and internal summaries. These are similar to the preview at the end of the introduction, but tend to be more condensed and work to keep the audience connected with the speech's thesis or argument. Let's look at how the body of a speech is structured within an outline.

Body

    I. Main point #1

    [Internal preview]

        A. Subpoint

        B. Subpoint

            1. Sub-subpoint

            2. Sub-subpoint

        C. Subpoint

[Transition]

    II. Main point #2

        A. Subpoint

            1. Sub-subpoint

            2. Sub-subpoint

        B. Subpoint

    [Internal summary]

[Transition]

    III. Main point #3

        A. Subpoint

            1. Sub-subpoint

            2. Sub-subpoint

        B. Subpoint

        C. Subpoint

[Transition]

There are several things to notice in this example. First, you see where internal previews and internal summaries are typically inserted. Internal previews fit at the start of a main point as a way to orient listeners to what they should listen for in the immediate future. Speakers do not need to insert an internal preview for every point, but rather should use them judiciously. The most effective time to provide the audience with an internal preview is when the upcoming topic includes terminology or topics that may be unfamiliar to the audience.

In the example above, also notice the internal summary placed in the outline. Recall that internal summaries are statements that recap the points just made. Internal summaries work best following an important or complicated point within your speech. You should add internal summaries to highlight the central components of the point you just made to the audience. Like internal previews, internal summaries are not necessary following every main point in your speech; rather, they should be employed when they are necessary in your speech. It is also

SPEAKING of CIVICENGAGEMENT

Three Lies
by J.C. Watts

Delivered to Students at Numerous Times and Places

Julius Caesar (J.C.) Watts was born in Oklahoma in 1957. Known as a football star at the University of Oklahoma, he went on to win MVP honors in the Canadian Football League's championship game, the Grey Cup.[3] Upon retirement from football Watts ran for office and was elected to Congress as a Republican in 1994, where he served four terms. Watts became known for his stance on family values and personal responsibility while in Congress.

Congressman Watts developed a speech about personal responsibility that he delivered to numerous audiences, but in particular student groups, around the country. His message was simple and contained three clear points. Additionally, Congressman Watts skillfully helped the audience understand the basic outline of his speech by verbally numbering his three points.

In the second line of the speech he clearly stated his first main point: "The first lie is this: 'I am entitled to one mistake.'"[4] He then told the story of the tragic death of NCAA basketball star, Len Bias, who died of a drug overdose soon after being the number one draft pick in the NBA draft. After completing the story Watts identified his second main point for the audience: "The second lie is 'It will never happen to me.'"[5] He then detailed Magic Johnson's confession of being HIV positive and that star's erroneous belief that it would never happen to him. Finally he identified his third point: "The third lie is this, and be careful that you understand this one: 'I've got plenty of time.'"[6] Here he told the students how lucky they were to have teachers and cautioned his audience regarding getting sidetracked from what is important.

In his conclusion, Watts again summarized his main points for the audience. Thanks to this type of structure Watts's speech was very effective and easy to follow.

important to note that internal previews and internal summaries are placed in brackets the same way transitions are and for the same reason: they are not main points, subpoints, or sub-subpoints.

Finally, in constructing the body of a speech, outlines can help with determining the number of main points. Most speeches that you will encounter will include 2-4 main points within the body. This is due to two factors: time and focus. The shorter the speech, the fewer main points you can include because they take time to develop and explain. Also, the more main points you include the harder it will be for you and your audience to focus on what is important. Speaking of focusing on what is important, once the body is complete, you have one last chance to reinforce your speech purpose and topic to the audience: the conclusion.

Conclusion

Conclusions are essential when it comes to making sure your audience understands the important concepts within your speech, and outlines are helpful here as well. Just like the main components of an introduction, the central tenets of a conclusion can be laid out properly in an outline. Conclusions contain three main elements. First, you need a signpost to indicate you are beginning to wrap up the speech. Typically, we place the signpost at the end of the body, with the transition from the final main point, but in some cases instructors place it within the conclusion. The important thing to remember is that it indicates the end of the speech is about to begin. Additionally, you should be aware that many instructors have a pet peeve about hearing "in conclusion," so it is best to avoid using that phrase as your signpost. After signaling the end of the speech, conclusions need to restate the thesis and summarize the main points of the speech. Finally, conclusions need to contain a clincher. Let's look at how conclusions are structured within an outline:

[Signpost/transition]

Conclusion

    I. Summary [restate thesis] and main points

    II. Clincher

In this example you move to the conclusion through the use of the signpost, which in the above outline is placed before the conclusion and at the end of your final main point. Then, the summary begins with a brief restatement of the thesis or argument and continues with restating the main points. This illustrates the principles of subordination and division in that restating the main points relates to the summary and thesis statement. It also shows there is more than one main point that needs to be restated. Finally, the clincher statement finishes the conclusion.

This structure is a very effective way of providing the audience the "take-away" elements of your speech one last time. It may sound very pedantic and boring, but it works, and for this reason, politicians often use this technique for constructing conclusions to their speeches. Take the example of former Republican Congressman and football star, J. C. Watts of Oklahoma, who on several occasions delivered a speech entitled, "The Three Lies," (see the nearby box). The speech is easy to follow because it follows a very clear outline and concludes with all of the elements of a conclusion mentioned in this chapter.

To recap, outlines are formal structures that allow you to organize the content of your speech in a logical fashion. The structure of an outline allows you to ensure that you have incorporated all the elements of an effective speech in an appropriate and logical way. In the next section we will move from the form of outlines to a brief discussion of their linguistic content and why outlines are more useful than drafts.

LANGUAGE AND OUTLINES

There are two reasons why you should avoid writing a draft and instead outline your speech. The first is that drafts tend to be free-flowing and less structured, allowing for the distinct possibility that you will lose your focus and go off on tangents in the middle of the speech. Drafts should be constructed only if the speech you plan to give is a manuscript speech, and even then only after you have outlined the address. The second reason drafts are a poor choice for a first step is that we write and speak differently.

When we write an essay for class we use different grammar, sentence structure, and vocabulary than when we speak, so if we write and deliver a draft, then we essentially read to the audience, as opposed to speaking to them. Writing calls for proper sentence construction where there is a subject, verb, and predicate, but oftentimes in speaking the best way to make a point to the audience and evoke emotion in them is not through this type of sentence construction. For example, when writing a letter to a subordinate, a boss may write, "Do not ask me for a raise, as your performance has not warranted it." When speaking, it might be delivered with more force this way: "Hello, Matthew. We will not discuss your pay. Do. Not. Ask. Me." This latter example does not contain properly constructed sentences, yet when spoken it makes sense and contains more emotional force than the written form.

When we write drafts we also try to vary the language, sometimes by consulting a thesaurus so the verbiage we use appears more formal and intelligent. In written communication finding synonyms and using them properly is perfectly acceptable and even encouraged, but in speech if you are using words that are not part of your normal spoken repertoire it may come across as awkward and unnatural. Look at these two examples. Which one seems more appropriate for written communication and which seems more natural in a speech?

> **Example 1:** *"There is a voluminous history of athletic accomplishment in the sport of soccer."*

Or: *"Soccer has produced its fair share of amazing achievements."*

Example 2: *"The daunting challenges presented will test the mettle and steadfastness of our citizenry."*

Or: *"Look folks, we have some tough times ahead and we need to stand strong."*

Both of the first statements get the same point across, but the first examples use more complex language than the second ones do, and therefore, are more suited for an essay than a speech. Speech uses terms and language we are comfortable using, and writing a draft encourages us to use the more formal written language than the more colloquial language we typically use when we speak. So, in addition to preventing tangents and keeping your speech focused, outlining also helps limit the use of formal language.

Despite the reduced emphasis on formal language, preparation outlines should use full sentences for each symbol. In fact, they should use one sentence per symbol to better illustrate the logic behind the placement of each sentence. If a sentence does not flow from the previous statement you should either move it somewhere else in the speech or eliminate it altogether. The only exception to this "one sentence per symbol" rule is when you are using a direct quotation. Then, and only then, should you include the whole excerpt next to the same symbol. Also, make sure to put quotation marks around the excerpt and properly document its source.

The preparation outline, however, is not the last step before your actual speech, although you will spend the bulk of your time before your actual presentation practicing from it, adjusting statements, moving points, and enhancing your language choices. When you are comfortable with the preparation outline it is then time to develop your speaking outline.

SPEAKING OUTLINE

After practicing with your full-sentence outline you will become more conversational in your delivery and will not need to look at your outline as much. Additionally, you will begin to remember the information in the full-sentence outline rather than needing to read it. So, to help you deliver your speech in a more natural and conversational style, you will want to use a *speaking outline*, or a truncated form of your full-sentence preparation outline that does not include complete sentences unless you are using direct quotations from another source. Speaking outlines are easy to develop from a completed full-sentence outline.

speaking outline
a truncated form of your full-sentence preparation outline that does not include complete sentences

The same format you used to create your full-sentence preparation outline applies to a speaking outline. When you create your speaking outline you still retain all the formatting elements of the full-sentence preparation outline in terms of Roman numerals, capital letters, and numbers, and you still follow the principles of outlining we discussed earlier. The only elements that do not appear on a speaking outline that appear in a full-sentence preparation outline are in-text citations, your stated general purpose, and your stated specific purpose.

PREPARATION (OR FULL SENTENCE) OUTLINE

I. Introduction
   A. Attention getter – How many of you are certified scuba divers?
      1. For those of you who are not, how many of you are interested in becoming certified?
   B. Credibility statement – I have been a certified scuba diver for a little over ten years, earning my certification after years of research and desire to become a diver.
   C. Thesis statement – Scuba diving is a great hobby that everyone should consider starting.
   D. Relevance statement – With over one million people getting certified everyyear,[1] it is time that you start to consider taking up this sport so that you are not left behind.
   E. Preview Statement – Today, I will introduce you to this fun, exciting sport by telling you exactly what scuba diving is, how you can become certified, and what important things to know once you have gotten your certification.
II. Body
   A. What is scuba diving?
      1. Let's begin by taking a look at what S.C.U.B.A. stands for.
         a. S.C.U.B.A. stands for self-contained underwater breathing apparatus.
         b. In layman's terms all this means is that you have the ability to breathe underwater thanks to the assistance of an oxygen tank.
      2. The origins of scuba diving date all the way back to 1535 when a diving bell was first created.
         a. This diving bell was an instrument that would cause air to become compressed in a bell when the bell was turned upside down, keeping water from leaking in as well.
         b. In 1865, the development of an underwater breathing apparatus made scuba diving much easier by making it possible for divers to breathe oxygen underwater from the water's surface. This allowed the divers to be able to move around like never before.[2]
      3. Scuba eventually evolved into the hobby that we know today.
         a. Present day divers carry all of their own equipment with them underwater, making any connection to the surface unnecessary.
      4. Transition statement – Now that you know what scuba diving is, let's explore how you can become certified to be a scuba diver.
   B. How to get your scuba certification?
      1. PADI, one of the world's leaders in scuba diving instruction and certification, recommends that in order to get certified you should start by doing research about different classes in your area.
      2. After you have found a school you like and sign up for classes, you should begin by studying the reading materials that your instructor provides you with when you first enroll.

3. The classes you take will cover everything from what to expect when you are diving to diver safety.
   a. The classes will be comprised of actual in-class instruction as well as time in the pool learning how to use the equipment to dive successfully.
4. Once your classes are complete, you will have to go through a two-step process to earn your certification.
   a. The first step of this process will require you to take a written exam.
   b. If you pass this part of the certification, then you will proceed to an open water dive, which will consist of you going through a series of exercises in open water, such as an ocean or lake, with your scuba instructor.[3]
   c. Transitional statement – Now that you know how to become certified, there are a few things that you might want to keep in mind to help you enjoy your new hobby even more.

C. What do you need to know once you are certified?
1. Once you have your certification, it is important for you to decide how much money you want to invest in your new hobby.
   a. If you do not anticipate going diving often, it would not pay off to purchase the more expensive equipment that you would need.
   b. It would be beneficial, however, for you to own your own mask, snorkel, and fins.
2. In order to get the most out of your certification, research different areas that are known for their diving or speak with the school where you got your certification for suggestions.

III. Conclusion
A. Now that you know what scuba diving is, how to become a certified diver, and what important things for you to consider once you are certified, you have been formally introduced to a great new hobby.
B. In addition to being loads of fun, scuba diving can be a great excuse to travel and meet new people.
C. Some of my fondest memories have been of me and my family scuba diving off the coast of Hawaii and seeing white tip sharks or exploring the caves of Belize.
D. So, now that you know a little bit more about scuba diving, how many of you are interested in getting your own certification?

Works Cited

[1] Belasco, J. (n.d.). How to be a scuba diver. Retrieved on April 29, 2010, from http://www.ehow.com/how-to_4845366_be-scuba-diver.html

[2] Aboutscubadiving.com. (2002). Scuba history. Retrieved on April 29, 2010, from http://www.about-scuba-diving.com/scuba-diving/history.htm

³ PADI. (n.d.). Scuba lessons, tips, training, and going pro. Retrieved on April 29, 2010, from http://www.padi.com/scuba/scuba-diving-guide/default.aspx

This example provides you with a better idea of what to include in your outline and how it should be formatted. Depending on the class and whether or not you will be turning your outline in for a grade, you might want to consider asking your instructors if they want the various elements: the attention getter, thesis statement, and so on, labeled the way they are in this outline. Be sure to notice that the sources for this speech were included both within the outline itself and in a separate reference section.

The core fundamental difference between the two outlines is that a speaking outline does not include full sentences unless you use a direct quotation, in which case getting the quote correct is of paramount importance. A speaking outline then includes a shorthand version of the full sentences within the preparation outline. Shorthand notes for speeches are not a new phenomenon. In fact, the speeches of Cicero were recorded using a shorthand system developed by one of his slaves who was later freed, Marcus Tullius Tiro. Tiro used what are now called Tironian notes, a shorthand system consisting of abbreviations for Latin words. Unfortunately, with the fall of the Roman Empire the system he devised fell out of use, but many copies of ancient texts transcribed through the use of Tironian notes were discovered in monasteries during the Protestant Reformation. Tiro and his shorthand note system allowed for many of the speeches of Cicero to survive the perils of history, thus making them available today. The idea of using shorthand to transcribe speeches is one of the fundamental precepts used in creating speaking outlines today.

shorthand

the process of shortening words or eliminating word clutter in the transcription process

Shorthand is the process of shortening words or eliminating word clutter in the transcription process. It allows for a document to contain the essence of what was said without taking it down word for word. As you can imagine, there are many words in every written sentence that you do not need to see in order to remember to say them. Let's look at this brief full-sentence example and see if we can identify unnecessary words:

Introduction

I. *Attention-getter:* Imagine yourself stranded, along with about 50 other people, on a desert island after a plane crash.

A. Well, that is the premise of the critically acclaimed television show *Lost.*

When looking to cut, look specifically at the full sentences. Obviously, the terms "with," "on," "that," "is," "the," "of," and "a" do not need to appear on a speaking outline because you could easily insert them when speaking without a prompt. But what else could you eliminate? What about the entire subpoint? It would make sense to delete the subpoint because it should flow naturally after the attention-getter. In fact, you might be able to deliver this attention-getter from a mere handful of words, such as this:

Introduction

      I. Imagine/stranded/50 people/island /plane crash. *Lost*

This is what a speaking outline contains: words and phrases from the original prose in the full-sentence outline separated by backslashes.

Speaking outlines can also contain delivery cues and directions for what to do during a speech. When practicing with the speaking outline you may notice certain points where you think a physical motion would help add emphasis. You also may want to remind yourself to pause or use a visual aid. If you are using PowerPoint, for example, you can put in a notation to change slides at specific points in the speech. The following example shows how you can effectively incorporate delivery cues into a speaking outline in a way that can enhance the delivery of your speech:

Introduction

      I. Imagine/stranded/50 people/island /plane crash. *Lost*

      II. Success/science fiction/ratings/critic reviews (change PowerPoint slide)

In this example the cue for the speaker to change the PowerPoint slide is embedded in the speaking outline. This serves as a reminder for a task many speakers often forget. One of the last things you want to have happen is to forget to change slides or pull out a visual aid during the speech, only to remember later and have to speed through slides for concepts you have already covered. This makes it seem like you did not practice and prepare, thus damaging your ethos with the audience. It also increases the likelihood you will become more cognizant of your nervous reaction to the mistake. Refer to Table 9.3 for some useful tips for creating an effective speaking outline.

Tips for Creating the Speaking Outline
Bold key terms
Write out quotes for accuracy
Do not have cluttered or congested text
Make main points easily recognizable
If using notecards, number them

Table 9.3

Cicero (106–43 B.C.)

Cicero is perhaps the second most important rhetorical figure in the age of classical rhetoric.[7]

Cicero was a brilliant lawyer and many of his judicial orations are available in a variety of contexts. He was a powerful force in politics and his speeches were known to rouse emotion and influence audience members. Cicero was also known for his writing on rhetorical theory. His most famous rhetorical work was *De Oratore,* or *On the Orator.* This book was more than simply a treatise on how to speak, but was also meant as an explanation of the power of persuasion. He used the book to make the point that the power of speech in the hands of men with no morals was one of the greatest threats to the community.

As an active politician, as well as writer, Cicero was quite outspoken in his support of the Roman Republic. As noted elsewhere, that outspoken support led to his death as the Republic gave way to the Roman Empire. He was killed by forces loyal to Marc Antony in a most gruesome way. He was decapitated, and his tongue and hands were cut off and nailed to the doors of the Senate in Rome as a warning to those who dared to criticize— through speech or the written word—the new leaders of the Empire. One of the most gifted rhetorical theorists and practitioners in history lost his life due to his insistence on standing up for and speaking his mind on political matters.

It is important to remember that you should move from practicing with your preparation outline to practicing with your speaking outline. In some cases, instructors may ask that you use notecards instead of a speaking outline. In this case it makes it all the more important to have a speaking outline done already. It provides the structure, emphasis, and cues you will want to transcribe to the notecards. Essentially, notecards can be more succinct, or even shorthand, versions of your speaking outline. It is essential though, that you practice a few times with the notecards. It is also important not to use the move to notecards as a reason to change the format from an outline to bullet points—a tempting but troubling idea. Doing so just runs the risk of damaging the format and delivery of what you have been practicing all along.

Even though we believe we have made a case for the use of outlines in this manner, some may still argue in favor of the use of bullet points instead of outlines. Bullet points do not visually display the logical hierarchy behind the speech and also create the danger of going off on tangents and not making your case to the audience as clear as possible. Bullet points are, for all intents and purposes, a list of items with no clear connection. Outlines provide that connection for the speaker and, consequently, the audience.

Others might agree with the use of an outline but object to the practice of indenting the tiers of information appropriately, arguing that it wastes space and the outline would make as much sense if the information were to appear on one side of the page. This, although better than bullet points, still does not clearly differentiate each level of information and its connection to the rest of the material in the speech for either the speaker or the audience. In short, it fails to properly employ the principle of subordination. So, the proper indentation of each level is essential for the speaker and the audience.

Outlining your speech begins early in the speaking process and continues until you deliver the presentation. It allows you to organize your thoughts and information into a coherent order. It provides you with something to practice from and thereby develop your speaking voice and rhythm, something altogether different from your written voice and rhythm. Most importantly, outlining is the manner by which a speaker arranges his speech from beginning to end.

OUTLINE TEMPLATE

Below is an example of what an informative or persuasive speech preparation outline should look like and where specific pieces we have discussed in this chapter should appear. Understand that certain parts of the template may change slightly due to the organizational pattern you use, but this should provide you with a strong head start in developing your speech's outline.

> ***General purpose:*** This is a simple statement and contains few words. It usually is "to persuade," "to inform," or "to celebrate."

> ***Specific purpose:*** This statement is narrower than the general purpose statement. It begins with the phrase, "After my speech, the audience will," or "My purpose is to inform (or persuade, or commemorate)," and it ends with the specific topic of the speech and how it will be addressed.

> ***Thesis statement (or argument):*** This is a single statement that encapsulates the overall argument and main points of the speech. It takes the specific purpose statement and recalibrates it to more specifically address the speech topic and main points in a manner that is suitable for speaking.

Introduction

I. *Attention-getter*: A brief story, quotation, or example that draws the audience into the speech. It captures their attention.

II. *Thesis statement (or argument)*: Encapsulates the entire argument or main point of your speech. This is where you make your introduction or insinuation clear. It introduces the topic and main points of the speech to the audience.

III. *Credibility statement*: Details your expertise on the topic of the speech.

IV. *Importance of Topic*: Establish relevance to audience.

V. *Preview*: A statement that broadly mentions the main point of your speech. It should begin with something like, "Today, I will discuss...."

   A. *Preview statement #1:* This sentence introduces the first specific main point you plan to address in your presentation, and it should begin with something like, "First, I will cover...."

   B. *Preview statement #2:* This sentence represents the second point you plan to cover in your speech. It should say something like, "Next, I will discuss..."

   C. *Preview statement #3:* This sentence represents the third point you plan to cover in your speech. It should say something like, "Finally, I will discuss...."

[*Transition:* This alerts the audience that the introduction is over and that you will now begin making your case by addressing the topic you mentioned in preview statement #1.]

Body

I. *First main point*: This statement declares the first main point you will discuss in depth. It is the same topic previewed in preview statement #1 in the introduction.

   A. *Subpoint #1:* This is the first piece of evidence regarding the first main point.

   B. *Subpoint #2:* A new piece of evidence regarding the topic of this section.

      1. *Sub-subpoint #1:* A further discussion of subpoint #2.

      2. *Sub-subpoint #2:* A further discussion of subpoint #2.

C. *Subpoint #3:* Another piece of evidence that relates to the topic of this section.

D. *Subpoint #4:* This may be another piece of evidence or a statement that illustrates to the audience how the main point you just covered relates to the overall thesis of your speech.

[*Transition:* Alert the audience that you are finished with the first main point and are now moving to a new main point.]

II. *Second main point*: This statement declares the second main point you will discuss in depth. It is the same topic previewed in preview statement #2 in the introduction.

[*Internal preview:* You may consider placing an internal preview at the beginning of a new main point to help orient audience members as to what is coming next in the speech.]

A. *Subpoint #1:* This is the first piece of evidence regarding the second main point.

B. *Subpoint #2:* A new piece of evidence regarding the second main point.

1. *Sub-subpoint #1:* A further discussion of subpoint #2.

2. *Sub-subpoint #2:* A further discussion of subpoint #2.

C. *Subpoint #3:* Another piece of evidence that relates to the second main point.

D. *Subpoint #4:* This may be another piece of evidence or a statement that illustrates to the audience how the main point you just covered relates to the overall thesis of your speech.

[*Transition:* Alert the audience that you are finished with the second main point and are now moving to a new main point.]

III. *Third main point*: This statement declares the third main point you will discuss in depth. It is the same topic previewed in preview statement #3 in the introduction.

A. *Subpoint #1:* This is the first piece of evidence regarding the third main point.

1. *Sub-subpoint #1:* A further discussion of subpoint #1.

2. *Sub-subpoint #2:* A further discussion of subpoint #1.

B. *Subpoint #2:* A new piece of evidence regarding the third main point.

C. *Subpoint #3:* Another piece of evidence that relates to the third main point.

D. *Subpoint #4:* This may be another piece of evidence or a statement that illustrates to the audience how the main point you just covered relates to the overall thesis of your speech.

[*Internal summary:* You may wish to consider an internal summary to remind audience members what you have already covered.]

[*Transition:* Alert the audience that you are finished with the third main point and are now moving to a new main point.]

[*Signpost:* This statement lets the audience know you are entering the conclusion. It usually begins with a phrase like, "Finally," or "To sum up."]

Conclusion

I. *Summary statement*: This statement summarizes your overall argument or thesis once again for the audience so they know what it was, generally, you spoke about.

A. *Summary statement #1:* This is a one-sentence summary of the first main point you covered.

B. *Summary statement #2:* This is a one-sentence summary of the second main point you covered.

C. *Summary statement #3:* This is a one-sentence summary of the third main point you covered.

II. *Clincher*: Here is where you again connect the speech to the audience. Sometimes, if your attention-getter was a hypothetical question, you answer it here. If the attention-getter was a story without an ending, you end the story here. It should be a statement designed to leave the audience with an emotional attachment to your speech.

SUMMARY

In this chapter we explained the concept of outlining and how its structure can help you organize the information you research into a speech that makes sense to both you and your audience. We discussed the philosophy behind outlining and the six major components of an outline: general purpose statement, specific purpose statement, thesis statement, introduction, body, and conclusion. We also explained the importance of and how to create a full-sentence preparation outline and then, after practicing with it, how to collapse it into an effective speaking outline replete with delivery cues.

KEY TERMS

coordination	specific purpose statement
division	speaking outline
general purpose statement	subordination
preparation outline	thesis statement
shorthand	transitions

REVIEW QUESTIONS

1. What are the components of an outline?

   _____

   _____

2. What is subordination and why is it important?

   _____

   _____

3. What is the difference between the two types of outlines?

   _____

   _____

4. Why do some students think outlines are a waste of time?

   _____

   _____

5. Can an outline save you time in preparing your speech?

   _____

   _____

THINK ABOUT IT

1. Can you prepare a good speech without an outline?

   _____

   _____

   _____

   _____

2. Can you devise another method to replace outlining?

   _____

   _____

   _____

   _____

3. Do you think that professional speechwriters use outlines? Why or why not?

   _____

   _____

   _____

   _____

ACTIVITIES FOR ACTION

1. Locate the text of any presidential State of the Union address. Comb through the transcripts and ascertain what the central idea and subsequent main points are for the different parts of the speech. Then, reconstruct the speech using the outline format provided in this chapter. You will hopefully see that many speeches are not as well structured as the ones you will deliver and hear in your public speaking class and that they would benefit from outlining.

2. Take a speech outline you developed and switch around the order of your main points. Does this change the meaning of the speech? Does it make it weaker or stronger? Why?

3. Find an outline of a speech either by creating it yourself, using one from the materials that accompany this book, or using one that a classmate or colleague developed. Cut it apart so that one sentence is on each slip of paper. Now, evenly distribute the slips of paper within the group with which you are working. Take a minute to learn your slips of paper, and then try to

engage the rest of the group to try and put the speech back in order. Did you find a better way of organizing the speech? Did you accurately recreate the speech?

4. Go to http://www.fountainheadpress.com/speaker.html and look in the right hand column under "Sample Student Videos." Select the "George Washington" video and watch it with the sample outline from the chapter (page 194) in front of you. Track the speech to see where there are deviations and where the speaker holds true to the form of the outline. This will help illustrate the connections between a preparation outline and the speech for which it is developed.

5. Take the sample outline on "George Washington" (page 194) and try to condense it to a speaking outline. What would you remove? What would you keep? Is there anything you would add, like notes for delivery? Why did you make those choices?

ENDNOTES

1. Jennifer J. McGee, "A Pilgrim's Progress: Metaphor in the Rhetoric of Mary Fisher, AIDS Activist," *Women's Studies in Communication* 26, 2003.

2. Quotation found on: http://www.famousquotessite.com/famous-quotes-614-pearl-buck.html (last accessed May 31, 2011).

3. Julius Caesar Watts, Jr., Biography: http://www.bookrags.com/biography/julius-caesar-watts-jr/ (accessed June 21, 2011).

4. www.americanrhetoric.com. J.C. Watts, "Three Lies," http://www.americanrhetoric.com/speeches/jcwattsthreelies.htm (accessed June 21, 2011).

5. Ibid.

6. Ibid.

7. Patricia Bizzell and Bruce Herzberg, *The Rhetorical Tradition: Readings from Classical Times to the Present* (Boston, MA: Bedford Books of St. Martin's Press, 1990), 31-33.

Informative Speaking

CHAPTER OVERVIEW

- Differentiates between the different types of informative speaking
- Covers the goals and strategies for each form of informative speech
- Discusses various situations where informative speaking is most likely to occur

Practically SPEAKING

In 2008 the U.S. economy slowed and then went into reverse, resulting in the significant loss of value in retirement accounts as well as the failure of numerous brokerage houses and banks. In March 2008 one of the oldest investment firms on Wall Street, Bear Stearns, collapsed and the Federal Reserve had to intervene and engineer a takeover by rival bank JP Morgan to ensure that people's assets would not completely vanish. In September another Wall Street firm, Lehman Brothers, also collapsed but the government did not intervene to save it. In the same month the government did, however, work to help Bank of America buy out Merrill Lynch. The result of all of these investment bank failures was an almost complete collapse of confidence in Wall Street. In fact, by October 9, 2008, the Dow Jones Index lost over one-third of its value from the beginning of the year.[1] That translated into huge losses for average Americans who invested in the stock market for their retirement.

Beginning with the Bear Stearns collapse, and accelerating with the events of September and October 2008, many Americans turned to CNN and other major news outlets for an explanation of what happened, how it happened, and how it would affect them. On CNN, chief business correspondent Ali Velshi became the network's de facto spokesperson for these explanations. He appeared almost daily on CNN to explain the complex world of global finance so people could better understand what happened. Oftentimes he employed graphs and charts to help him explain things. What he did the majority of the time was inform the American public on the state of the economy and how the economy functions. His aim was not persuasion, but rather he sought to provide people with information.

Despite Velshi's goal, words are inherently persuasive, even though persuasion may not be the general purpose of a speech. Some speakers like Velshi seek to inform an audience about something, but that information still may change the way the audience views the topic in question. Similarly, audiences may listen to a speech intended to persuade them only to gather information about a topic. This reality makes it nearly impossible to construct and categorize a speech as purely "informative." The purpose may be to inform, but even pure information has some level of influence over an audience. In Velshi's case, his explanation of the crash may have influenced people's decisions to keep money in the market or take it out, even though that was not his goal.

Informative Speaking Overview

We need to think of informative and persuasive speaking as lying on a continuum, rather than as two mutually exclusive boxes. On the one end of this spectrum lies the persuasive speech, where the purpose of the speaker is to persuade and the audience's purpose is to create an opinion based upon what is offered. On the other end of the continuum exists the theoretical informative speech. See Figure 10.1.

Informative speech   Persuasive speech **Figure 10.1**
Informative vs.
Persuasive Speech

Continuum

We say theoretical because, as we have pointed out, information does not exist in a vacuum and will influence people, even in a small way.

Even though information always persuades on some level, there are those speeches that come close to the theoretical *informative speech*, and they provide information in as neutral an environment as possible, where both the speaker and the audience typically seek to teach and learn. Informative speeches are also structured differently than persuasive speeches and employ different vocabularies. For these reasons, it is important to define the purpose of your speech and know as much about the audience as possible when constructing your presentation.

informative speech
provides information in as neutral an environment as possible, where the speaker and the audience typically seek to teach and learn

An example of what we mean by this differentiation can be found on campuses throughout the country. Schools often bring in researchers to talk about their work with students in a variety of forums. These lectures provide information to the students and faculty in attendance, but they also may inspire new interest in topics for those audience members. A lecture by noted historian Doris Kearns Goodwin on her research on President Abraham Lincoln's cabinet primarily provides information to the audience. It also may very well influence the audience to study that aspect of history in even more detail or spark

Historian
Doris Kearns Goodwin

an interest in history for some students. So, as you can see, it is not a purely informative speech, but neither is it a truly persuasive type of speech.

One other difference between informative and persuasive speaking is the ability of an informative speech to occasionally use language very specific to a certain field. Persuasive speeches, because they seek to move entire audiences to action, necessarily use less field-specific language so more people can understand and follow the speaker. When informative speeches are geared toward people in a very specific field and use disciplinary-specific language, we refer to them as technical speeches. This chapter, however, focuses on informative speeches rather than the more advanced version of technical speeches.

In this chapter we will help you better identify a speech with an informative purpose. We begin by explaining the four different types of informative speeches and then move to a discussion about the goals and strategies that best achieve the purpose of informative presentations. We conclude with a brief chat about different situations where you might find yourself asked to deliver an informative speech. Regardless of the situation, it is always important to keep your purpose at the forefront of your mind and remember that all information influences audiences, even when you do not intend for it to do so.

TYPES OF INFORMATIVE SPEECHES

There are four different types of informative speeches, each designed to convey a unique set of information to an audience. Each one lends itself to different topics and organizational strategies. In this section of the chapter we will discuss the four different informative speeches: speeches about objects, speeches about processes, speeches about events, and finally, perhaps the most difficult to construct as a speaker, speeches about concepts.

Speeches about Objects

speech of self-presentation
···············
a speech where the speaker's topic is introducing himself or herself to the audience

Speeches about objects are the simplest form of informative speeches. One of the most common informative speeches about an object is a *speech of self-presentation*, where a speaker's topic is the introduction of herself or himself to the audience. Often these types of speeches are the first that a student delivers in an introductory speaking course. They are typically not long and touch upon the highlights of the speaker's life. They often include important events, individuals, and achievements by the speaker. Sometimes speeches of self-presentation cover elements of the person's philosophy and belief systems, but each speech is unique and what the speaker chooses to present tells you as much about the person as what they choose to leave out. After all, these are personal narratives constructed by the speakers, and whether or not they mean it, the story is always biased and incomplete, making these speeches fascinating in their own right.

Objects can also include people other than the speaker. Take the example of Doris Kearns Goodwin mentioned at the start of this chapter. Goodwin spoke about people in President Lincoln's cabinet, clearly not making herself the topic of the speech. These speeches differ from self-presentation speeches in that Goodwin

SPOTLIGHTING THEORISTS: G. THOMAS GOODNIGHT

G. Thomas Goodnight

G. Thomas Goodnight is currently a full professor and director of doctoral studies at the prestigious Annenberg School for Communication at the University of Southern California. Before joining USC he taught in the doctoral program at Northwestern University. The American Forensic Association recently named Goodnight one of the top five scholars in argumentation over the past 50 years for his contributions to the field. He has developed and taught courses on the Rhetoric of War, Science Advocacy, Risk Communication, Contemporary Rhetorical Theory, Rhetorical Criticism, and the Public Sphere. Additionally, his research has appeared in a variety of well-respected journals in the field of communication studies.

One of Goodnight's contributions is his work on the relationship between the technical and public spheres of argument. He pointed out that in the hard sciences (biology, physics, etc.) argument has different goals, aims, and even structure than it does in rhetoric, the humanities, and the social sciences (psychology, counseling, sociology, English, etc.). His work also has shed light on why public speaking courses typically separate speech types into the categories of informative, persuasive, and epideictic/special occasion when all ultimately have a persuasive effect.

The transmission of information is seen as a neutral effort in the hard sciences, while the social sciences see it as persuasive regardless of the intent of the speaker. But due to the disciplinary differences between the hard sciences and social sciences, speeches are typically separated into the categories we have today. Technical, rather than informative, however, is the better way to label those speeches that typically take place in the hard science fields.

Goodnight still conducts research in rhetoric and argumentation. Currently he explores issues related to deliberation in postwar society, science communication, argument and aesthetics, public discourse, and reason in controversy.[2]

does need to mention herself and her research to establish her credibility on the topic, but then her focus returns to the other individuals. In speeches about other people as objects, the topics the speaker chooses to cover are of the same variety as those in the self-presentation speech with the exception that they apply to others.

Another informative speech about an object involves places. These types of speeches are presented on tours. When visiting Boston, Massachusetts, on vacation you may decide to take a Duck Boat Tour of the city, during which the

A Duck tour boat

guide will speak about the history of the city, making special note of important historical locations along the route. Although this speech provides information, people on the tour may want to then learn more about places the tour guide has mentioned, prompting them to make another trip after the tour ends, again demonstrating that there is differentiation between informative and persuasive speaking.

The final type of informative speech about objects involves things. These can include something as meaningful as a memento or heirloom, or something as simple as a television or movie. Informative speeches about objects that are things encompass tangible objects that do not fall in the previously discussed categories. For examples of the three types of informative speeches about objects, see Table 10.1.

Table 10.1

Thesis Examples about Objects	
Speech Topic	**Thesis Statement Example**
Michael Jackson	"The three main periods of Michael Jackson's life are his youth, his reign as the King of Pop, and the tragedies late in his life."
New Orleans	"The three primary areas of interest in New Orleans are the French Quarter, the Garden District, and the industrial area."
Buying a used car	"When purchasing a used car you should consider factors such as age, quality, and price."

Speeches about Processes

Another common type of informative speech is a speech about a process. Process speeches are delivered using a chronological organizational pattern because that is what allows the topic to make the most sense to the audience. Process speeches traditionally are reserved for delivering information about tasks an audience may need to complete. They are, for all intents and purposes, "how to" speeches.

Consider the following hypothetical example. Elaine is a mechanic and has been asked by her local church to deliver a speech to the Women's Club on simple ways to save money on car maintenance. She chooses what she believes to be the simplest but most effective way for her audience to save money: How to change the oil in their cars. In order to adequately explain how to accomplish this task Elaine needs to proceed in sequential order and detail what needs to be done in language everyday people who are not mechanics can understand. Other process topics vary from the sequence of building a house, to describing the process of how wine is made, and even, as in Ali Velshi's case earlier, explaining how the economy works.

The final type of process speech we will cover involves neither a job-specific task like changing oil, nor an everyday activity such as cooking; rather, these speech topics relate to social processes. Common to this category are political, economic, religious, or cultural procedures. Such speeches might cover "how to get elected," "how to celebrate a Catholic Mass," or "how interest rates work." These are more complicated and deal with social processes rather than task procedures, but they are still informative speeches about processes. Because of their complexity, these types of speeches often are the most interesting process speeches to hear. If you want to write such a speech just think of some type of social process and research how it operates.

Informative speeches about processes are excellent examples of the blurred line between informative and persuasive speaking. People hearing these speeches might be more inclined to do exactly what the speaker has described now that they know how. That influence could be branded persuasive rather than informative, but if the speech is presented simply as a "how to" speech it becomes much more of an informative address than a persuasive appeal. See Table 10.2 for examples of the different types of informative speeches about processes.

Table 10.2

Thesis Examples about Processes	
Speech Topic	**Thesis Statement Example**
Brewing beer	"To brew beer you must have an initial fermentation, then a secondary fermentation, and finally, bottle it."
Health plan	"To live a healthy life requires a balance of nutrition, exercise, mental stability, and good lifestyle choices."
Applying for Communication graduate school	"To successfully apply for graduate school one must have at least a 3.0 GPA, an appropriate undergraduate degree, an official GRE report, official transcripts, and letters of recommendation."

Speeches about Events

The third form of informative speeches, those that cover events, combines elements of both speeches about objects and speeches about processes. Events can include objects, in particular people, but they are more complex than simply detailing a singular item. They can also include a process, or the unfolding of the event, but the focus is not on explaining the process; rather it is on detailing the importance of the event itself. Your goal is to provide information to an audience; what they do with it is up to them. This illustrates yet again the subtle difference between informative and persuasive speaking.

Artist: Francis Bicknell Carpenter

First Reading of the Emancipation Proclamation of President Lincoln

Think back to the example of the hypothetical lecture by Doris Kearns Goodwin on President Lincoln's staff during the Civil War. We illustrated how this could be an informative speech about an object, the individuals in the staff, but it also could be a speech about an event. Change the topic ever-so-slightly to "The President and the Civil War" and the speech becomes more about the event and the individuals become secondary.

Informative speeches about events can cover things that have happened in the past, are happening now, or may happen in the future. Like the Civil War example, an informative speech about an event can cover something from the past. These speeches can also cover events occurring in the moment, such as a public address by a public official during a hurricane or natural disaster. Event speeches can also discuss things that will happen, such as a speech opening a business convention that lays out the schedule, topics, and important organizational members for the ensuing meetings.

Informative speeches about events can employ several organizational patterns. Often the primary organizational pattern is chronological, but there are cases when event speeches can utilize topical and even spatial patterns. For example, the above speech about the Civil War could be set up as a chronological history of battles leading to the surrender at Appomattox. It also could focus on the leaders of the Civil War on both sides, making the primary organizational pattern topical. A third option for organization involves a discussion of the states and their participation in the war, thus encouraging the use of a spatial organizational pattern. See Table 10.3 for examples of the different types of informative speeches about events.

Table 10.3

Thesis Examples about Events	
Speech Topic	**Thesis Statement Example**
1942 WWII Pacific naval campaigns	"Three major naval operations in 1942 were the raids into the Indian Ocean, the Battle of Coral Sea, and the Battle of Midway."
Weddings	"The major events of a wedding ceremony are the exchange of vows, the wedding toasts, the cutting of the cake, and the first dance."
9/11	"The September 11, 2001, terrorist attacks on the United States included two airplanes hitting the Twin Towers, the attack on the Pentagon, and the crash of United Flight 93 in Pennsylvania."

Informative speeches about events can be used to inform audiences about occurrences in the past, present, or future. They are organized in a variety of different ways, but they also contain elements common to both informative speeches about objects and informative speeches about processes. The fourth and final type of informative speech, however, is unique.

Speeches about Concepts

Informative speeches about concepts focus on informing an audience about beliefs, values, or theories. These speeches do not seek to convert an audience to a particular point of view, but instead seek simply to explain a given philosophy. Informative speeches about concepts also almost exclusively employ the same organizational pattern, regardless of what concept they explicate.

One potential informative speech about a concept covers belief systems, such as a particular religion. Religions are not tangible objects, sequential processes, or fixed events, despite the fact elements of each may play a part in the belief system. For example, in Judaism, the Star of David is a prominent object, weekly service follows a specific regimen, and the conclusion of the annual reading of the Torah is a celebratory event. Each of these would make terrific topics for informative speeches about an object, process, or event, but none of them cover the beliefs of Judaism. An informative speech about a concept that conveys information about the beliefs of Judaism would cover its notion of the afterlife, its understanding of God, or its approach to keeping kosher.

Religion is only one example of a concept, and it is grounded in a specific worldview. A different way to approach beliefs would be to cover more abstract ideas such as love, hate, affection, or depression. The definitions for these concepts vary from culture to culture. An informative speech about a concept would attempt to convey an understanding of any one of those emotions, but in doing so the speaker would have to acknowledge the various ways different places define those feelings.

A third type of concept covered by this type of informative speech addresses theories. Take, for example, Dina, who wants to give a speech to her science class that defines the theory of evolution. She can cover who developed the theory and mention the controversy surrounding it, but the focus of her speech is to explain how evolution works. She can provide examples of how the theory proposes that large hairy mammals evolved into human beings, but again her focus is on explaining the concept to the audience. Examples essentially become data and evidence, where the main points are the theoretical propositions themselves.

One final category of concepts covered in an informative speech of this type are political or economic concepts. Like religious beliefs, political and economic belief systems may have important people, defined processes, or singular events that have contributed to their development, but the focus of the speech is to describe the core facets of the system. A speech of this type on communism, for example, might mention Karl Marx and Friedrich Engels as the pioneers of the philosophy, their expulsion from Germany as an event contributing to the creation of their worldview, and the explanation of the five epochs of history as a process that will eventually lead to the world adopting communism, but the focus is on explaining the tenets of a communist society. How is workload handled in a communist society? What is the role of money? How are leaders selected? These and other questions get at the central concept of communism and thus qualify the presentation as an informative speech about a concept. Table 10.4 provides examples of informative speeches about concepts.

Table 10.4

Thesis Examples about Concepts	
Speech Topic	**Thesis Statement Example**
Pillars of Islam	"The five pillars of Islam are the profession of faith, prayers, giving of alms, fasting during Ramadan, and pilgrimage to Mecca."
Ethics	"The two major categories of ethical principles are teleological and deontological ethics."
Psychological Egoism	"The theory of psychological egoism states that altruism is a myth and that all acts are self-serving."
Free Market Economy	"A free market economic theory is based upon competition and no government intervention."

Like each of the other types of informative speeches, speeches about concepts also provide information that may influence an audience. What qualifies them as informative rather than persuasive speeches is the speaker's goal of providing information in a neutral fashion to an audience that wishes to learn that information. Movement to action and changes in the audience as a result of this information are inevitable, but they are not the goal. As you can surely imagine, constructing an informative speech without calling people to action or asking them to change their beliefs and values can be difficult. In the next section we will provide some helpful tips on how to craft informative speeches about objects, processes, events, and concepts.

GOALS AND STRATEGIES FOR INFORMATIVE SPEAKING

As we have emphasized throughout the chapter so far, informative speeches seek to convey information in as neutral a fashion as possible, despite the fact people may be influenced by that information. Yet another distinction can be seen in the nature of the audience. Audiences for informative speeches are relatively passive and seek to receive information. In contrast, those who listen to persuasive speeches are more active audiences, cognitively processing the information to formulate opinions and make decisions regarding calls to action. In this way audiences for informative speeches often employ comprehensive listening, which, you may recall from Chapter 2, involves listening to understand a message.

The speakers who deliver informative speeches also need to have strong initial and derived credibility. This makes sense because if an audience seeks to understand something from a speaker then they must believe that the person to whom they are listening knows about the topic. As they deliver information, speakers must continue to demonstrate their expertise and knowledge about the topic.

It is also important for speakers delivering information to behave ethically. Because they know more about the topic than the audience, they must not abuse the trust the audience has placed in them by skewing the information in favor of one interpretation. To do so would be to present a persuasive appeal under the pretense of an informative speech.

Strategies for Informative Speeches about Objects

One of the reasons you would deliver an informative speech about an object is that the object is complex and hard for the audience to understand. This fundamental appreciation of the speech purpose is the basis for three strategies for effectively presenting speeches about objects.

First and foremost you must spend a significant amount of time detailing the object and explaining its purpose. These details should cover subjects relevant to the audience's understanding of the object. Such topics might include the history of the object, its purpose, and various ways in which it can be used (if indeed, it can be). Take, for instance, an object as simple as a baseball. While explaining the object you might want to explain how it is constructed, what role it plays in a baseball game, and how many different ways it can be thrown.

When detailing the object for the audience it is also essential for the speaker to use language the audience will understand. Oftentimes, when we are experts on a subject we talk about it as if everyone around knows the *jargon*, or terminology that relates to a specific activity, associated with the topic. When conveying information to an audience seeking to learn something we need to avoid using jargon without explaining the terms and phrases to the audience so they can follow along. Verbal explanations, however, are sometimes not enough to adequately explain a topic to the audience.

jargon
terminology that relates to a specific activity

Sometimes topics about an object require visual as well as verbal representation for the audience to understand. Visual aids are often effective tools when delivering informative speeches about objects, especially when the objects are large and complex. If the object you are discussing is a person, her life may be complex and therefore a timeline may be a useful visual aid for the audience; however, a bust of the person's head would not be. Recall two of the rules of using visual aids: do not create a distracting visual aid, and do not create visual aids for tangential aspects of the speech. A bust, or picture of the individual, violates both of those rules and does not help the audience better understand the topic of the speech. The timeline, on the other hand, does. Variations of timelines also might be helpful as a visual aid with our next subject: informative speeches about processes.

Strategies for Informative Speeches about Processes

As we mentioned earlier, informative speeches about processes typically follow a chronological organizational pattern, and as such the sequence is important. In order to create an effective speech about a process you need to adequately explain not just each sequential step in detail, but how each step leads to the next one.

Especially important in that description are the starting and finishing points in the process. Another important aspect of informative speeches about processes is that they need to detail the practical applications of the process being described; in other words, what can it be used for?

Each step in a speech should build upon the previous one. Beginning with the first step you should explain what is needed to complete the process and then the order in which the steps should be executed to successfully complete the task at hand. For example, a speech about how to fish should begin by explaining what tools are needed to go fishing. Simply listing the fishing pole, lure, and line, though, should be avoided as it engenders boredom in the audience. Describe not just what is needed, but how to determine its quality and where it can be located so the audience does not have to guess.

SPEAKING of CIVIC ENGAGEMENT

Comments Before the Credentials Committee by Fannie Lou Hamer

Delivered August 22, 1964, at the Democratic National Committee, Atlantic City, New Jersey

Fannie Lou Hamer, the granddaughter of slaves, was born in 1917 in Mississippi. She became a sharecropper on a plantation, and in 1962 when members of the Student Nonviolent Coordinating Committee (SNCC) came to town to hold a voter registration meeting, Hamer didn't even know that she had a constitutional right to vote. Once she knew she could, she volunteered to help register others to vote and was later jailed, beaten, and driven from the farm where she was a sharecropper as result.[3]

Hamer went on to become secretary of the SNCC and traveled to various places registering people to vote, spoke about voting rights, and co-founded the Mississippi Freedom Democratic Party (MFDP). The Credentials Committee of the 1964 Democratic Convention asked her to speak about racial injustice.[4]

Hamer told the committee of the treatment she had received from the police, how the plantation owner had pressured her to withdraw her registration request, and that when she refused he told her to leave his property. She also recounted the resistance at registration drives and how she and others with her were not allowed to eat in some restaurants or use restrooms.[5] She told of black prisoners ordered to beat her with blackjacks and of the terrible names the police called her. Here is an excerpt from her informative and emotional testimony:

"I was carried out of that cell into another cell where they had two Negro prisoners. The State Highway Patrolmen ordered the first Negro to take the blackjack. The first Negro prisoner ordered me, by orders from the State Highway Patrolman, for me to lay down on a bunk bed on my face. As I laid on my face, the first Negro began to beat me. And I was beat by the first Negro until he was exhausted."[6]

After describing what is needed in terms of materials, you should proceed to describe each step in the process. Using our fishing example, you should tell them that the next step is determining where to fish, renting a boat, and then setting a time for the trip. Be descriptive and tell the audience how to decide on each of these issues and describe what you would recommend doing for maximum success. Remember from our discussion of language earlier in the book that vivid language is a very effective way of maintaining audience interest and attention.

When you are finished describing all the steps in detail for the audience it is also important to let them know about the practical applications of the process so they will know when to use it. For the fishing example, you might suggest trying this activity on a vacation. Process speeches have a much greater effect when audiences believe they apply to their own lives. Otherwise, process speeches become simple instructions instead of a creative and eloquent way to invite an audience to learn something.

Strategies for Informative Speeches about Events

Delivering an address informing an audience about an event requires different elements than a speech about objects or processes. For one, you need to set the parameters of the event to focus the speech for the audience. You must explain who the key players are and clearly establish the background on the event so the audience can identify the topic. To be effective you also need to make a conscious effort to deliver the speech in an active voice with vivid description.

Setting the parameters of the event you are talking about means providing the audience with the proper context. *Context*, or the conditions surrounding the event, includes who the prominent figures are, when the event occurred, and other relevant circumstances. It is important when talking about an event that you place it in the proper context by establishing a clear beginning and ending. Clearly, events do not exist in a vacuum and there are a multitude of factors that influence them, but as a speaker you must make decisions about which are pertinent to the event in question, and which elements are not essential for understanding the event.

context
the conditions surrounding the event

Take the case of Fannie Lou Hamer, a former sharecropper who helped register African Americans to vote during the Civil Rights movement in the 1960s. In 1964 the Democratic National Convention asked her to provide personal testimony on racial injustice in the South. To do so, she needed to provide the context for her experience in vivid detail so that the legislators and leaders at the meeting would not only understand what happened, but actually be able to visualize how it took place. Hamer did just that. See the nearby box.

When making such decisions you should remember your ethical responsibility to provide balanced and neutral information to the audience and not shape the speech so as to promote one particular interpretation. This may seem difficult, and sometimes even impossible, but so long as you keep ethical considerations in the front of your mind when constructing the speech, you will be doing your duty to the subject and the audience.

One of the more difficult tasks in any informative speech remains ensuring it is interesting. To accomplish this feat you should try to always speak about the event in an active voice and use vivid language. A good example of this can be found in the address given by former Senator Fred Thompson at the 2008 Republican National Convention. In his speech he discussed nominee Senator John McCain's time as a POW, stating:

> After days of neglect, covered in grime, lying in his own waste in a filthy room, a doctor attempted to set John's right arm without success... and without anesthesia.
>
> His other broken bones and injuries were not treated. John developed a high fever, dysentery. He weighed barely a hundred pounds.
>
> Expecting him to die, his captors placed him in a cell with two other POWs who also expected him to die.
>
> But with their help, John McCain fought on.
>
> He persevered.
>
> So then they put him in solitary confinement... for over two years.
>
> Isolation... incredible heat beating on a tin roof. A light bulb in his cell burning 24 hours a day.
>
> Boarded-up cell windows blocking any breath of fresh air.
>
> The oppressive heat causing boils the size of baseballs under his arms.
>
> The outside world limited to what he could see through a crack in a door.[7]

Former Senator Fred Thompson

In this passage Thompson describes the event with language that encourages a specific picture in the mind of the audience. Notice that, despite the fact that the event has already occurred, not once does Thompson use passive voice through the terms "was," "would," "has," "is," or "have." Doing so provides the speech with an engaging feel while still conveying information about an event to the audience in an ethical manner. This skill is equally important, if not even harder to employ, within informative speeches about concepts.

Strategies for Informative Speeches about Concepts

Concepts may be the most difficult thing to inform an audience about because they are so abstract. Objects, processes, and events are often very easy for a speaker to concretize for the audience, but concepts are not so simple for a speaker to describe. Concepts also are sometimes difficult for an audience to relate to, so finding a way to connect the audience to the speaker and the topic is essential when delivering an informative speech about a concept. One of the simpler components of constructing these speeches, however, is that you can effectively organize them only one way.

As a speaker trying to convey a concept to an audience you need to give the concept as concrete a foundation as possible. Employing examples of the concept in practice helps to provide that foundation. Take the topic of gravity which, as a law of physics, fits the definition of a concept. Merely describing what gravity is and how it operates keeps the speech on the abstract level, but by introducing examples of objects performing according to the law of gravity, the speech becomes more concrete and the concept becomes easier for the audience to visualize.

In addition to providing imagery illustrating the concept, you must also make the idea you are speaking about relevant to the audience. This can be done in several different ways. You can show how they might need to understand the concept to perform some of their daily activities. In the case of gravity, you can explain that when things fall it is because of this concept. This connects the concept to a person's daily life because people can fall, or objects around the house can fall and hurt them, thus making understanding gravity more important and relevant to the audience. You can also call upon the inherent curiosity of the audience regarding subjects and theories, thereby asking them to learn the idea you are speaking about because of their curious nature.

Regardless of how you hook the audience, any informative speech about a concept is likely to be organized in a topical fashion. Concepts do not follow an order, otherwise they would be a process. They also are not tangible and therefore cannot be organized according to space. They are abstract, and because they are abstract it is difficult to determine the logic by which they should be organized within a speech. It is most instructive then to proceed with constructing the speech in a topical fashion, covering the various topics of the theory, idea, or belief.

For example, consider an informative speech about Hinduism. The religion itself is a concept and invites the possibility of structuring a speech in a variety of different ways. For instance, you could start with the various gods in the religion, then move to sacred symbols, and conclude with its belief regarding life and death. You also could pick entirely different topics relevant to the concept of Hinduism and structure the speech around them. It is, by and large, entirely up to you as the person constructing and delivering the address. In the next section of this chapter we will briefly discuss various situations in which all four types of informative speeches might occur.

SITUATIONS FOR INFORMATIVE SPEAKING

Informative speaking occurs in a variety of different situations, but there are three that are the most prevalent. The first, and perhaps most common situation in the professional world, is the internal business setting. As students, though, you encounter informative speaking all the time as it is the primary mode of delivery in education as well. Finally, any time you attend an orientation program you will hear informative speeches. In this part of the chapter we will briefly discuss these three rhetorical situations and discuss which informative speeches are most likely to occur in each.

Informative Speaking in the Business World

Professionals in the business world deliver two types of speeches, but they are each audience-specific. When the speech is internal, that is, given to employees and shareholders of the company, the majority of the time it is an informative address. When the speech is to an external audience of potential clients and investors then the speeches are more overtly persuasive in nature. Internal informative business speeches often occur at board meetings, planning sessions, and company conventions.

Board meetings often contain a report to the board on the state of the company. These speeches contain facts and figures regarding revenue, profit, company costs, and the performance of divisions within a company. These speeches often employ visual aids to deliver statistics regarding the success or failure of parts of the company in order to paint an overall picture of the current state of the corporation. These informative speeches also detail future plans of action for the company and the strategies going forward.

Planning sessions also contain informative speeches and occur in the business world as well. Planning sessions are far more common than board meetings and can occur within divisions of the company, not simply at the top of the administrative ladder. In these planning sessions the state of the department is usually described, followed by an account of available resources and concluding with the goals of the planning session. The idea is for everyone in the room to start off on the same page in terms of the available information and to then generate as many ideas as possible for how to achieve the goals of the division or company.

Most companies also have yearly conventions where the company's leadership delivers a state of the company address, or something similar. This address and others during the conference focus on the goals and plans for the next year. They address what succeeded and what failed during the previous year and lay out what still needs to be done. Of the three addresses we have discussed with regard to business settings, these speeches occur in front of the largest audience and are potentially the longest as well.

Informative internal business speeches often use visual aids and follow a topical organizational pattern, but by no means do all of them follow these two maxims. The context largely determines the topics covered in the speeches for businesspeople, but again the organizational pattern focuses on topics more often than it doesn't. Some exceptions might include planning meetings where a chronological path might need to be laid out for the group, or during conventions if the focus is on how the company developed over the past year. These are, however, exceptions.

Informative Speeches in Education

A professor's lecture in a classroom is a perfect example of an informative speech, and depending upon the course content, it can take the form of any one of the four types of informative speeches. A lecture is not persuasive and instructors design them to deliver information to students using a variety of different methods. Courses also sometimes require students to issue reports to the class on research they conducted; again, these types of speeches are not persuasive but are meant to transmit information to an audience. In any event, you can hardly find performances that lean more toward the informative side of the continuum than a lecture.

Instructors talk about objects, processes, events, and concepts quite often. Every time they step in front of a class they attempt to help students learn about famous people, items of interest, important events, biological processes, philosophical ideas, and much more without advocating a specific position for students. In fact, *critical thinking*, or the ability for students to evaluate on their own the material they learn, is often stated as a course goal of many instructors. To facilitate critical thinking the lectures must not advocate or persuade, but rather provide data for students so they can make their own evaluations.

critical thinking
the ability for students to evaluate on their own the material they learn

Students also present reports to classes, thereby granting them the role of instructor-for-a-day. They are often evaluated on these reports based on the information they deliver and how well they deliver it. As with instructors delivering a lecture, students also often use PowerPoint to assist them in delivering the material. These reports range in length but almost always cover the same elements of any speech: introduction, body, and conclusion.

Informative speeches are common to academia, regardless of whether you are a student or an instructor. The speeches spell out information for an audience seeking to learn, and do so without any persuasive goals.

Informative Speeches in Orientation Programs

The final common realm where you might encounter informative speeches is during an orientation or training program. Although one of the aims of these programs is to get you to perhaps do something a specific way, they are designed to provide information on how to do it. They do not advocate a belief, attitude, action, or value; rather they seek to describe a process or concept.

Orientation programs, such as a Sexual Harassment Orientation program required by many companies and organizations, often describe concepts through a systematic process. They go step by step ensuring audiences receive specific information when they are supposed to. People often consider such programs dull because speakers rarely incorporate context into their delivery of material.

Training programs are slightly different because sometimes the context is readily recognizable. For instance, if you attend a training program for how to use Microsoft Excel, you will most likely be placed in front of a computer and walked through the steps of how to use the program. Orientations cover concepts, whereas training programs cover processes, like learning a computer program.

SUMMARY

There is no such thing as a purely informative speech; rather, there are speeches that focus on providing information which audiences can then do with as they wish. Informative speeches exist in four different forms: those about objects, those about processes, those about events, and those about concepts. Each requires different strategies and organizational patterns, but all simply attempt to convey information. These types of speeches occur most frequently in internal business settings, the classroom, and within training and orientation programs. The key to remember is that persuasion is not the goal of informative speeches.

KEY TERMS

context   229

critical thinking   233

informative speech   219

jargon   227

speech of self-presentation   220

REVIEW QUESTIONS

1. What is the difference between an informative speech and a persuasive speech?

   _____

   _____

2. What are the four types of informative speeches?

   _____

   _____

3. What are the three common situations where informative speeches occur?

   _____

   _____

4. What are the best ways to organize each type of informative speech?

   _____

   _____

5. Which speaking situation calls for all four informative speeches, depending on the topic?

_____

_____

1. Can information be truly objective and neutral?

_____

_____

_____

_____

2. Does even the choice of evidence make a speech persuasive?

_____

_____

_____

_____

3. Why do we separate informative speeches from persuasive speeches if they all influence people?

_____

_____

_____

_____

4. Do you think commemorative speeches are mainly informative or persuasive?

_____

_____

_____

_____

ACTIVITIES FOR ACTION

1. Identify a commercial that tries to convince an audience to change its attitude about something or purchase a product. After examining the content of the advertisement, turn that persuasive appeal into an informative speech using the same evidence.

2. Find a famous person with whom you either strongly disagree or who you dislike. Create a list of information about that person that is corroborated with documented evidence. Be sure the information you use is factual and not colored by your own opinions.

ENDNOTES

1. Prieur_du_Plessis, "Stock Market Crash 2008 Market Round Up," *The Market Oracle,* available: http://www.marketoracle.co.uk/Article6728.html (last accessed April 5, 2009).

2. Information contained in this segment was obtained through G. Thomas Goodnight's faculty web page at the Annenberg School for Communication at: http://annenberg.usc.edu/Faculty/Communication/GoodnightG.aspx (accessed September 6, 2008).

3. Fannie Lou Hamer of the NCCC, http://www.ibiblio.org/sncc/hamer.html (accessed June 13, 2011).

4. Ibid.

5. Fannie Lou Hamer testimony before the Credentials Committee, http://americanradioworks.publicradio.org/features/sayitplain/flhamer.html (accessed June 13, 2011).

6. Ibid.

7. Fred Thompson, "Fred Thompson's Address to the RNC," September 2, 2008, available: http://www.realclearpolitics.com/articles/2008/09/fred_thompsons_address_to_the.html (accessed September 3, 2008).

Crafting an Informative Speech

PracticallySPEAKING

On March 20, 2003, the United States and a coalition of over 40 countries invaded Iraq in an effort to oust dictator Saddam Hussein. The war itself was brief, but the occupation that followed went on for years. The ensuing presence of U.S. forces and the inability of Iraq's new government to quickly establish control across the country infuriated elements of the population and drew al Qaeda to what has become the primary front of the War on Terror.

With casualties mounting for both U.S. and Iraqi forces, many in the United States started to call for a change in tactics. In fact, several prominent members of Congress referred to the effort in Iraq as "lost." Facing mounting pressure to address the Iraq issue on January 10, 2007, President George W. Bush announced a new military policy for Iraq. He temporarily increased the number of troops in Iraq by 20,000 to assist the Iraqis with securing neighborhoods, protecting the local population, and training the Iraqi security forces to handle these duties moving forward. The policy was largely well received, especially given the fact it was the brainchild of General David Petraeus, commander of the multinational forces in Iraq and a counterterrorism expert.

In September 2007, Petraeus appeared before Congress to provide a report on the security situation and the effect of the surge in Iraq since its implementation. Petraeus informed Congress that the situation was vastly improved and that civilian and military deaths had been dramatically reduced as evidenced by the 70% drop in Baghdad civilian deaths from their peak the previous year.[1] He also noted that local tribes and neighborhoods had begun to reject al Qaeda and work with the U.S.-led coalition to secure Iraq.

The purpose and structure of Petraeus's speech are worth noting. The report to the House of Representatives committee was aimed at providing them with information, not persuading them one way or another on a particular policy. He began his testimony with a summary of the situation before and after the surge. He then reviewed the nature of the conflict in Iraq because it was different than any conflict the United States had been involved in over the last 200 years. His speech concluded with a report on his recommendations for moving ahead in the coming months. He approached the speech in a topical fashion, as you might surmise from your readings in the last chapter.

In this chapter we will discuss how to formulate a speech like the one given by General Petraeus in 2007, though you are likely to have a much different topic. We will first begin by discussing the elements of an introduction for an informative speech. Next, we will cover the different ways you can construct the body of an informative speech. Finally, we will explain the way in which you conclude an informative speech. You will then be ready to apply these elements using outlining information.

11

Informative Speech Introductions

Introductions are, as the saying goes, your last opportunity to make a first impression on the audience. Many people believe that informative speeches are necessarily boring because they are not calling on an audience to do anything, but they need not be dull. What they do need to be, however, is clear and complete. As stated previously, in order to create a strong introduction, you must first identify two things. The first is the general purpose of the speech. In the case of an informative speech, your general purpose is simply "to inform." The second is your specific purpose, which is a narrower version of the general purpose in that it identifies specifically what you are speaking about. For instance, a specific purpose for an informative speech about greenhouse gases would be: "To inform my audience about greenhouse gas emissions."

Once you identify the general and specific purposes of the speech you can start to work on the speech itself. In this section we will discuss the five main components of an introduction in an informative speech and illustrate how you can enhance an audience's interest in your speech using creativity.

Attention-Getter

The first element of an introduction for an informative speech is the *attention-getter*, or a device that immediately attracts the audience's interest to the subject that the speaker plans to discuss. You can choose from a variety of different attention-getters when creating the introduction, but keep in mind that regardless of which type you use, your goal is to attract the audience's attention to the subject. In this part of the chapter we will outline four common attention-getters that you might employ.

attention-getter
a device that immediately attracts the audience's interest to the subject that the speaker plans to discuss

The first, and perhaps the easiest, attention-getter technique is the *rhetorical question*, or asking the audience a question related to the subject that does not require an answer from them. For example, if you plan to give a speech informing the audience about the history of the Philippine Islands you might begin the speech with the hypothetical question: "Did you know that the United States once occupied the Philippine Islands?" If your speech was designed to teach the audience how to play the game of tennis you might begin by saying: "Have you ever watched a tennis match and thought, 'How can I do that?'" These questions

rhetorical question
asking the audience a question related to the subject that does not require an answer from them

draw the audience in by orienting them toward a question which will likely be answered within the body of the speech.

famous quotation

actual statements closely related to the topic of the speech made by individuals the audience will easily recognize

A second popular form of attention-getter is the use of a *famous quotation* to begin the speech. Famous quotations are actual statements closely related to the topic of the speech made by individuals the audience will easily recognize. For instance, if you gave a speech to inform an audience about America's history with slavery, you might want to begin by saying: "Frederick Douglass once observed, 'I didn't know I was a slave until I found out I couldn't do the things I wanted.'" Or, if your purpose was to inform the audience about the landing on the moon, you might begin with, "'That's one small step for man, one giant leap for mankind.' Those were the words Neil Armstrong uttered when he first landed on the moon." In both of these examples you would pique the audience's interest in your topic by associating it with famous individuals who others recognize.

The third form of attention-getter we will describe is the use of startling statistics. People value statistics, and if you find some numeric data that might shock the audience into listening to your speech it might serve as an appropriate attention-getter. Think about a speech about how to change the oil in your car. The average oil change costs $25, and car owners need to have about four oil changes a year and about 40 if they keep their car for 10 years. So, to start a speech on this subject you might attract an audience's attention by beginning this way: "I am going to tell you how you can save $100 a year for 10 years, or $1,000." If your topic is informing an audience about a historical battle, you might want to provide them with the casualty count upfront in the attention-getter. Statistics are very good ways to get an audience's attention.

The fourth type of attention-getter is a short story or narrative that helps introduce your topic. The narrative cannot be too long because you risk beginning with a tangent and losing the audience's ability to focus on your speech topic. Suppose a student wanted to give an informative speech about the famous cycling race, the Tour de France. A short narrative about Lance Armstrong would be a good way to introduce the topic and would help garner the interest of the audience. See Table 11.1 for a summary of these four types of attention-getters.

You might recall our discussion of tangential information when thinking about these particular attention-getter strategies. Tangential information is often a very good source of attention-getters for a speech, so be sure to hold onto that type of data throughout the research process. However, despite the fact that attention-getters are important, and the first thing an audience hears, they are not the most crucial element of an introduction.

Getting the Audience's Attention		
Topic	Introduction Function	Example
Shooting a bow and arrow	Getting attention by asking a question	"Do you know what the primary weapons for hunting and war were before the advent of gunpowder?"
Community service	Getting attention by using a quote	"President John F. Kennedy once stated, 'Ask not what your country can do for you, ask what you can do for your country,' and today I plan to tell you the same thing."
College dropout rates	Getting attention with statistics	"Look around you; research shows that 50% of you will never graduate from college."
Safety on campus	Getting attention with a short narrative	"I want you to imagine a young woman who wakes up in her campus living quarters and notices a shadowy figure standing above her."

Table 11.1

Thesis Statement

Once you have your audience's attention with a creative attention-getter, you need to tell them exactly what you plan to discuss. This is done through the delivery of the thesis statement, or a single sentence that articulates the significance and relevance of the information you present in the speech. The thesis statement is the anchor for the rest of the speech because it is what all the main points and evidence presented throughout the body support or explain.

Proper thesis statements flow from the purpose of the speech and the information that you will present. As we mentioned previously, the general purpose of an informative speech is to inform, and the specific purpose explains the specific topic you will inform the audience about. Although some speakers can get away with delivering thesis statements without the word "I," we suggest that as beginners you do not try that strategy.

Take the case of Carrie, whose specific purpose is "to inform the audience about the history of Christmas." Carrie used a creative attention-getter by using a hypothetical question. She asked the audience if they were aware Christmas has pagan roots. She then delivered her thesis statement: "Today, I will explain how Christianity co-opted pagan rituals and called it Christmas to attract more converts." This one sentence establishes the significance of the topic by linking Christianity to paganism, and it implicitly lets the audience know all the information that follows will unpack that statement in greater detail. For examples of possible thesis statements, see Table 11.2.

Whereas attention-getters attract the audience's interest, thesis statements begin the process of grounding the audience's focus on a more particular topic—your topic. But getting attention and focusing the topic are not the only goals of an introduction. In the next section we will elaborate on the next part of an introduction—establishing your credibility as a speaker on the topic.

Table 11.2

Developing the Thesis Statement	
Speech Topic	**Thesis Statement**
Framing a house	"Today I will explain that to build a house you need to pour the foundation, create the subfloor, frame the building itself, and then finally form the roof."
Appealing a grade	"The grade appeal procedure starts with the professor, then the department chair, then the dean, and finally, if not resolved at one of these levels, the university provost."
Wine	"Wine can come in four different types: red, white, blush, and champagne."

Establishing Credibility

Even though you have gotten the audience's attention and told them the main point of your speech, they still need a reason to believe you. In an introduction for any type of speech—and especially in an informative speech—it is important to establish your credibility on the topic about which you are speaking. This will help enhance your ethos and will also aid in maintaining the attention of the audience. Everyone enters their speech with some level of credibility, and this is called your *initial credibility*. This can come from past work with which the audience is familiar, degrees you may have earned, or experiences you have had that the audience knows about.

initial credibility
the level of believ-ability a speaker has before beginning his or her speech

Audiences see you as more or less credible entering a speech based upon a variety of factors. First, if you are an expert on the topic on which you are presenting and the audience knows this, then you will have high initial credibility. For instance, a designer for General Motors would have high credibility when discussing how to build a car engine. Perhaps, however, you are not a General Motors mechanic but have worked on cars before. Such experience heightens your credibility, regardless of the fact you do not have an official pedigree. Maybe you have delivered several addresses on the topic but have never actually built a car; if your audience is aware of these speeches then you may also enter the occasion with a relatively high amount of initial credibility.

You can also establish your credibility by referring to your research early in the introduction. Let's say Marcus is addressing his classmates for the first time and his goal is to persuade them to buy a home security system. Marcus is neither an expert in home security systems, nor does he own one at the time of his speech. In order to convince his audience that they should hear and believe what he has to say, Marcus could make a direct reference to his research into home security systems early in his introduction. This reference can take the form of something like: "I have spent the last few weeks examining various ways of protecting a home from burglars...." This statement immediately cites a reason why Marcus should be trusted speaking on this topic, thereby providing him with credibility on the topic.

Perhaps you have some experience with your topic that should be mentioned. By telling the audience that you have had this experience first-hand you become a more credible speaker. Think about the scene in the movie *My Cousin Vinny* where Marissa Tomei's character is interviewed by her fiancé about her automotive knowledge. After saying she is a hairdresser (not providing any credibility on the topic) she then goes on about her experience with her family—all of whom were mechanics. This experience makes her a more credible speaker on the stand.

One final way you can influence your credibility is through your appearance. Well-dressed speakers tend to be more confident, and as we have mentioned, confident speakers appear more believable to audiences. When you do not dress the part, the audience focuses on your appearance instead of your message, and this damages your credibility and your ability to get your message across to your audience. Poor dress, however, is not in itself a death knell for your credibility. That said, it is important to know what can influence your believability before you begin your presentation and establish your credibility in your introduction. For some examples of how speakers establish credibility, see Table 11.3. Once your credibility has been established, you can preview how you plan to explain your topic to the audience.

Table 11.3

Establishing Speaker Credibility	
Speech Topic	**Credibility Example**
Writing a software program	"I know about designing software as I am a computer science major, and I have a part-time job writing software programs."
Genetically modified food	"I have thoroughly researched genetic food in our library and online."

Previewing the Body

At this point, you have the audience's attention, you have them focused on the topic of your speech, and you have given them a good reason to listen to what you have to say on the subject. The next thing to do is to let them know what points you plan to discuss and the order in which you will cover them. Introductions need to provide audiences with a roadmap for the remainder of the speech, and a good preview does this by explicitly identifying the main points to come and the order in which you plan to cover them. Previews also alert the audience as to how you have chosen to organize the speech, making it easier for them to follow you throughout the presentation.

A preview can be either one sentence or a series of sentences that touch upon what will be the main points of the speech. Previews do not give out any specific information, but rather focus on introducing topics. For a good example of a one-sentence preview, let's look at the speech General Petraeus delivered to Congress on Iraq. At the close of his introduction he issued the following one-sentence preview of the rest of his speech: "I would like to review the nature of the conflict in Iraq, recall the situation before the surge, describe the current situation, and explain the recommendations I have provided to my chain of command for the way ahead in Iraq."[2]

In this excerpt Petraeus clearly outlines the points he will cover and the order in which they will be delivered. First, he plans to review the form and type of fighting going on in Iraq. Second, he will discuss the situation on the ground in Iraq in terms of how it was before the surge, and then how the surge affected it. Finally, he plans to inform Congress on the recommendations he made to his staff for moving forward. This preview lets his audience know what he plans to address and when they can expect to hear it. This excerpt serves as an example of a one-sentence preview, but it could have easily been a multisentence preview. This could be done by simply breaking the component elements into separate sentences—much like we did in our explanation of the quote in this paragraph.

Previews are an essential part of any informative speech introduction, but there is one more aspect of a good informative speech introduction we have yet to cover: the transition to the body of the speech.

Transitions to the Body

We have referred to introductions as the roadmap for the speech, but without a starting point any map is useless. The last part of an effective introduction is a transition, which is a statement that connects the introduction to the first main point of the speech. As noted previously, transitions are one form of connective statement. There are several others which we will discuss later, but a transition is the only type of connective statement that works at the end of an introduction. A *transition* signals that you are done with one point, in this case the introduction, and that you are moving on to another.

transition
· · · · · · · · · · · ·
a connective statement that signals you are finished with one point and moving on to another

When to Write the Introduction

As you can see, introductions are an essential part of any speech. They include various elements that capture an audience's interest, focus their attention, and preview the rest of the speech. One thing we have yet to mention about introductions, however, bears particular attention: Introductions are not the first part of the speech you construct. The introduction is not first because the "meat and potatoes of a speech," the body, might change form repeatedly during the development of the speech, depending upon what information you find and how you decide to present it to an audience. Obviously, the roadmap will change along with the body, so why keep changing the introduction? Instead, create one introduction when you are happy with the finished body of the speech. In the next part of this chapter we will discuss various ways to organize the body of your informative speech.

INFORMATIVE SPEECH BODY

As you may have surmised, there are several different ways you might decide to organize the main points in the body of an informative speech. To a great extent, your particular topic and specific purpose will point you toward the best organizational pattern to employ in your speech. The information you collect through research needs to be organized in the manner best fitting your speech purpose and audience.

In this section we will discuss five different ways in which you can organize your main points in an informative speech. We will also cover some options for connecting those main points through the use of a variety of connective statements, like the transitions we just covered.

Chronological Organization of Main Points

The first possible organizational pattern for informative speeches we will discuss is chronological. *Chronological order* involves arranging points in the order in which they occur, or occurred, from start to finish. When your specific purpose is to inform the class about an event or a process, then the vast majority of the time you will arrange your points in chronological order. This only makes sense because these two topics lend themselves to speaking about them in time order.

chronological order
arranging points in the order in which they occur, or occurred, from start to finish

Informative speeches about events often cover what happened at a particular moment in history, or what will happen at a specific time in the future. Take the case of Kylie, whose specific purpose is to inform her audience about the Battle of Thermopylae, where 300 Spartan warriors fought against hordes of invading Persians. This topic encourages a chronological organizational pattern. It would make sense for her to structure her main points like this:

> Body
> I.   Main point: How the Battle of Thermopylae Started
> II. Main point: Repelling the Persian Army
> III. Main point: The Defeat of the Greeks

his sequence follows the order in which the events occurred and makes it easy for Kylie to achieve her specific purpose and the audience to learn about the Battle of Thermopylae.

Some lectures also are organized chronologically. For example, media mogul Rupert Murdoch was invited to speak about the state of the newspaper industry during the Boyer Lecture Series, an event sponsored by the Australian Broadcasting Commission. Murdoch addressed the industry by providing a chronological history of newspapers and his own experiences with them. It was more than just a sequential list of events, as he engaged the audience with both facts and personal testimonies that made the address quite engaging. Events, however, are not the only speech topics that invite chronological sequencing.

The Future of Newspapers
by Rupert Murdoch

Delivered November 14, 2008, at the Boyer Lecture Series

Australian media mogul Rupert Murdoch has spent much of his life in the media business. Murdoch knows about the media both past and present, so with many concerned by the shrinking of newspaper subscriptions, he addressed the future of the industry by discussing its origins.

Murdoch used a chronological organizational pattern to address several different topics in his rather complicated but informative address. When discussing his own history with media, he signified a chronological pattern with phrases such as: "When I was growing up...," "Over many decades," and "I became an editor and owner."[3] He also began one particular main point within his speech with, "When I took over the *News*..."[4]

Murdoch also spoke about implications for the industry from resources to technology changes, its challenges and opportunities, and the importance of brands. Murdoch completed his speech by reemphasizing the chronological development of his speech with this statement:

> "But I don't think I will be proven wrong on one point. The newspaper, or a very close electronic cousin, will always be around. It may not be thrown on your front doorstep the way it is today. But the thud it makes as it lands will continue to echo around society and the world."[5]

Informative speeches about processes also engender constructing main points in chronological order. For instance, Trevor's specific purpose is to inform his audience about how to apply for student financial aid. To accomplish the task of applying for financial assistance it is important to do things in order, and so his organizational pattern is chronological and looks something like this:

Body
I. Main point: Determining your Eligibility
II. Main point: Obtaining the Correct Forms
III. Main point: Submitting Materials

Like Kylie, Trevor needs to lay out the task at hand in the best way for people to understand it, and since it is an informative speech and he is trying to teach them about something, the best way for them to learn is through receiving the main points in a time sequence so they know what to do and when to do it.

Cause and Effect Organizational Pattern

Chronological patterns for organizing main points are not the only method of ordering ideas in an informative speech. A second method is *cause and effect arrangement*, which orders your points first by discussing the cause of something that occurred, and then moving to an explanation of the impact of its occurrence. Although there are similarities with the chronological pattern in that the cause must necessarily precede the effect in the speech, this is a much more specific structural pattern as it pertains only to causes and their subsequent effects. Cause and effect arrangements are typically used in informative speeches about events, as both causes and effects are events.

cause and effect arrangement
orders your points first by discussing the cause of something that occurred and then moving to an explanation of the impact of its occurrence

An informative speech structured according to cause and effect typically will have two main points: the cause, followed by the effects. If there are multiple causes and/or multiple effects, however, it is possible for there to be more than two main points. As a means of an example, let's look at Wanda's informative speech in which the specific purpose is to inform the audience about the Great Depression. If she chose to deliver this speech using a cause and effect arrangement, then her main points would look like this:

Body
I. Main point: Cause #1: Speculation
II. Main point: Cause #2: Stock Market Crash
III. Main point: Effects: Unemployment, Deflation

In this speech the first cause (speculation) leads to the second cause (stock market crash), and both ultimately have the effect of increased unemployment and deflation. This approach follows a time sequence, but that order is predicated only on causes and their subsequent effects.

Problem-Solution Organizational Pattern

Another organizational pattern for informative speeches that also relates to the chronological sequencing of main points is problem-solution arrangement. *Problem-solution arrangement* orders points by first discussing a problem and then explaining how it was addressed. This organizational pattern is chronological, and when employed in an informative speech it discusses events of the past. If a speaker advocates for a solution to a current problem, then he veers dangerously close to changing the purpose of the speech from conveying information to changing an audience's perception about an issue. In an informative speech it is best to use this form of chronological ordering to explain events of the past or available solutions in the present, rather than discussing current issues that do not contain a resolution. It is also essential not to advocate or label a particular solution "the best way" to solve a problem. Later in the book we will discuss how this organizational pattern can be effectively employed in a persuasive speech, but for now our focus remains on its use in an informative presentation.

problem-solution arrangement
orders points by first discussing a problem and then how it was addressed; a subset of chronological order

When using the problem-solution arrangement in an informative speech it is essential to present the problem as what happened and the solution as how it was corrected. For example, take Leslie, whose specific purpose for her informative speech is to tell the audience how to fix a reservation error that involves an online booking agent, like Priceline. Here the problem is simple—an error in a submitted online reservation—and she wants to teach her audience how to fix that error. Using the problem-solution arrangement for her main points, her speech would look like this:

Body
I.   Main point: Problem: Making an Error on an Online Reservation
II. Main point: Solution #1: Call the Agency
III. Main point: Solution #2: Call the Airline

Here, Leslie effectively orders her points by laying out the problem and then describing the available solutions for fixing the problem. In this speech there is no space for advocating for a specific solution, merely an explanation of ways a person could solve the problem. Remember, her general purpose is to inform; what her audience does with that information is entirely up to them.

Map of the Battle of Gettysburg

Spatial Organizational Pattern

Sometimes informative speeches do not need to be sequentially ordered, but rather the best way to achieve your specific purpose might be by organizing your main points according to space. *Spatial order* arranges points according to geography or logical movement through an area, so it is easy to see how certain topics could be covered in this manner. Spatial ordering of main points is typically applied to informative speeches about events and objects, as we will now demonstrate.

The spatial ordering of main points can be encouraged through a simple change in a specific purpose statement. For instance, Roland plans to deliver an informative speech with the specific purpose of informing his audience about the battlefield at the Battle of Gettysburg. This specific purpose is subtly different from a speech designed to inform an audience about the Battle of Gettysburg, but the simple adjustment encourages a spatial, rather than chronological, ordering of the main points. With Roland's specific purpose in mind, his speech would probably best be structured in the following manner:

spatial order arranges points according to geography or logical movement through an area

Body
I.   Main point: Little Round Top
II. Main point: Big Round Top
III. Main point: Cemetery Hill

Roland organizes his points so that he goes around the battlefield at Gettysburg to discuss the layout of each particular area where fighting took place. It is not organized according to chronology, but rather according to the landscape of the battlefield, thus making it a spatial ordering of main points and not a chronological arrangement.

Informative speeches about objects also can call for a spatial arrangement of main points. The specific purpose of Gwyneth's speech, for example, is to inform her audience about the chain of islands in the Caribbean called the Lesser Antilles. She might structure her speech by separating the islands into groups according to their location in the chain so it would look something like this:

Map of the Lesser Antilles Islands

Body
I.   Main point: Northernmost Islands
II. Main point: Central Islands
III. Main point: Southernmost Islands

This structure allows her to categorize the islands and move down the Lesser Antilles chain in the order of the islands' geographic location. This helps the audience make sense of where the islands are, and it allows Gwyneth to achieve her specific purpose in a logical manner.

topical arrangement the organization of main points by subpoints that do not naturally fit together in another way

Topical Organizational Pattern

If your informative speech does not fit one of the four organizational strategies discussed above, do not fear, there is one other option that remains open to you. The *topical arrangement* of main points works when your specific purpose encourages the division of main points into logical subpoints. These subpoints do not fit together in a chronological or spatial way and have certain characteristics that differentiate them from each other; however, they still share enough in common so as to logically relate to the topic of the speech. This organizational pattern could be applied to any of the four types of informative speeches except, typically, processes.

Informative speeches about concepts can be arranged in a topical fashion. Carlos wants to deliver a speech with the specific purpose of informing an audience about the four food groups, and so his speech topic does not invite any pattern we have discussed so far. Instead, he separates the concept of the four food groups into their distinctive categories and structures his speech accordingly:

> Body
> I.   Main point: Dairy
> II. Main point: Vegetables
> III. Main point: Grains
> IV. Main point: Meats

These main points are the categories of the four food groups, and thus, they provide four logically related areas to cover in the speech. Rather than a distinct chronology, spatial arrangement, or problem or cause, this speech is organized around logical subsets of information.

Crafting an informative speech about an event can also employ a topical arrangement of main points. Take, for example, a speech with the specific purpose of informing the audience about the Revolutionary War. This speech can cover the individual generals, the major battles, and the ramifications of the war. Those points are not chronologically or spatially related, and thus they provide an opportunity for using a topical organizational pattern like this:

> Body
> I.   Main point: Major Generals of the Revolutionary War
> II. Main point: Battles of the Revolutionary War
> III. Main point: Results of the Revolutionary War

Here a topic that one might think would only be covered using a chronological pattern has been shifted to fit a topical pattern. It is a perfect example of how the organization of a speech can be adjusted simply by reformulating the specific purpose.

Finally, informative speeches about objects can be constructed using the topical arrangement pattern. Take the example of the islands we used a little while ago. Gwyneth could easily have chosen a topical organizational pattern by discussing aspects of the island chain instead of their location. For instance, she could have focused on their colonial history, weather differences, and tourist destinations. Again, these aspects of the islands are not related by time or space, but they are worthy of discussion, and so if Gwyneth wished she could have structured her speech in this way:

Body
I. Main point: Colonial History of the Lesser Antilles Islands Chain
II. Main point: Weather of the Lesser Antilles Islands
III. Main point: Tourist Destinations in the Lesser Antilles Islands

These main points can be structured to logically flow into each other. For example, colonial history introduces interesting aspects of the islands that might attract visitors, information on the weather suggests when to visit, and the tourist destinations segment provides information on popular attractions to visit.

Choosing the proper organizational pattern makes all the difference in a speech. It demonstrates logical thinking on behalf of the speaker and allows an audience to follow the main points of a speech, thus enabling speakers to achieve their specific purpose. Arranging the points in the body of the speech is only one part of the equation. The other half is seamlessly connecting them so the speech stays fluid and smooth by using connective statements (recall our discussion of the transition statements used at the end of an introduction). In the next section we will discuss several strategies for connecting main points and creating smooth movement between the points of an informative speech.

Connective Statements within the Body

Determining your main points and how to arrange them is only half the task of developing a good body for your speech. The other half is connecting the points in a coherent fashion. There are several ways in which you can signal your speech is about to move to a new main point. In this part of the chapter we will discuss two methods, in addition to transitions which we mentioned earlier, that you can use to move from one point to another.

The first type of connective is an *internal preview*. Internal previews often work in conjunction with transitions by using two statements to segue between the two points:

> "Now that we have covered the scoring rules of baseball let's look at how those rules relate to other professional sports. First we will examine football, then we will discuss hockey, and finally we will conclude by showing the differences between baseball and soccer scoring."

internal preview
serves as an outline of what is to come next in a speech and is often combined with transition statements

The first sentence serves as the transition and the second provides a preview of what is to come.

Internal summary, the second type of connective we will discuss, is a statement that summarizes what you already covered and precedes transitions. Like internal previews, this summary serves as a roadmap for you and your audience and is most useful when you are covering several different main points in the body of your speech. For instance, consider this internal summary:

internal summary
a statement that summarizes what you already have covered and precedes transitions

"We have explored the early cultures of Latin America and what happened when the Spanish discovered South America. The history of South America, however, did not end with the arrival of the Spanish."

Notice how the summary of what has been covered occurs before the transition to a new main point. This is the inverse order of an internal preview, but it can have the same effect.

Once the body is complete you must still use one last connective to signal the conclusion. In the next section we will discuss that particular device as well as how to structure the conclusion for your informative speech. Before moving on, review the checklist for preparing the body of the speech provided in Figure 11.1.

Figure 11.1
Checklist for Preparing the Speech Body

✔ Have a clearly worded specific purpose

✔ Ensure your thesis does what you want it to

✔ Choose the proper organizational design that fits your specific purpose

✔ Have transitions between each main point

✔ Use connectives for speech clarity

INFORMATIVE SPEECH CONCLUSIONS

Informative speeches conclude in a slightly different way than other speeches. It is important to remember, however, that even an informative speech can have a persuasive impact, especially if loaded words are used. Rhetorician Richard Weaver (see the nearby box) noted the use of "god terms" and "devil terms" that can affect the meaning of a speech. With that in mind, it is important to carefully consider word choices within conclusions so as not to change the purpose of the entire speech from providing information to calling an audience to action.

In this section we will explain the dimensions of an informative speech conclusion, beginning with the signal that the speech has entered its final phase. We then lay out how to construct a summary, and finally, how to conclude with a strong statement.

Signposts

signpost
a connective that lets the audience know what is next; most effective form of connective for moving from the last main point to the conclusion

Once you completely cover all the main points you previewed in the introduction you need to let the audience know the presentation is about to wrap up. This is done with a statement called a *signpost*. These statements typically let the audience know you are moving from the body to the end of the speech, although they also can appear within the body of a speech. A signpost itself is a connective, but it is best suited for the move from the last main point to the conclusion.

SPOTLIGHTING THEORISTS: RICHARD M. WEAVER

Richard M. Weaver (1910–1963)

Richard Weaver was born in North Carolina. Five years later his father died and his mother moved the family to Lexington, Kentucky. Weaver worked his way through school at the University of Kentucky and graduated with a degree in English in 1932. Upon graduating, Weaver was unable to find work given the poor economic climate created by the Great Depression. The young graduate was bitter and joined the Socialist Party, but after a few years its ideas fell out of favor with him and he left the party.

He eventually received a scholarship to Vanderbilt University and studied under John Crowe Ransom, where he was introduced to southern agrarianism, an anti-progress movement. In 1942 Weaver achieved a Ph.D. at Louisiana State University and began a career teaching and writing about rhetorical theory and composition.[6]

Weaver was very interested in the nature of human beings and how language was used in expression. Weaver became known for describing such ways of knowing as argument by definition. He was enthralled with orator Edmund Burke and the Lincoln-Douglas debates of 1858. Weaver was also interested in understanding how orators could use loaded words to make a point. He labeled those "god terms" and "devil terms." Weaver noted that god words, such as science, progress, freedom, and democracy, had positive cultural connotations, whereas devil words, such as communist and fascist, had negative connotations.[7] Weaver later declared that no words are value-free, because each contains a worldview.[8]

Weaver also wrote about culture and rhetoric's place in it. He felt that society in general was declining. Weaver noted that scientific progress was not all that should be considered when analyzing culture. He pointed to things such as scientism and cultural relativism as warning signs in the structure of societies.

Weaver died at age 53 in 1963.

Acceptable signposts include phrases such as "Finally," "To wrap up," and "So, what is the point of all of this?" to name a few. When used within the body of the speech they might take the form of "Next," "First," or "Secondly." These signal a previously established order in which you planned on addressing certain topics. Each of these phrases allows the audience to catch up to the speech and get ready to absorb, once again, the main points of the presentation. Once you state the signpost, you can then move to the remainder of the conclusion.

Speech Summaries

Once you let the audience know that you are about to conclude your speech, you need to provide them with a summary of what you just told them. The *summary* is the central part of the conclusion, and it is where you reiterate the speech's

summary

the central part of the conclusion; it is where you reiterate the speech's thesis statement and recap the main points you addressed throughout the body thesis statement and recap the main points you addressed throughout the body. There are a few key aspects of the summary that require discussion.

Whereas a speech preview in the introduction clearly states the thesis before the preview of the main points, many conclusions do the opposite—although that is not required. The restatement of the thesis needs to occur either before or after the summary of main points and it also must be phrased differently than the original thesis statement in the introduction. Do not simply "cut and paste" the thesis into the proper slot in the conclusion. The same goes for the summary statements of the main points.

Again, you have options with regard to the summary statements for the main points. You can either combine them into a single complex statement or address each one individually. Choose whichever method makes the most sense and is clearest to the audience. Look at the following example of two different ways to summarize a speech:

> **Option #1:** "Today we learned about the history of the city of New York (restatement of thesis). First, I explained how the Dutch bought part of what is now New York for a box of trinkets. Then, I detailed the controversial group of politicians that ran the city for years, Tammany Hall. Finally, I sketched an overview of the city in the years following the attacks of 9/11."

> **Option #2:** "Today we learned about the history of the city of New York (restatement of thesis). We covered the early days with the Dutch, the years under Tammany Hall, and finally the more recent state of affairs since 9/11."

Both of these options equally reiterate the central thesis and main points in a way the audience can understand. The main points also are addressed in the order in which they appear in the speech, again emphasizing a symmetry that is easy for listeners to follow.

A signpost and good summary are not, however, the only components of an effective conclusion.

Clinchers

clincher
....
the final statement of
your speech

After reminding the audience of what they just heard it is time to issue the final statement of your speech, the *clincher*. Clinchers for informative speeches are very different than clinchers for persuasive or epideictic speeches as they do not really have an emotional dimension. There is no call to action as there might be in a persuasive speech conclusion and no recognition of the importance of the moment as there might be in an epideictic address. Rather, informative speeches end with a statement regarding the topic itself.

Clinchers for informative speeches might refer to a short story you used as your attention-getter. They may also be a quotation from another source, so long as you have not already used one as your attention-getter. These quotations also need to relate to your speech topic. So, if you informed your class about D-Day and World War II, you might quote Britain's Queen Elizabeth, who said:

> *"There are only a few occasions in history when the course of human destiny depended on the events of a single day. June 6, 1944, was one of those days."*[9]

Or perhaps you spoke about how to paint, in which case you might end with the following quotation from Leonardo da Vinci:

> *"Painting is poetry that is seen rather than felt."*

Clinchers also could simply be a statement regarding the knowledge you just provided the audience. Due to the nature of the speech, clinchers need to let the audience know what they learned and alert the audience that the speech has concluded.

One effective way of crafting a clincher is to end with a signpost in much the same way the conclusion itself began with one. Think of using phrases such as, "So, I will conclude by saying," "I wish to leave you with this," or "The last thing I wish to say." These phrases let the audience know the words you are about to utter are the final words of the speech.

SUMMARY

In this chapter we explained how to use the information from the previous chapter to construct an informative speech. We discussed the elements of an informative speech introduction, the various ways it can be organized, and the components of an informative speech conclusion. These tools, along with a properly constructed speech outline, will help you create an effective and interesting informative speech.

KEY TERMS

attention-getter	problem-solution arrangement
cause and effect arrangement	rhetorical question
chronological order	signpost
clincher	spatial order
famous quotation	summary
initial credibility	topical arrangement
internal preview	transition
internal summary	

REVIEW QUESTIONS

1. What are the three types of attention-getter devices discussed in this chapter?

   _____

   _____

2. What are five different ways you can organize the main points in an informative speech?

   _____

   _____

3. What are the four types of connectives you can use to smoothly move from one main point to the next?

   _____

   _____

4. What are the five important elements of a speech introduction?

   _____

   _____

5. What are the three important dimensions of a speech conclusion?

   _____

   _____

THINK ABOUT IT

1. Is there such a thing as a purely informative speech?

   _____

   _____

   _____

   _____

2. Are there any other ways to order points in an informative speech without affecting the purpose of the speech?

   _____

   _____

3. Can you think of any ways to creatively and excitingly craft a clincher without calling an audience to action?

1. Choose a topic which you know little about but would like to know more. Write out a series of questions about the topic you want answered, then place them in order according to one of the organizational patterns discussed for informative speeches. After you determine which pattern of organization you will use, figure out one or two additional ways of organizing the speech. After you have done that, determine the pros and cons for each organizational method.

ACTIVITIES FOR ACTION

2. Take all the objects from your bookbag and lay them on a table. Select an object and then write down all the major characteristics of the chosen item. Next, practice organizing an informative speech by developing the main points for an informative speech about the object you chose.

ENDNOTES

1. General David Petraeus, "Opening Statement to the Joint House Committee on the Situation in Iraq," http://www.americanrhetoric.com/speeches/wariniraq/davidpetraeusoniraq.htm (accessed April 9, 2009).

2. Ibid.

3. Rupert Murdoch at Boyer Lecture, http://www.abc.net.au/rn/boyerlectures/stories/2008/2397940.htm#transcript (accessed June 25, 2011).

4. Ibid.

5. Ibid.

6. Karen Foss, Sonja Foss, and Ronald Trapp, *Contemporary Perspectives on Rhetoric* (2nd Ed.) (Prospect Heights, IL: Waverland Press, 1991).

7. Richard Weaver, *The Ethics of Rhetoric.* (Davis, CA: Hermagoras Press, 1985). (Original publication was in 1953 by Regnery/Gateway, published by permission).

8. Patricia Bizzell and Bruce Herzberg, *The Rhetorical Tradition: Readings from Classical Times to the Present* (Boston, MA: Bedford Books of St. Martin's Press, 1990).

9. As quoted in a speech by Reverend Billy Graham entitled, "Leadership in the Third Millennium." For transcript see: David Edmison and Edward P. Badovinac (Eds.), *The Empire Club of Canada Speeches 1995-1996,* The Empire Club Foundation, Toronto, CA, 1996, 81.

Crafting a Persuasive Speech

12

CHAPTER OVERVIEW

- Discusses the Classical Greek and Roman approaches to structuring persuasive speeches
- Explains how to combine classical and contemporary approaches in developing introductions and conclusions for persuasive speeches
- Describes the various organizational patterns for persuasive speeches

Practically SPEAKING

In 1924 at a small YMCA in Santa Ana, California, a small group of people got together to help each other become better public speakers and have a little bit of fun in the process. Over the years, that small group expanded and became a group called Toastmasters International, a non-academic leader in helping people develop oral communication skills. This nonprofit organization now boasts nearly 235,000 members in over 11,700 clubs like the one in Santa Ana that started it all, in 92 different countries.[1]

Toastmasters begins by using a manual to help members develop certain speaking skills. It focuses on the use of humor, gestures, and eye contact. Once the initial manual is completed members then progress to more advanced manuals that narrow the skill's focus considerably. Thousands of corporations, companies, and civic organizations encourage their employees and affiliates to participate in Toastmasters because of the practical benefits gained from the group.

Toastmasters International also contributes much in the way of community service. It promotes youth programs designed around developing oral communication and leadership skills. It supports "Gavel Clubs" where it brings speech training inside prison walls. It works with community organizations and businesses to help them tell their story to the community in which they reside. Additionally, it offers short courses on crafting a speech.[2]

One of the central focuses of the Toastmasters International programs on crafting a speech is organization. In fact, it makes a point to tell people one of the ten most common errors in public speaking is lack of preparation and organization. When you do not organize your thoughts in a logical manner and then present them to an audience, it makes it at best difficult and at worst nearly impossible for your audience to follow what you are saying and ultimately get anything out of your presentation.

Persuasive speeches must be carefully arranged to ensure the speaker achieves his or her specific purpose. In fact, persuasive speeches were the foremost concern of the Greeks and Romans. In the first part of the chapter we will discuss the ways in which Classical Greeks and Romans taught students how to construct persuasive speeches. Then, we will discuss how you can incorporate aspects of the model for developing an informative speech. Finally, we will offer several different organizational patterns you can use for the various types of persuasive speeches identified in the previous chapters.

CLASSICAL SPEECH STRUCTURE

It should come as no surprise that the Greeks and Romans were among the first to break down a speech into its component parts. Today, we use different terminology, but the segments of the speech are essentially the same. It appears the most effective way to organize a persuasive speech has changed very little over the course of the last 2,500 years! As the saying goes, "if it ain't broke, don't fix it." In this part of the chapter we will discuss the three sections of a persuasive speech as identified by the Greeks and Romans: the exordium, the narrative, and the conclusion.

The Speech Exordium

The introduction is your best opportunity to establish a rapport with your audience, which is very important in persuasive speeches as your goal is to get them to listen and respond to your position. This importance was not lost on the Greeks and Romans either, so perhaps the best way to understand how to craft an effective introduction to a persuasive speech is to begin with an examination of classical speech structure. In this section we will discuss introductions using the terminology of the Greeks and Romans, who called it a speech exordium. We will explain why they saw it as important and then detail the elements of an exordium.

The Greeks and Romans referred to the start of a speech as the *exordium*, as they understood it as the place in the speech where you convince an audience to listen to your position. In fact, Quintilian stated that the purpose of the exordium is to prepare the audience to listen intently to the remainder of the presentation.[3] One of the ways you accomplish this task is by capturing the interest of the audience and the other is by establishing your credibility as a speaker.

exordium
the place in the speech where you convince an audience to listen to your position; Latin label for the introduction of a speech

A good exordium captures the interest of the audience almost immediately by connecting the topic to something the audience might be interested in. Aristotle argued that this process included an effort to make the audience hold a favorable impression of the speaker and the topic. After you gain their interest with your opening statement using an attention-getter, you need to begin the case for why the audience should listen to what you have to say on the topic. You do this by demonstrating knowledge of the subject matter.

Although the exordium was considered one of the most important parts of a speech by the Greeks and Romans, they felt it should not be the first part of the speech you prepare, for two reasons. First, Cicero warned his students that it was impossible to effectively introduce arguments yet to be crafted. You may know what you want to say, but until you write it down you don't know how you will say it or the order in which you will present the points. Essentially, Cicero suggested writing the bulk of the speech before creating the exordium.

The second reason classical speakers felt the exordium should be composed last also illustrates a key difference between an introduction for an informative and a persuasive speech. Cicero stated that the quality of the case the speaker presents should determine the type of exordium created. He proposed two ways to begin a speech, although he also pointed out that there are rare situations when exordiums are not necessary; however, those rare instances do not exist for informative speeches. The first type of exordium Cicero discussed he called an introduction.

introduction
one form of exordium where speakers use plain language to lay out their case in an effort to get a confused and ill-informed audience to pay attention

insinuation
a form of exordium reserved for cases made about disputed topics to audiences with animosity toward the topic or the speaker

Cicero defined the *introduction* as an exordium that lays out the speaker's case in plain language so that the audience becomes receptive and attentive. They are often most useful when an audience is confused or ill-informed and when the topic is not controversial. Introductions today are often understood as the only way to start a speech, whereas for Cicero they were simply one way to do so. That is why this method of crafting an exordium seems familiar—it's similar to how we described starting an informative speech a few chapters ago.

Cicero reserved the other form of exordium, *insinuation*, for cases made about disputed topics to audiences with animosity toward the topic or the speaker. A common insinuation exordium promises the audience you will be short and to the point when you know they are tired of hearing about the issue on which you are speaking. These work to reduce the reluctance of an audience to listen and allow speakers to make their case. Unlike introductions, insinuations do not need to unpack information for the audience to relieve confusion, because the audience is already informed—in fact, possibly overinformed!—about the subject matter.

Regardless of which type of Ciceronian exordium you might use to begin your persuasive speech, there are various ways to gain the attention of an audience while making them more receptive to your speech by enhancing your credibility. The first way involves stressing the importance of the topic of your speech and connecting it to the lives of the audience members. For example, if you deliver a speech arguing to update the technology of a factory in a town, you might also stress the importance of your topic to the community at large, telling them that the plant is outdated and may close if the technology isn't improved and thus the expensive update will actually save jobs for the community. Either way, you need to connect the audience to the topic in a personal way that increases the likelihood they will listen to what you have to say. This is something typically not necessary with informative speech introductions because the audience is there to learn something and thus wants to be there.

One final piece of advice offered by the Romans on exordiums is important to note. Cicero believed, as did his Roman counterpart Quintilian, that exordiums must be serious in nature, as this lends gravity and importance to the topic of the address. Cicero maintained that when a topic already has the support of the audience before the speech begins, then a rhetor might best eliminate the exordium because it could make the speaker seem condescending. In such situations speakers still previewed their speech, but they did away with the elements of the exordium that attempted to raise the interest of the audience. Quintilian additionally advised that if a speaker entertains doubts about the audience's knowledge of the issue under consideration then he or she should briefly review the situation in the exordium. Both of these suggestions underscore ways for you to lend gravity to your speech and increase your ethos within the exordium.

The Greeks and Romans understood that the exordium is the first impression a speaker makes on an audience but the last part of the speech to be composed. Its content is driven by the topic and the disposition of the audience toward the speaker, and its goals are to get the attention of the audience, establish a speaker's credibility, and ensure receptivity to the speaker's message. Once these goals are accomplished they taught students to move to the body, or what they called the narrative.

The Speech Narrative

Aristotle argued that the introduction was one of only two elements of a speech, referring to the second component as the argument proper. The Romans taught that the body of the speech that followed the exordium contained three parts: the statement of facts, the argument, and the refutation. In this way they expanded Aristotle's approach to arranging a speech. In this section we will discuss the elements of the narrative of the speech, or what we now call the body, by addressing the three areas identified by the Romans.

When we use the term "narrative" today we think of a coherent story, or even fiction. Our understanding of the term differs from that of the Classical Greeks and Romans when applied to constructing a speech. For them the narrative of the speech consisted of several parts arranged in a coherent order. They did not provide an exact recipe for that order, acknowledging that each speaking situation called for a different response and thus a need for the speaker to arrange his or her points differently. The first of these parts they called the *statement of facts*, an explanation of what the audience needs to know in order to appreciate the main argument of the speech.

statement of facts
an explanation of what the audience needs to know in order to appreciate the main argument of the speech

The statement of facts helps speakers familiarize their audience with the relevant details about their topic. Cicero and Quintilian both recognized that this portion of the narrative might not be necessary all the time, while at other times it might be the only part of the narrative required of a speaker. If an audience is familiar with the case you present, then a brief statement of facts might be all that is needed. For instance, if you plan to convince the student body at your school that they need to build a new recreation center through an additional student fee, you may not need to explain why since the students might be well aware of the need.

When your goal is simply to inform an audience, then the statement of facts is the only element of the narrative you need to develop. Here, an audience is confused or ill-informed about your topic and your goal is to convey information to them. The facts of the case are all you need to present an informative speech, as you are neither making an argument nor countering any opposition to your point of view. In persuasion, however, arguments flow from the facts of the case—even when they are not explicitly outlined in the narrative by the speaker.

The Greeks and the Romans believed that the argument was the core of any speech, and this is certainly true when your purpose is persuasion. The *argument*, also called the *proof* or *confirmation*, is the portion of the speech that validates your position on the issue laid out in the statement of facts. It is, for all intents and purposes, the central idea of your speech laid bare for the audience. Whereas in an informative speech the thesis statement is a one-sentence sum of the goal of your speech, the Greeks and Romans taught that in a persuasive speech the argument portion of your speech details all of your evidence and claims regarding your topic.

argument
....
also called the *proof* or *confirmation*; the portion of the speech that validates your position on the issue laid out in the statement of facts

The argument portion of the speech often contains more than one claim, and choosing the way to organize these claims to maximize your ability to persuade your audience is tricky. The Greeks and Romans both taught their students not to start with their strongest, most persuasive claim; rather, they suggested that in many cases you should end with it. This allows your argument to end on its highest and best note, rather than a weaker, less persuasive point. Quintilian suggested spending more time developing the strongest point than the weaker arguments, which he proposed should be lumped together if at all possible. On the latter suggestion he famously wrote, "They may not have the overwhelming force of a thunderbolt, but they will have all the destructive force of hail."[4] After you organize your claims in the argument portion of your speech, you still must be aware of the opposition.

refutation
....
response to potential opposition to your argument

The third component of the narrative part of the speech according to the classical speech teachers is where you attempt to anticipate opposition to your argument. The *refutation*, or the response to opposition to your argument, is only relevant for persuasive speeches and, even then, situational factors largely determine where you place it. For example, if your audience prefers the position opposing yours, it might be best to lay out the refutation as reasons not to agree with the opposition before you even detail your argument. In this instance, moving the refutation to a position immediately following the exordium might be wise. However, when an audience is hostile toward either you or your argument, even Quintilian would encourage you to hold the refutation for as long as possible.

The Greeks and Romans believed the refutation is an important part of any speech for two reasons. First, it demonstrates that you have thought about and researched the issue on which you are speaking, thus enhancing your own credibility. Second, it makes you appear more objective, making it easier for people to listen to your point of view. In other words, if people don't view you as partisan about an issue, then they will be more likely to be persuaded by your arguments.

12

Determining the order of the statement of facts, argument, and refutation is the first of a two-step process. The second step in constructing the narrative involves connecting each to the other, in other words, providing the glue that enables your argument to make sense. You can accomplish this by using one of the several different connective statements. Connective statements are common to both informative and persuasive speeches.

All told, for the Greeks and Romans, the narrative, or body, of a speech is the most time-consuming and difficult to develop. Placing the three elements of the narrative—the statement of facts, the argument, and the refutation—into the best possible order and making that arrangement seem natural and smooth takes time. Additionally, determining that order is significantly influenced by situational factors like audience disposition. Cicero, Quintilian, and others would argue that it is important to approach constructing the narrative not as an inflexible recipe for success, but rather as a guide for helping you determine the best way to arrange the main points of your speech. Later in this chapter we will discuss some tried and true organizational patterns that may further help you develop and arrange your persuasive speech, but for now we need to finish discussing the third part of a persuasive speech: the conclusion. As you are leaving the narrative, you should signal your audience that you are moving into the conclusion with a signpost, just as you would for an informative speech.

The Speech Peroration

If the narrative, or body, is important because it contains the core point of the address, then the conclusion is important because it summarizes that idea for the audience. Aristotle and Cicero both contributed to our understanding of the content and goals of a conclusion, or as they called it, the *peroration*. Conclusions represent the last opportunity for a speaker to present his or her case to the audience and leave the audience with something to remember.

peroration
speech conclusion

Think about the last speech that you heard. What do you remember? The evidence? A statistic, perhaps? More than likely, you remember how that speaker finished the speech, the last words spoken. This is illustrative of the *principle of recency*, or the idea that the last message you heard is most likely to be the one you remember. For this reason it is important to finish a persuasive speech with a bang, and not a whimper. You want the audience to leave knowing what you want them to do or believe and why.

principle of recency
the idea that the last message you heard is most likely to be the one you remember

Aristotle taught that conclusions accomplish four things. First, they need to leave the audience with a positive impression of you as the speaker. Failing that, they need to at least leave the audience with a less than enthusiastic view of your opponent. Second, conclusions need to both augment the force and presence of your arguments while diminishing the power of those that may be offered by your opponent. Third, Aristotle argued conclusions must incite the proper emotions in an audience. Finally, he believed conclusions should restate the arguments and supporting facts central to the speech's goal.

Cicero followed up on Aristotle's approach by advocating three distinct things speakers could do in their conclusion. First, like Aristotle, he stated speakers should summarize their ideas. This summary should briefly review the statement of facts and take a moment to encapsulate each of the main points the speaker presented. Second, Cicero called for speakers to use the conclusion to cast anyone who disagreed with them in a bad light through emotional appeals. Finally, where Aristotle argued conclusions must incite the proper emotions, Cicero gave the emotion a name: sympathy. He also said that the audience's sympathy should be toward the speaker and the topic, not one or the other. In fact, in his book *De Inventione*, Cicero provided quite a number of specific ways to accomplish this (for a few examples, see Table 12.1).

Table 12.1

Emotional Appeals	
Goal	**Emotional Appeal Example[5]**
Invoke authority	"As a 10-year cancer survivor I am proof of the benefits of this treatment."
Point out the effects of success or failure	"When we took this approach in a similar situation my plan worked, while my opponent's failed."
Show what will happen if the state of affairs remains unchanged	"Just look at what happened three years ago when we faced a similar challenge, and we did nothing. It is time to act decisively."
Demonstrate that the state of affairs violates community values	"The current crisis in our area goes against everything most of us believe in, against what our parents taught us, and against the ideals with which we grew up."
Ask the audience to identify with those injured or insulted	"My friends, think how you and your family would feel if you were treated in such a shabby manner. Put yourself in their place and ask yourself how you would feel."

The classical construction of a speech in this manner, however, has not been lost to history. In fact, we can find many examples of speeches structured this way. One of the more famous classically structured speeches in modern times came from one of the most eloquent and inspiring leaders of the twentieth century: Winston Churchill. Shortly after taking the position of prime minister in May 1940, Churchill delivered his now famous "Blood, Toil, Tears and Sweat" speech to Parliament (see the nearby box). In it he provided a brief exordium, a statement of facts, and a peroration all worthy of praise from Cicero and Quintilian, thus demonstrating to students of speech that what was true about speech over 2,000 years ago is still true today.

Both Cicero and Aristotle noted the importance of conclusions in persuasive speeches. They knew that just as exordiums, or introductions, were the first opportunity to make a strong case to the audience, perorations, or conclusions, were the last best chance to win the audience over. In the next part of the chapter we will explain some ways in which the classical approach to crafting a persuasive speech can be incorporated by you when developing your persuasive presentations.

Contemporary Speech Introductions and Conclusions

Now that we have illustrated the importance of persuasive speeches to the Greeks and Romans and discussed how they understood the practice of persuasive speaking, we need to show you how these ideas translate to you and your efforts at creating persuasive appeals. In this section we will provide you with some strategies for developing effective introductions and conclusions (or, as the Greeks and Romans called them, exordiums and perorations). We will then spend the final portion of the chapter exploring several different organizational strategies for the body of a persuasive speech.

Strategies for Persuasive Introductions

The Greeks and Romans noted the uniqueness of introductions in providing several different options for developing them, and these observations also illustrate the differences that exist between persuasive and informative introductions. That said, there are similarities between the two types of speech introductions. This section will note the similarities while also providing you with ways to effectively construct an introduction appropriate for a persuasive speech.

Cicero and Quintilian's recommendation that the introduction be the last part of the speech you write is true with persuasive as well as informative speeches. You should not set up the introduction until you know what you are going to say and have an idea of the knowledge level and disposition of your audience. This information is key to making sure you effectively preview your speech's main points, capture the audience's interest, establish credibility, and focus the audience's attention.

Those four goals of an introduction, you may well remember, are the same for informative as well as persuasive speeches. You need to get an audience's attention, but as Cicero and Quintilian noted with regard to persuasive speeches, you must be sure to do so without offending the audience. You must be attuned to the audience's feelings about the topic or the occasion and determine whether a traditional introduction or Ciceronian insinuation would benefit the speech most. You also need to establish your credibility almost immediately by stating why an audience should listen to you on a particular subject. Finally, you need to preview your speech's main points in much the same way you would do so for an informative speech. See Table 12.2 for a summary of tips for an effective persuasive introduction.

One thing you should note from Cicero and Quintilian is their belief that introductions are serious. Many people believe that today the best way to get an audience's attention is with a joke, but that is not something the Romans, or we, would recommend—especially for persuasive speeches. Telling a joke is very risky, because if people do not laugh you start off on a poor note, and you might

Blood, Toil, Tears and Sweat
by newly elected Prime Minister Winston Churchill

Delivered May 13, 1940, to the British House of Commons

Prime Minister Winston Churchill delivered a terse, yet powerful call to action shortly after becoming prime minister of Great Britain in May 1940. As if the war was not a large enough complication for the new leader, outgoing Prime Minister Neville Chamberlain received a boisterous round of applause, while Churchill was greeted with a subdued reaction from members of the House of Commons, thus illustrating the fragile coalition supporting Churchill and his government.[6]

At the time of the address Adolf Hitler's Nazi war machine was crushing opposition everywhere it went. Britons were concerned that their country's safety, freedom, and sovereignty were at risk. Churchill rose to the task of inspiring confidence in both his leadership and the country itself with this brief (only 688 words) address to parliament.

In his statement of facts, Churchill noted he selected a five-person war cabinet that contained diverse political views. He pointed out that Britain was already fighting in Norway and Holland, that the Mediterranean was a concern, and that the air battle over the remainder of Europe was "continuous." He argued that these facts required that "many preparations have to be made here at home."

Churchill proclaimed the famous line: "I have nothing to offer but blood, toil, tears and sweat"[7] as part of his rebuttal, and aimed it at those who might criticize the swift creation of the cabinet without "ceremony." In fact, his phrase made it seem like he pled with them to accept it because he was essentially trying his best.

In his peroration the prime minister closed with a clarion call to action after admitting the country faced "many, many long months of struggle and suffering." These words, his declaration of a policy of victory, and his concluding statement of, "Come then, let us go forward together with our united strength"[8] all created emotional connections between the initially divided audience, himself, and his policies.

also unintentionally offend someone in the audience, thus damaging your ability to move the audience to action. Instead of a joke, make use of an attention-getter.

Finally, students delivering a persuasive speech should be aware of what their instructors expect in an introduction. Some instructors may, for instance, also require students to state their name or the title of their speech. Be sure you know what is expected before you write your introduction.

Tips for an Effective Persuasive Introduction	**Table** 12.2
• Develop the introduction last	
• Capture the attention of the audience	
• Establish your credibility	
• Focus the audience's attention	

Strategies for Persuasive Conclusions

Just as with introductions, there are elements common to both informative and persuasive conclusions. After reading how the Greeks and Romans approached perorations we now realize there are differences between informative and persuasive speech conclusions. In this section of the chapter we will discuss the similarities and differences while also providing tips on how you can create a strong conclusion to your persuasive speech.

One of the aspects of conclusions shared by both informative and persuasive speeches is the need for a signpost at the start of the conclusion. Signposts serve the same function for persuasive speech conclusions that they do for informative speech conclusions: They let the audience know the speech is almost over.

Similarly, both informative and persuasive speech conclusions should summarize each of the main points in the speech and demonstrate how they connect to and support your argument. You should never introduce new evidence in a conclusion, but rather re-emphasize the fundamental points of your speech. This allows the audience to walk away from your presentation understanding your central point and how you got there. Rarely will an audience recall the specific evidence you lay out, but they will remember your main points. With regard to persuasive speeches this summary also enables you to build up your clincher, which can be a much more powerful statement than in an informative speech.

Although both informative and persuasive speeches have clinchers, in a persuasive speech there is much more room for creativity and direct calls to action. The reason for this is simple: The general purpose of a persuasive speech is to persuade, so the last thing the audience should hear should be a call to action.

The success of your persuasive speech conclusion often depends on your ability to channel and incite the proper ethos through this clincher. This is where Aristotle and Cicero's goal of creating audience sympathy toward the speaker or topic should be accomplished. The clincher should not take long to state, and there are a variety of ways to construct an effective clincher for a persuasive speech. Most importantly, however, in persuasive speeches it is essential for you to find a way to issue a call to action that the audience can reasonably and realistically accomplish.

A common error novice speakers make in their persuasive speech conclusions is reserving their persuasive effort for the clincher. Do not wait until the last statement to persuade the audience. The clincher should be the last push and a logical next step based on the case you have made throughout the speech. In short, the conclusion should feed off of the body and accentuate your case and its significance for the audience.

One final note about conclusions bears mentioning. Conclusions should not be very long. In fact, they should take about as long as your introduction and thus typically account for no more than 20% of your speech. If your conclusion rambles on it loses its effectiveness and you lose your audience. If it is too short, your audience may never truly understand the point of your speech. Remember, your conclusion is the last chance you have to underscore your case and its importance for your audience. Table 12.3 provides a summary of tips for creating persuasive speech conclusion.

Table 12.3

Tips for a Persuasive Speech Conclusion
• Provide a signpost at the beginning of the conclusion
• Summarize the main points
• Do not present new evidence
• Emphasize the fundamental points
• Build up the clincher
• Do not wait until the conclusion to present persuasive appeals
• Accentuate the speech body and case
• Make it approximately the same length as the introduction

Conclusions are essential elements of any good persuasive speech. They involve letting the audience know you are almost finished, restating your argument and main points, and clinching your appeal with a call to action. They share some similarities with conclusions for informative speeches, but there are key differences you must be aware of when putting together your speech. Developing strong introductions and conclusions is only two-thirds of the process of crafting a successful persuasive appeal. In the next section we will explore the various methods that you might use to properly organize the "meat" of your persuasive speech.

ORGANIZATIONAL PATTERNS FOR PERSUASIVE SPEECHES

The general and specific purpose statements of a persuasive speech differ from those of an informative address, but they too help you determine how to arrange your points. A closing argument in a courtroom is a persuasive speech where the general purpose is "to persuade" and the specific purpose is tied to the facts of the case. For example, the lawyer for Kelly, who was accused of stealing money from a CVS pharmacy, gave a closing argument where the specific purpose was "to persuade the jury that Kelly did not steal the money because she had no motive or opportunity to commit the crime." This specific purpose statement encouraged the lawyer to use a particular organizational pattern to accomplish his speaking goals. In this section of the chapter we will detail some of the common organizational strategies you can effectively employ for persuasive speeches.

Although persuasive speeches have very different general and specific purposes than informative/technical speeches, the two types of speeches are similar in that the specific purpose often dictates what organizational pattern should be used. Persuasive speeches can be directed at a specific problem or the problem's fundamental cause. They also can be focused on arguing that one option is better than another. Finally, there are persuasive speeches that attempt to move people to immediate action. Depending on which of these purposes is your goal, you may choose any one of four potential organizational patterns.

Problem-Solution Order

If you seek to convince an audience that a specific policy or action will solve an existing problem, the *problem-solution order* might be best. In this arrangement you first convince the audience that there is a problem and then make the case that the solution you propose will alleviate that problem. To effectively arrange this speech

problem-solution order
a means of organizing a persuasive speech in which you discuss the problem first and follow with a discussion of your preferred solution

you must first establish a clear specific purpose that states exactly what you want your audience to do. Then you must consider several important questions to evaluate the merits of your case as you develop it and prepare to present it to your audience.

The first question deals with the definition and scope of the problem. You need to establish how you see the problem at hand and convince your audience to see it that way as well. If they disagree with your definition of the problem then you will never get the audience to buy into your solution; you will be stuck arguing over what Quintilian called definitive stasis. So, before even offering a solution you need to clearly establish the scope of the problem you plan to address. In explaining the scope of the predicament you may wish to inquire as to whether any party has been harmed by the problem and allow them to explain. This can help create an emotional connection between the audience and the issue, thus enabling you to add some pathos to your appeal.

Once the dilemma that faces the audience has been established you need to move on to the solution. The initial part of this portion of your speech should answer the question of evaluative criteria. In other words, establish by what criteria a potential solution to the problem should be judged. After constructing this list of criteria for evaluating a solution you should check your proposed solution against it to ensure that what you propose actually resolves the problem. If it does not, then your solution is unlikely to be adopted by the audience.

Finally, you need to explain to the audience how your solution can be put into effect. The "how" element is important because it is the prescription for action that you want the audience to follow. It should contain practical and specific steps for the audience to take that will actually enact the solution and solve the problem facing the community.

Let's look at the hypothetical case of Lionel to illustrate how a simple problem-solution speech might be approached. Lionel is tired of the potholes in the road in front of his house, so he attends the city council meeting and addresses the members. First he explains that the road in front of his house contains 10 potholes in a three-block span, and then he informs the council that these potholes have caused several thousand dollars in damage to the cars that drive that road in the last month alone. He then proposes that they use city funds to fill the potholes with macadam to avoid further damage.

In this speech, Lionel details the problem and proposes a solution once the problem has been made clear to everyone. Using the problem-solution order this speech roughly looks like the following:

> Body
>
> Main point: State of the road in front of the house *(problem)*
>
> Main point: Funding road repairs *(solution)*

This can be an effective way of convincing an audience to support your plan; however, it is not always the most compelling way to propose a solution. Sometimes, you need to do more.

Problem-Cause-Solution Order

Problems, be they public or personal, always have a root cause and to effectively resolve the problem you need to address that root cause, otherwise the symptoms will recur. To this end you must look at the situation to determine the causes of the problem facing the audience and then decide whether or not the cause can actually be addressed. If it can, then the speech needs to recognize the problem faced by the community as well as add a discussion of why the problem exists—its cause. In short, you must convince the audience not only that a problem exists, but that the problem exists because of a root cause and that addressing that root cause is the most effective way to handle the situation. Let's return to Lionel and see how this works.

Does it not make even better sense to not just fix the potholes, but to make sure they don't happen again? This would involve changing the specific purpose and, as a result, the organization of the main points in the speech. Lionel's specific purpose would change to reflect his new goal, and it would be something like this: "To persuade the audience to redesign the street where potholes have damaged cars so that they will not occur again."

The goal for Lionel now is to address the problem (potholes) by providing a solution to it and its cause (poor design of the street).

> Body
>
> Main point: The state of the road in front of his house *(problem)*
>
> Main point: The poor street design *(cause)*
>
> Main point: Funding for proper road repairs *(solution)*

His speech arrangement now is ***problem-cause-solution order***, where he first discusses the immediate problem, then explains what caused it, and finally provides a solution that addresses both the potholes and the poor street design.

Comparative Advantages

More often than not, you will not be the only one offering solutions to a problem. In fact, having multiple ideas about how to fix something or address an issue is commonplace. The important thing to remember is to research and evaluate all the other potential solutions that might be offered to the problem. After doing so, if you believe yours is the best approach, then it might be helpful to recognize the fact you are aware of other potential solutions, but that they would not be the best option. This approach looks at the strengths and weaknesses of other solutions and compares them to your own. Such an approach can help increase your ethos with the audience and make your case even stronger.

Continuing with the example of Lionel and the dangerous potholes, perhaps he is not the only one who has brought this issue to the attention of the city council. In fact, the council already knows about and agrees there is a problem and its cause is poor street design. Let's say that the day before Lionel arrives to give his speech the council comes out in favor of a plan to fill the potholes but not redesign the street because it would be cost prohibitive to do so. Lionel, aware of this alternate plan, needs a different specific purpose and organizational pattern than in either of the two previous scenarios. Now his specific purpose is "to persuade his audience that paying the money to fix the street now is a better solution than simply fixing the potholes."

He then structures the body of his speech by using a ***comparative advantage*** organizational pattern, in which every main point in the argument explains why redesigning the street is better than just fixing the potholes and not addressing their root cause.

> Body
>
> Main point: Fixing potholes is temporary; a proper repair job will be permanent
>
> Main point: Fixing the road will create a smoother surface
>
> Main point: Fixing the road correctly will be less expensive in the long run

problem-cause-solution order
••••••••••••••
a means of organizing a persuasive speech in which you discuss the problem first, then its root cause, and then your preferred solution that addresses both the problem and its inherent cause

comparative advantage
•••••••••••••
an organizational pattern that uses each main point to explain why the speaker's solution is better than another proposed solution

The case of Lionel and his topic illustrates several different ways of organizing persuasive speeches. Each one helps to establish a strong case for taking a particular policy. There is, however, one more organizational pattern for persuasive speeches we need to discuss and it is particularly useful when seeking immediate action from an audience.

Monroe's Motivated Sequence

The fourth organizational pattern for your main points we will discuss provides a way to effectively arrange a speech designed to incite immediate action in your audience. Alan Monroe, a professor at Purdue University, developed what we call *Monroe's Motivated Sequence* in the 1930s. The five-step sequence combines psychological elements with speech persuasion in an effort to move an audience to action. First, Monroe advocated something the Greeks and Romans also called for: getting the attention of your audience. Then he argued a speaker should clearly lay out the need for change, something again advocated by the classical philosophers we discussed earlier. Once you clearly establish the problem you satisfy the need by providing a solution to that problem. Fourth, Monroe's sequence calls for you to intensify the audience's desire for your solution to the problem by visualizing its success. This involves the use of imagery and asks the audience to actually see themselves doing what you call for—at least to see it in their mind's eye. Finally, once you state your case and get your audience to visualize your solution's success, you can use emotionally stirring language to tell them how to act.[9]

As an example, suppose a student wants to persuade his audience to get involved in cleaning up a park on his college campus that is strewn with trash and debris. He then composes the following order for his points using Monroe's Motivated Sequence:

Attention:	"Do you think we should have a pleasant outdoor place to enjoy nature, to hang out with friends? To take walks, play sports, have cookouts, and entertain?"
Need:	"We do not have that on our campus, and there is a nearby park we could use, but it is overrun with weeds and trash and is currently unacceptable." (Pictures would be a good visual aid at this juncture.)
Satisfaction:	"We could all pitch in, share the work, and it would not be that big of a burden on anyone."
Visualization:	"A place to hang out, play ball, walk, enjoy fresh air and nature, and have cookouts—and we would have made that possible." (Visuals of a beautiful outdoor setting would be effective at this point.)

Monroe's Motivated Sequence

a five-step organizational pattern that combines psychological elements with speech persuasion to move an audience to action

SPOTLIGHTING THEORISTS: ALAN H. MONROE

Alan H. Monroe

Alan H. Monroe served as a member of the faculty at Purdue University in Indiana beginning in 1924. He was initially hired as an instructor in English to teach basic courses in the English department. He quickly infused the English curriculum with classes such as Principles of Speech and Debating in English. Today, we recognize these topics as Communication rather than English courses. Through Monroe's efforts Purdue University established a strong Communication department known for teaching and research.[10]

In 1927 Monroe became the head of the Speech faculty in the English department at Purdue, but he was not formally recognized in that role until 1941. Along with other members of the then English department at Purdue, Monroe led efforts during the 1930s to expand the curriculum, specifically adding courses in oral interpretation, public address, and debate. In 1935 Monroe published the first edition of his book *Principles and Types of Speech*, which is now in its 16th edition, a testament to the ingenuity and importance of what Monroe accomplished while at Purdue.

In 1948 Purdue inaugurated its own Ph.D. program in Speech Communication, largely through Monroe's efforts. Monroe worked using relationships he had developed in the Purdue Department of Psychology to help push the Speech Communication department toward a Ph.D. program. He resigned as head of the department in 1963, after successfully creating an independent Communication department, separate from English, with its own robust undergraduate and graduate curriculum.

As a researcher, Monroe is best remembered for the development of the Monroe's Motivated Sequence model for persuasive speeches that seek immediate action. This model is still taught today, and if you look closely you can see it at play in things as varied as commercials and political speeches. Alan Monroe truly made a mark on the campus of Purdue University as well as the discipline of communication and public speaking education.

Action: "Will you join me in making this dream come true? Again, the work will be shared, and we will have made an improvement for all to enjoy."

Let's take a moment and look at each one of these elements.

The first step, gaining the audience's attention, is nothing new; it simply employs a rhetorical question to raise the audience's awareness of the speech topic. Any form of attention-getter we covered earlier in the book would be acceptable for this stage of Monroe's Motivated Sequence. The second step of establishing need is a way of presenting a problem to the audience, but it differs slightly from the way we discussed it when we explained the problem-solution order.

Of course, the need for the audience may be to solve a problem. In fact, solving a problem is a terrific motivator when the audience recognizes there is a dilemma that affects them and that needs to be resolved. That said, for Monroe's Motivated Sequence establishing a need can also include constructing, or illuminating, a need of which the audience may not be aware. For instance, in the above example, students on the campus may not really notice the need for the clean park because they may just have adapted to using other facilities for enjoying nature and entertaining.

Also consider persuading an audience to purchase a particular product. The audience may not see a real need for making the purchase at the time, so the speaker needs to explain why the need does in fact exist. Not all problems that exist are obvious to an audience, and so sometimes speakers need to work extra hard to establish a need before persuading an audience to act. In short, Monroe's Motivated Sequence recognizes that a speaker needs to both raise awareness of a problem and create a need to address it.

Once the need has been established, you next must produce a way to satisfy the need. It would be tremendously awkward, if not unethical, to tell people there is a problem but not give them a way to solve it! Monroe labels this step "satisfaction" because it is the point in the speech where the solution is provided and couched in a way that firmly satisfies the need. This can be through the proposal of a solution to specific policy or through encouraging an audience to take a particular course of action. Here is where you must offer solid reasoning and evidence to illustrate how your proposed solution will satisfy the need and why it is an appropriate and effective remedy for the problem facing the community. We must be mindful, however, when doing this that we do not fall into the trap of using reasoning fallacies in an effort to achieve our goal. The means of satisfying the need, and the tools we use to tell the audience about those means, are just as important as the end goal of attaining audience support and action. So, let us look at how we might go about accomplishing the satisfaction step in Monroe's Motivated Sequence.

In the example regarding the dirty park on campus, satisfaction is achieved through a group effort to clean the park. In the case of seeking to convince an audience to purchase a product, the speaker needs to show how the product will fulfill a personal need or desire for the audience. For example, if you tell an audience that bad breath is both unhealthy and unattractive and thus they need to keep it from occurring, then you need to tell them that the path to satisfying that need to avoid bad breath can be fulfilled by purchasing and using Colgate toothpaste.

Monroe's Motivated Sequence does not stop at satisfaction, however, as the next step is getting the audience to visualize fulfilling the need. Visualization uses concrete language and calls upon the audience to actually see themselves as the instruments of satisfying the established need. It helps the speaker further connect the audience with the issue, its solution, and the speaker by getting them to picture a future where the need has been fulfilled. Such efforts employ both emotional and logical appeals to the audience. Ultimately, when the audience can see themselves taking part in an action that effectively satisfies a need for either themselves or the community, it becomes a simple task to call them to action—the final step of Monroe's Motivated Sequence.

All told, Monroe's Motivated Sequence represents a modernized pattern of organization for a balanced persuasive appeal to an audience. It's five steps are easy to follow as both a speaker and an audience and are most effective when immediate action is sought.

Whether you are debating policy positions, factual accuracies, the value of one solution over another, or calling an audience to act, there are a wide variety of organizational patterns you can use in a persuasive speech. Just like informative speeches, persuasive speech arrangement largely depends on the formulation of your specific purpose, but once that is crafted the speech can quickly take shape. Knowing the main parts of a speech and how to organize your main points can help you get ready to prepare your presentation. The most crucial step in speech creation remains organizing the product of your research in a cogent, coherent, and persuasive manner. For a summary of the organizational patterns for persuasive speeches covered in this chapter, see Table 12.4.

Table 12.4

Organizational Patterns for Persuasive Speeches
• Problem-solution
• Problem-cause-solution
• Comparative advantage
• Monroe's Motivated Sequence

SUMMARY

The Greeks and Romans separated persuasive speeches into a variety of different parts: the exordium, the narrative, and the peroration. They paid particular attention to the narrative and broke it down into several component parts, including the statement of facts, argument proper, and refutation. Today we use terms like introduction, body, and conclusion to describe the elements of a speech, but the ideas about what must be done in each part to achieve a persuasive purpose are the same. In this chapter we also identified some of the common elements between informative and persuasive speeches, while elaborating on their differences; most notably, those differences relate to the various ways you can organize a persuasive speech. Finally, we encourage you to refer to Chapter 9 on outlining for models that can help you develop your persuasive speech.

KEY TERMS

argument

comparative advantage

exordium

insinuation

introduction

Monroe's Motivated Sequence

peroration

principle of recency

problem-cause-solution order

problem-solution order

refutation

statement of facts

REVIEW QUESTIONS

1. What are the three components of persuasive speeches according to the Greeks and Romans?

   _____

   _____

2. What are the two types of exordiums proposed by Cicero?

   _____

   _____

3. What four things did Aristotle say a peroration should do?

   _____

   _____

4. What are the four ways you can organize the main points in a persuasive speech?

   _____

   _____

5. What are the five parts of Monroe's Motivated Sequence?

   _____

   _____

THINK ABOUT IT

1. Would it ever be a good idea to present your strongest argument first?

   _____

   _____

_____

_____

2. How do you measure whether your credibility increases or decreases during a speech?

_____

_____

_____

_____

3. Is it ethical to induce emotions in a conclusion or in any part of the speech? Why or why not?

_____

_____

_____

_____

4. How could you use Monroe's Motivated Sequence in everyday language?

_____

_____

_____

_____

ACTIVITIES FOR ACTION

1. Working in a group of three members, develop several different ways to get an audience's attention. Then, state several ways you could establish credibility. Finally, figure out a way that statements could both get the attention of the audience and establish credibility, thereby killing two birds with one stone.

2. In this chapter we discussed Monroe's Motivated Sequence. Divide into groups of three and assign each group a product on the market right now. Give each group 10 minutes to create a "commercial" where Monroe's Motivated Sequence is used to sell the assigned product. The catch is every person in each group must have a speaking role in the skit.

Endnotes

1. Toastmasters International, "What Is Toastmasters?" http://www.toastmasters.org/MainMenuCategories/WhatisToastmasters.aspx (accessed September 19, 2008).

2. Toastmasters International, "Community Service," http://www.toastmasters.org/MainMenuCategories/WhatisToastmasters/CommunityService.aspx (accessed September 19, 2008).

3. Quintilian, *The Institutes of Oratory,* translated by H. E. Butler, Loeb Classical Library (Cambridge: Harvard University Press, 1980), IV, i, 5.

4. Ibid., V, xii, 5.

5. Sharon Crowley and Debra Hawhee, *Ancient Rhetorics for Contemporary Students*, 4th Ed. (New York: Pearson Education, 2008).

6. Winston Churchill, "Blood, Toil, Tears and Sweat," Speech to the British House of Commons, http://www.historyplace.com/speeches/churchill.htm (accessed June 13, 3011).

7. Ibid.

8. Ibid.

9. Raymie E. McKerrow, Bruce E. Gronbeck, Douglas Ehninger, and Alan H. Monroe, *Principles and Types of Speech Communication,* 15th Ed. (New York: Longman: 2003).

10. W. Charles Redding, "An Informal History of Communication at Purdue," http://www.cla.purdue.edu/communication/graduate/informalhistory.pdf.

Constructing an Epideictic Address

Practically SPEAKING

One occasion that calls for an epideictic speech is a death. This practice was as common in Classical Greece as it is today, perhaps even more so. In fact, after wars prominent statesmen and public figures were chosen to give speeches to the public in honor of the dead. One such figure who gave at least two funeral orations after wars was Pericles of Athens, considered by many historians to be one of the greatest city leaders during that period.

Although we do not have the actual texts of his speeches verbatim, we have transcriptions from the Athenian historian, Thucydides, who attempted to capture the essence of Pericles's speeches in his notes. In what we now refer to as Pericles's *Funeral Oration*, the Athenian leader not only honored the dead from a recent war, but used the occasion to articulate what he understood as the appropriate relationship between the individual and the state. In short, he used the speech to connect the people to their government through the meaning he ascribed to the occasion.

When Pericles spoke to the public, rather than referring to the dead as individuals, he chose to provide their deaths with a larger meaning. He recognized the immense sadness and possible reduction of faith in the state that can come from so much loss of life, so he used his *Funeral Oration* to remind the audience that the nation was worthy of such sacrifice. In effect, he praised both the fallen of the city and the city itself.[1]

The *Funeral Oration* itself is organized into four distinct parts, with an introduction and conclusion accounting for two of them. The body is topically separated between honoring the dead and honoring the city. The speech was, obviously, a speech of praise and Pericles's organization allowed him to do just that.

We may not think that these types of public eulogies occur in today's society, but they are, in fact, more common than we might think. Lincoln's speech at Gettysburg was a public eulogy, for instance. Also, when former presidents pass away there is broadcast coverage of their funerals where state officials, and often the current president, give eulogies. An even more recent example came when President Barack Obama eulogized those who lost their lives when a gunman opened fire at an event sponsored by Congresswoman Gabrielle Giffords at a Tucson, Arizona, supermarket on January 8, 2011.

In his speech, Obama did much the same thing as Pericles in terms of using the moment to honor the deceased and praise the country. So, as you can see, public eulogies are just as common and just as potent as they were in ancient Greece and they serve the same purposes.

Eulogies are just one type of epideictic address, but the organizational structure and style of each form of epideictic speech is relatively similar. In this chapter we will discuss those common attributes in terms of how to construct an introduction, body, and conclusion for an epideictic speech.

13

EPIDEICTIC SPEECH INTRODUCTIONS

From their very beginning, epideictic addresses are very different from informative and persuasive forms of speech. In this section we will elaborate on those differences by explaining how to craft an effective introduction for an epideictic address. First, we will discuss the formulation of the specific purpose statement for an epideictic address. Then we will explain the elements of an introduction, as it requires different things than introductions for informative and persuasive speeches.

Formulating the Specific Purpose

In his discussion of epideictic speeches, Aristotle described them as speeches designed to "praise or blame" something or someone. Although a bit simple, this is a rather accurate account of what these types of speeches do and how they differ from informative and persuasive speeches. That said, it is important for us to understand the complex nature of these speeches in a bit more detail. In this part of the chapter we will discuss how to articulate the complex nature of an epideictic address from the very start.

First, let's take a look at determining the general purpose. This is a relatively simple task for informative and persuasive speeches as the general purpose flows from their labels. That is to say, the general purpose for an informative speech is "to inform," and the general purpose for a persuasive speech is "to persuade." This, however, is not the case with epideictic speech. It makes no sense to have a general purpose stated as "to epideictic." Instead, the general purpose is a bit more varied depending on the occasion. It could be, for instance, "to celebrate," "to praise," or "to commemorate," just to name a few. Understanding the general purpose of an epideictic speech is essential for developing the speech in an effective manner, but then so is knowing what the specific purpose is as well.

The specific purpose for an epideictic speech is always tied to the moment or the occasion on which you give the speech. It also needs to articulate the value or idea that the occasion represents, because with epideictic speech the event or person is not the most important element of the speech; rather, celebrating the value or idea that person or thing represents is the core purpose of an epideictic speech. For instance, Candy's general purpose is to commemorate, and her specific purpose is to commemorate the new Gordon P. Goodspeed Library on her campus. The building was named after a person who graduated from the college, went on to write 15 national best-selling novels, and then donated the funds to build the library. If that is the context, then her specific purpose statement might be: "To commemorate the opening of the Gordon P. Goodspeed Library in honor of a distinguished graduate who valued education." This specific purpose ties the event to a value and captures the essential points in Candy's speech by providing an explanation of the person and event, as well as the importance of education represented by this building.

In short, the specific purpose of epideictic address is to discuss the larger meaning inherent in an event, person, or thing. This is quite different from an informative speech in which the specific purpose is to describe, define, or teach an audience about something. When starting to write an epideictic address, it is important that you identify the larger value represented by the topic of your speech in your specific purpose (see Table 13.1). Think back to the example of Pericles in the opening of the chapter. He used the funeral for soldiers to talk not about what happened to them but about the ideas they represented and for which they fought and died. After developing a clear specific purpose for your epideictic address, you can then move on to crafting the speech itself, and that begins with the introduction.

Table 13.1

Specific Purpose Examples for Epideictic Speeches	
Eulogy	"To present to the audience the major achievements and characteristics of the deceased"
Acceptance speech	"To thank all those who made my winning the award possible"
Toast	"To inform the audience of my intent to honor the person at the event"

Strategies for Epideictic Introductions

As you might guess, epideictic speeches have quite different introductions than informative and persuasive speeches. First, the types of attention-getters they use are different, simply because of the nature of the speech. In terms of establishing a thesis or an argument, there again is a difference between the three speeches. Finally, in an epideictic speech, previews are either not used at all or they are very subtle. It may be that the only real common element between the three different speeches and their introductions is the need for a clear and appropriate transition to the body.

Attention-Getters

Attention-getters serve an important function for both informative and persuasive speeches, and they are central to an epideictic address as well, although not in the same way. Audiences for epideictic addresses typically want to be there to hear the speech, and as such you do not need to fight to get their attention immediately. Instead, you should use the attention-getter to reinforce for the audience why they (and you) are in attendance. As a means of illustrating, let's return to the speech being given by Candy. Everyone at the dedication of the new library has chosen to attend and expects to hear a speech, so getting their attention is not the main purpose of the attention-getter in her speech; rather, her attention-getter is designed to remind them of the importance of that choice to attend. So, beginning her speech with a statement to that effect helps achieve those ends: "Thank you for coming here today to dedicate our new library, a building that will serve as the foundation for future student education here at the university." This statement captures the audience not by startling them or telling them something they did not know. Instead, it reminds them of what the library represents to the university (education), thus reinforcing the importance of the event and by extension their attendance.

Reinforcement Statements

You might recall that in other speeches, once you have delivered your opening line you need to quickly move to your thesis or argument. Although you need to establish your central idea in the introduction of an epideictic speech, it is not entirely a thesis in the informative speech sense, nor is it an argument as described for persuasive speeches. Epideictic speeches use what we will call a ***reinforcement statement***, or an expression of the connection between the event and the social value it represents. We call it reinforcement because members of the audience typically share the value and so, as a speaker, you simply reinforce the importance and power of that social value. This relationship between the speech, the event, and the social value it represents is illustrated in Figure 13.1.

reinforcement statement

an expression of the connection between the event and the social value it represents

The main point of an epideictic speech varies depending on the type of speech it is, but it always includes two elements. The first is an emotional dimension. For instance, if you are accepting an award, your reinforcement statement should express humility and/or gratitude. If, however, you are introducing someone for an award, it should contain a level of pride and happiness. In terms of eulogies, grief should be there but it should be tempered with hope. Providing the emotional dimension for understanding the event/person/thing that the speech is about is a central component of the reinforcement statement in the introduction of an epideictic address.

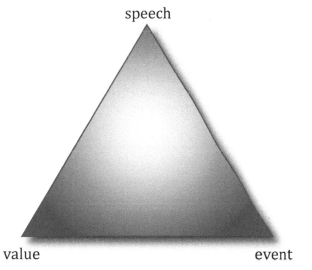

Figure 13.1
Epideictic Elements

The second component of a reinforcement statement is the connection between the value and the event itself. Not only must the statement evoke an emotional appreciation for the moment, it also must articulate the value the moment represents. In short, it must create an image of the event as a symbol for something larger. What is the meaning behind the occasion that has brought everyone together to hear your speech? For instance, Coach Parsons is about to announce the winner of the "Most Improved Player" for the high school basketball team. His reinforcement statement is as follows: "This guy worked harder than any player I have ever coached, always asking for extra practice time and always pushing himself in the weight room." Here the topic is clear (the winner of the award) and the value the individual and the award represents is also clear: hard work.

The purpose of a reinforcement statement in an epideictic speech is the same as the purpose of a thesis statement in an informative speech and an argument in a persuasive speech. All three share some qualities but they are different in two primary respects. First, a reinforcement statement contains a strong degree of emotionality. Second, a reinforcement statement connects the occasion to some higher shared social value. Once you have developed an introduction and a reinforcement statement, it is time to finish the introduction of your epideictic address.

Remainder of Introduction

As we have discussed in previous chapters, informative and persuasive speeches contain a clear and deliberate preview in their introductions immediately following the thesis statement or argument. Epideictic speeches contain no such previews. In fact, if an epideictic speech contains a preview it is very subtle. We will not discuss how to construct such previews, but rather emphasize the need to move from the reinforcement statement to the body of the speech in a smooth fashion that does not take away from the heightened expectations and meaning established in your reinforcement statement.

Rather than previewing the stories that support the value inherent in the moment, the introduction needs to move directly to those stories. You do this by using a carefully crafted transition; often, this same transition serves as both the notice that the brief introduction is over and the introduction of the next topic. For example, in Pericles's *Funeral Oration,* he begins the first main point of his speech by stating, "I shall begin by speaking about our ancestors, since it is only right and proper on such an occasion to pay them the honor of recalling what they did."[3] In this transitional statement, Pericles moves from his opening discussion about what values and principles the deceased stood for to a discussion that connects the past to the present moment. It thus serves as a marker for the audience that something new is coming next.

Do not be fooled into thinking that because the introduction to an epideictic address is shorter it is therefore easier. In many ways it is harder because it needs to establish an emotional connection between the occasion, the speaker, the audience, and a shared social value in short order. This requires more elaborate language, as well as a clear understanding of the audience and the scene. Different occasions, however, call for different epideictic addresses, and in the next part of the chapter we will discuss how to organize and develop a body for various epideictic addresses.

EPIDEICTIC SPEECH BODY

The body of an epideictic speech, regardless of the occasion, is also quite different from the bodies of informative and persuasive speeches. One primary difference is in the form of evidence. Epideictic speeches are a series of stories that serve as examples of the connection between the topic of the speech, the occasion, and the shared social value represented by the event. These stories are narratives and often do not include much in the way of startling statistics or testimony. What is essential when telling these stories is that the connection between the story and the shared social value is clear to the audience.

These stories are typically organized in one of two different ways. The first is chronological, like in the case of Pericles. Following this pattern you would be telling stories of the past in sequential order, but always connecting the purpose of the story to the shared social value that belies the speech. The other organizational pattern is topical, which works if there are multiple stories that illustrate different parts of the shared social value. Each part then becomes a topic, and the topics, not the chronology, dictate in which order the stories are presented. In this part of the chapter we will provide suggestions for the types of stories that might be used in the bodies of some common forms of epideictic speeches.

Eulogies

Eulogies are often believed to be sad speeches, but they need not be. A good eulogy takes time and focus to develop because you need to determine the emotion you wish to convey to the audience, as well as identify the value the departed's life represented for everyone in attendance. Start the process of figuring this out by looking inward and seeing what the person meant to you. In terms of emotions, sadness is a natural part of a eulogy, but hope and happiness can also be part of the emotions of the day. After all, it is important to see a eulogy as a chance to celebrate the person's life and what they meant to those who were close to them.

The stories within the body of a eulogy should be examples of the shared value and feeling the person represented. You should not treat the stories as a simple chronology of their life, because then you reduce the meaning of the person to what they did, rather than what they represented. For example, Kassandra was asked to deliver a eulogy of her grandfather and in it she wanted to express the

Remarks at the Tucson Memorial Service
by President Barack Obama

Delivered January 12, 2011

On January 8, 2011, a deranged gunman, Jared Loughner, opened fire into a crowd seeking to meet U.S. Representative Gabrielle (Gabby) Giffords. Six people died, among them a federal judge and a nine-year-old girl, and many more were wounded. Representative Giffords suffered head wounds from the shooting and it was feared that this popular politician would also die (as of this writing, Representative Giffords is making a recovery that can only be labeled miraculous).[3]

This tragedy was shocking to the nation, but much more so to the community in which it occurred. It was only fitting that the President of the United States address the large crowd at the memorial service.

President Obama began his speech with these poignant words:

"To the families of those we've lost; to all who called them friends; to the students of this university, the public servants gathered tonight, and the people of Tucson and Arizona: I have come here tonight as an American who, like all Americans, kneels to pray with you today, and will stand by you tomorrow."[4]

He assured the audience that the nation stood with them, and he quoted comforting scripture.

He then gave a brief biography of each person who was killed, noting some had given their lives to save others. One of the most emotional segments was dedicated to the young girl who perished:

"And then there is nine-year-old Christina Taylor Green. Christina was an A student, a dancer, a gymnast, and a swimmer. She often proclaimed that she wanted to be the first woman to play in the major leagues, and as the only girl on her Little League team, no one put it past her. She showed an appreciation for life uncommon for a girl her age, and would remind her mother, 'We are so blessed. We have the best life.' And she'd pay those blessings back by participating in a charity that helped children who were less fortunate."[5]

The loss of anyone is a tragedy, but even more so when the unnecessary death is one who is so young. President Obama's story about Christina celebrated the energy of youth, and reinforced the idea that Americans of any age value and appreciate life. Later in this speech he said that heroes are found in everyday life and noted that the acts of the heroes in this tragedy were a challenge to everyone else to use the tragedy to make themselves become better. The speech celebrated lives in a personal way but did so while showing how those lives represented values larger than themselves—values every member of the community shared and celebrated.

idea that he represented the importance of generosity. With that as her goal, she told three stories that showed her grandfather giving his time, donating his money, and offering to help a friend in need. These stories were organized topically, not chronologically, but each allowed for a celebration of the individual and a reinforcement of the shared value of generosity.

The need for a story that provides some value or feeling shared with the person or group being eulogized is also apparent in public eulogies, like the one President Obama delivered in Tucson in 2011. Although he did not know any of the deceased victims, Obama crafted an artful story extolling the virtues of American society through the individuals who lost their lives in that horrific attack. He did this topically rather than chronologically because he did not know those who were killed and also did not want to spend time on what happened; rather he wanted to use what happened to help the community celebrate the lives of the individuals and turn them into a synecdoche for values cherished by Americans everywhere. In this speech, there is a clear connection between the eulogized, the stories told about them, and the values they represented; as such, it is good example of an epideictic address.

Eulogies do not always need to contain three main points; in fact, often they contain more. What is more important than the number of stories contained in the eulogy is that they are all related to the shared value you wish to express in the speech. Next, we will turn our attention to a happier form of epideictic address: wedding toasts.

Wedding Toasts

Wedding toasts share some similarities with eulogies, but there are also some obvious differences. Both are epideictic in that their purpose is to express emotionality and a shared social value through the discussion of an event or moment. Both often include a celebration of love. One key difference, however, is in the brevity of wedding toasts compared to the sometimes extensive nature of eulogies. That brevity makes it even more important to have a tight focus and concise summary of the stories you tell in the body of the speech.

The best organizational pattern for a good wedding toast is topical. People in the audience already know the bride and groom (presumably) so you do not need to recount their lives to the audience. What you need to do is identify the shared social value you believe their partnership exemplifies. Often, people choose love or kindness, but other values could also work, like perseverance and a sense of community. Ask yourself, when you think of the couple, what value comes to mind? What does a marriage represent to you?

Your stories should then be illustrations of how the couple individually and/or together exemplifies that value. The stories should be short and you should use vivid language whenever possible. For example, if you wish to tell the story of when you first saw the couple together, which of the following versions do you think works best?

>*Example A:* "I met Sandy and Charles together at a bar downtown."
>
>*Example B:* "I first saw Sandy and Charles together at a swanky bar in downtown Seattle where we went to see a Coldplay concert."

Obviously, Example B has much greater detail and is more vivid for the audience. It also allows you to make a swift move to connecting that moment to the value represented by the two individuals.

Brevity is important with wedding toasts, so however many short stories you tell, make sure they are not so lengthy that they cause the speech to drone on and lose its meaning. In a perfect scenario, you can begin with a story about each of the individuals, followed by a story in which they are a couple, because that topical progression illustrates the event: two separate people joining as one in marriage. Next, we will discuss how to organize speeches delivered at award ceremonies.

Award Ceremonies

Much like wedding toasts, award ceremony speeches are often expected to be short. There are some exceptions, such as when an entire event is in honor of one individual, but more often than not these speeches are only a few minutes at best. So, like wedding toasts, it is important to know what shared social value you wish to get across and select brief stories that will help demonstrate that value to the audience. This process is quite different when presenting and when accepting an award. In this part of the chapter we will discuss both.

Academy award winner Sandra Bullock

When presenting an award, the focus should be on the value that the award itself represents, not on yourself or the individual receiving the honor. Again, the organization of the body should be topical or, in some circumstances, chronological. If you are to present one of many different awards (like the Oscars or Emmys), focus on values by sharing one or two brief stories. For instance, you might choose to recall the previous winner of the award and link their story to what the award represents. You also might focus on the namesake of the award and link their activities to the shared social value you believe the award demonstrates.

If, however, you are presenting an award to the sole honoree of the event (i.e., Person of the Year) then you have more time to build up the award winner and the moment. In this speech you might wish to focus on telling a chronology of stories from different stages of the honoree's life and tie each story to the shared social value. You also might use the tried and true topical method of picking certain aspects of the person's character that illustrate the shared social value, but do not necessarily come in sequence. Either way, these speeches must connect the moment, the honoree, and the value for the audience. When receiving an award, however, your body is slightly different.

There are two types of award acceptance speeches you might deliver. First, if you are the only honoree of the evening, or if you are the main honoree of a ceremony, then you will potentially deliver a long address. The other type of award acceptance speech occurs when you are one of many people receiving an award. In this instance you will give a very brief address. In each case it is important to know how much time you have to speak because that will determine the number of stories you will be able to place in the body of your speech.

In the event you are lucky enough to be the honoree at an event where you get to give a long speech, there are certain things you should consider when crafting your acceptance speech. First, what is the core value of the award or the group who is bestowing the award on you? Second, what stories can you tell that connect you to that mission or shared value? Let's look at an example.

Lionel Fox was being honored by United Cerebral Palsy, a nonprofit group that advocates for people with disabilities, for his hard work helping people with cerebral palsy in his neighborhood. In fact, the organization held a fundraiser around the event where Lionel was to be honored, and he was expected to deliver a speech accepting the award. He was told he would have about 10 minutes, and so he decided on four stories he wanted to tell, each about individuals with cerebral palsy with whom he worked. Each story reinforced the central mission of United Cerebral Palsy and exemplified the value of service to one's community. Because he had the time, Lionel was able to relay his stories in a very effective manner, but time is not something everyone has when they give an acceptance speech.

Award acceptance speeches are more often than not very short. Think about the amount of time people have to speak when accepting Oscars, Emmys, or Tonys. Usually they have a minute or less at those award ceremonies to deliver their speech, and in most instances you will have only a few minutes. This means you need to maximize the time you spend connecting the occasion to the shared value you wish to express. And as we have repeatedly mentioned, that value should be related to what the award represents.

The trick with a short acceptance speech is to find one or two examples that convey what you want to convey. Simply listing "thank yous" is an awful way to spend your time in the speech, but making the thank you part of a story that helps augment the meaning of the moment is a good way to structure the body of the speech. Acceptance speeches are very hard to deliver because of how short they are, which means even more care must go into creating them.

In the next part of this chapter we will discuss how to properly construct a conclusion to an epideictic address.

EPIDEICTIC SPEECH CONCLUSIONS

Much like conclusions for informative and persuasive speeches, there needs to be a clear transition to the conclusion of an epideictic speech. One thing that is different, however, is that there is no definitive summary in an epideictic speech like there is in an informative or persuasive speech. Finally, the clincher of an epideictic speech is unique in that, in many cases, it does not refer to the topic but to the shared social value the topic represents. In this part of the chapter we will discuss what should be done instead of a summary and how to construct a good clincher for an epideictic speech.

Summary

As we have mentioned, epideictic speeches do not contain summaries in the sense that informative and persuasive speeches do. Much like the preview in the introduction of an epideictic speech, the summary should be subtle and not defined. In short, do not say "First, we spoke about...then we discussed." This type of approach destroys the emotional dimension of the speech and does little to reinforce the shared social values you have spent the rest of the speech discussing. So, in lieu of a traditional summary, in an epideictic speech conclusion you should concentrate on the shared social value. Let's look at some examples in common epideictic speeches.

Eulogies do not conclude by simply restating the stories you relayed about the deceased. Instead, they conclude by stressing what those stories represented. For instance, if you tell a story about how the person always made you laugh when you were around them, then in the summary you might summarize that by stating how you learned to love life from the way they lived theirs. The focus, then, is not on the individual or their death, but rather on the meaning of their life.

As you might guess, wedding toasts do not lend themselves to the traditional summary either. These speeches typically end by connecting the shared social values the wedding represents to an expression of hope and luck for the future. For example, if you are concluding a toast to newlyweds, you might summarize a story you told in the body about how they met by saying something to the effect of, "May the spark you felt when you first met become the fire that fuels your relationship every day." Here passion and love become what is summarized, instead of what actually happened in the story.

Award speeches also do not allow for typical summaries in their conclusions. In presenting an award you need to use the conclusion to build toward the announcement of the award winner, and simply recapping the main points of the speech does not allow you to do this. In accepting an award, you also do not want to recall all the stories you just told the audience. In both instances, the summary should help the audience reconnect the shared social value being celebrated with the award and then, by extension, the award winner.

Summaries for epideictic addresses are much more subtle than in informative and persuasive speeches. Clinchers are also different in epideictic speeches, as we will discuss next.

SPOTLIGHTING THEORISTS: KATHLEEN HALL JAMIESON AND KARLYN KOHRS CAMPBELL

Epideictic speeches are the most common type of speech we encounter. As you discovered in this chapter, they come in the form of wedding toasts, award speeches, and eulogies. All of those are speeches any individual might give or hear, but two scholars, Kathleen Hall Jamieson and Karlyn Kohrs Campbell, have focused some of their research on epideictic speeches delivered by presidents. In fact, their book on the genre of presidential rhetoric, *Deeds Done in Words*, contains several chapters on different forms of epideictic address delivered by various presidents of the United States. They point out that presidential inaugural addresses in particular help define the principles that guide our government and call on our commonalities in the wake of divisive elections. These important tasks are only accomplished through the use of epideictic address.

Dr. Kathleen Hall Jamieson (1946–)

A noted rhetorical and political scholar, Hall Jamieson is the Elizabeth Ware Packard Professor of Communication at the Annenberg School for Communication and Walter and Leonore Annenberg Director of the Annenberg Public Policy Center on the campus of the prestigious University of Pennsylvania.[6] As director, she also supervises FactCheck, a nonprofit organization housed at Annenberg that looks into the factual accuracy of U.S. political advertisements.

Among many other awards and honors, she was awarded the Speech Communication Association's (now the National Communication Association) Golden Anniversary Book Award for *Packaging the Presidency* (Oxford, 1984) and *Eloquence in an Electronic Age* (Oxford, 1988).

Jamieson has often been interviewed on political issues on both public television and public radio and has been interviewed by Bill Moyers on PBS's NOW program.[7] She has researched and written on numerous political and rhetorical topics, focusing primarily on presidential discourse. She is known as one of the country's foremost experts on political advertising and campaigns.

Dr. Karlyn Kohrs Campbell (1937–)

A professor in the Department of Communication Studies at the University of Minnesota, Campbell specializes in studying feminist and political discourse.

Since earning her Ph.D. from the University of Minnesota in 1968, Campbell has won many awards, chief among them the National Communication Association's Scholarship Award and an Honorary Doctorate of Humanities from Michigan State University.[8]

In addition to her current and previous work at Minnesota, she has also served in several different capacities elsewhere. She was a fellow with the Joan Shorenstein Center on the Press, Politics, and Public Policy at Harvard University's Kennedy School of Government in 1992. She was also the director of the Women's Center at the University of Kansas.

Jamieson and Campbell have been highly instrumental in our understanding of the uses of epideictic oratory, particularly as it pertains to presidential discourse.

Clinchers

Clinchers serve different purposes in different epideictic speeches. In eulogies, they recall the meaning of the deceased's life for everyone in attendance. In wedding toasts, they express well wishes for the new bride and groom. Clinchers for award presentation speeches announce the winner, while those for award reception speeches thank the audience by expressing again how much the award means. In this part of the chapter we will briefly discuss the characteristics of an effective clincher in each of those types of commemorative speeches.

When you deliver a eulogy you spend quite a bit of time using stories to connect the audience with the meaning inherent in the life of the deceased. The clincher represents your last opportunity to stress that connection to the audience. It should strike a somber, yet hopeful, tone and concentrate more on the undying quality of the shared social value you connected the person to, rather than on the person himself.

Wedding toasts must strike a happy and hopeful tone, something quite different from a eulogy. As is typical with these occasions, the shared social value usually is love or passion, and that should be stressed again in the clincher while also wishing the newlyweds luck in their future together. Unlike some conventional approaches, it is inadvisable to have a humorous clincher for a wedding toast, as it should be a serious expression of happiness and hope.

Award introduction speeches represent unique epideictic speeches and as such their clinchers are also unique. The clincher for an award introduction speech is almost always the same, in that it is the time when you name the award recipient for the first time. Just naming the recipient, however, is not enough because you have spent a great deal of time in your speech establishing a connection between the individual, the award, and a shared social value they both represent. It is important to creatively introduce the individual so the audience carries the connection of the three elements (award, recipient, shared social value) into the person's appearance and subsequent acceptance speech. The key point to remember with these speeches is that the name of the person is what the audience has waited to hear.

When accepting a speech, clinchers must again carefully continue to connect the shared social value with the award. This is done through using the clincher to express a deep appreciation for the meaning of the award and your subsequent reception of it. Thanking the audience is not enough in a clincher for an award acceptance speech, you must also express your understanding of what the award means to you and to those in attendance.

A Final Note on Epideictic Speeches

Although we have focused on three primary forms of epideictic addresses in our discussion of introductions, bodies, and conclusions, there are a variety of other types of commemorative speeches, and many of these speeches are not only known to you, but are subjects of significant critical analysis. For instance, many scholars have paid a lot of attention to presidential inaugural speeches. In fact,

Kathleen Hall Jamieson and Karlyn Kohrs Campbell have examined inaugurals and developed five characteristics that every inaugural shares (see the nearby box). The point is, epideictic speech is more common than you might first believe and an important part of our lives. It is much more than speech for special occasions; it is the speech that makes mundane occasions special.

SUMMARY

In this chapter we extended our conversation about epideictic address by providing you with more concrete ways to develop an effective commemorative speech. We began by exploring the elements of a good epideictic introduction, specifically by showing how it does not contain a traditional preview. We then explained that most, if not all, epideictic addresses are topically organized around stories that exemplify the shared social value that underlies the speech's purpose. Finally, we discussed the different elements of epideictic conclusions and showed that, among other things, they do not contain traditional summaries.

KEY TERMS

reinforcement statement

REVIEW QUESTIONS

1. What is the thesis statement or argument called in an epideictic speech?

   _____

   _____

2. What component(s) of an introduction is not in an epideictic speech but is in informative and persuasive speeches?

   _____

   _____

3. What is the primary way of organizing the main points in an epideictic speech?

   _____

   _____

4. What are the three elements that need to be connected in an epideictic speech?

_____

_____

5. What component(s) of a conclusion is not in an epideictic speech but is in informative and persuasive speeches?

_____

_____

THINK ABOUT IT

1. What other forms of epideictic speeches are common in society?

_____

_____

_____

_____

2. Can you imagine an epideictic address not tied to a shared social value?

_____

_____

_____

_____

3. How do you determine the stories you use as main points in an epideictic address?

_____

_____

_____

_____

4. Which type of epideictic address would be most difficult for you to perform? Why?

_____

_____

1. Think about your best friend, and then prepare and deliver a wedding toast as the maid of honor or best man at his or her wedding.

2. Imagine you are nearing the end of your life at some point in the future. Think about all those things you had hoped to accomplish in your life and the things for which you would like to be remembered. Now, write an obituary that would appear in a local paper following your untimely death. Then, write a eulogy that you would like someone to deliver for you at your own funeral. Finally, look at both the obituary and the eulogy and identify the similarities and differences between the two.

ACTIVITIES FOR ACTION

ENDNOTES

1. Richard A. Katula, "Seven Greek and Roman Speeches," in *A Synoptic History of Classical Rhetoric* (2nd Ed.), edited by James J. Murphy and Richard A. Katula with Forbes I. Hill, Donovan J. Ochs, and Prentice A. Meador (Davis, CA: Hermagoras Press, 1995), 221-223.

2. Katula, 221.

3. "In Attack's Wake, Political Repercussions," http://www.nytimes.com/2011/01/09/us/politics/09giffords.html (accessed June 14, 2011).

4. Text of President Obama's Memorial Speech, http://www.nytimes.com/2011/01/09/us/politics/09giffords.html (accessed June 14, 2011).

5. Ibid.

6. http://www.asc.upenn.edu/ascfaculty/FacultyBio.aspx?id=129 (accessed April 28, 2009).

7. http://www.pbs.org/now/politics/jamieson.html (accessed April 28, 2009).

8. http://www.comm.umn.edu/faculty/profile.php?UID=campb003 (accessed April 28, 2009).

Appendix A

SPEECH EXAMPLES

Persuasive Speech: "Finish Your Degree"

I ran into a high school friend of mine the other day, a person who finished in the top 10 percent of our class but decided to drop out of college in the middle of sophomore year. She is now working as a manager at a local department store—the same store she worked at in high school. This person makes about $12 an hour and has some benefits as a full-time employee—but no more room for growth at the company. I don't tell this story to get you to pity her, but rather to illustrate the difference between finishing a college degree and not doing so. As a college student with dreams of my own that involve more than managing a department store, I decided to research some more concrete information on why we should all finish our degree programs. Even though there is nothing you can do to guarantee success in life, I want to encourage you to get that degree, and today I am going to tell you why. First, I will share the economic benefits of finishing college. Then I am going to explain the other benefits you can earn in the job market with a college degree. Finally, I am going to detail the health and wellness incentives for finishing your degrees. So, let's get started so that we can finish our degrees.

Our professors think a degree makes us a more rounded person, but let's be honest, we want the degree for financial reasons. The United States Census Bureau shows that an associate's degree recipient will make approximately $1.2 million

This short story serves to capture the audience's attention by making the topic of the speech real for them.

his statement establishes e speaker's credibility y citing his/her osition as a student nd explaining that the eaker did research the pic.

Here is the speaker's argument, clearly stated for the audience.

hese sentences preview ow the speaker plans n making his/her case o the audience.

This is an effective, if simple, transition to the main body of the speech.

Here is proper verbal attribution of the source of the evidence the speaker used to support his/her claim.

more than a person with just a high school degree throughout his/her working career, and it gets even better for those who complete their BA. Listen to this: A person with a bachelor's degree will earn around $2.1 million more in his/her career than a worker with just a high school degree.[1] My friends, does that sound significant to you? It does to me.

The economics don't just stop with total earnings. In 2007–2008 the U. S. economy went into recession and we all heard the gloomy forecasts about investments, and most especially the high unemployment numbers. Fox News reported in December 2008 that those without a college degree had a jobless rate of 7.2%, but those with a degree had a jobless rate of 3.7%.[2] That report quoted Lawrence Mishel, president of the Economic Policy Institute in Washington, D.C., as saying: "College grads have a privileged position in the labor market.'"[3] One of the reasons is that a person with a degree earns more and has a more secure job, but it is also much easier for a person with a college degree to take a demotion.[4] Essentially, a college degree gives you more security. Now that I have provided you with evidence that the college degree is worth the effort economically, let's look at some other benefits to getting that degree.

With a college degree you get more money, and with that you also get better benefits. A report by Collegeboard.com in 2007 noted that college graduates are more likely to have a job that provides health insurance and retirement benefits. College grads also are noted as having better overall health, probably because of their health insurance.[5] Degreeadvantage. com noted that studies show that a college graduate's children had a better life, were able to save more money, made wiser decisions on purchases, and had improved time off work. It also noted that research found that college grads are more rational thinkers, more willing to accept other opinions, more consistent in their application of logic and ethics, and better managers."[6] Additionally, grads "pass on" those positive things to future descendants.[7]

Here is proper verbal attribution of the source of the evidence the speaker used to support his/her claim.

Not convinced to stick with your degree program? Well here is more evidence. The collegeboard.com report I mentioned earlier noted that college grads are less likely to smoke, pay more in taxes to society, and are less likely to need government assistance. Additionally, college grads are more likely to be involved in civic activities, volunteer, vote, donate their own blood, and be tolerant of the opinions of others.[8] All in all, in addition to the doors of financial opportunity a college degree opens, what those college professors tell you about becoming a well-rounded citizen through your college education is also true. There really is a reason why getting a college degree is so coveted by our parents, families, and society.

In summary, there are significant financial advantages to getting a college degree. With a college degree you will earn an average of over $2 million more than if you dropped out, and you are much more likely to have a job in a down economy like the one we face today. Then there are the quality of life issues for both you and your family. You will be more likely to have health insurance; you will live a happier life; you will be more open-minded; and, you will be more likely to get involved in the community. Yeah, it may take awhile, but we are all here anyway so let's finish that degree to improve our lives. As Nike has said for years: "Just do it."

ENDNOTES

1. Jennifer Cheeseman Day and Eric C. Newburger, "The Big Payoff: Educational Attainment and Synthetic Estimates of Work-Life Earnings," *Current Population Reports, Special Studies*, 23-210, Washington, D.C.: Commerce Dept., Economics and Statistics Administration, Census Bureau. [Online], 2002, http://www.census.gov/prod/2002pubs/p23-210.pdf (accessed December 3, 2009).

2. Christopher Leonard, "College Grads Avoid Brunt of Layoffs," *Foxnews.com*, January 10, 2009, http://www.foxnews.com/wires/2009Jan10/0,4670,MeltdownCollegeGraduates,00.html (accessed December 3, 2009).

3. Ibid.

4. Ibid.
5. Sandy Baum and Jennifer Ma, "Education Pays: The Benefits of Higher Education for Individuals and Society," *College Board* (2007), http://www.collegeboard.com/prod_downloads/about/news_info/trends/ed_pays_2007.pdf (accessed December 3, 2009).
6. Larry L. Rowley and Sylvia Hurtado, "The Non-Monetary Benefits of an Undergraduate Education," University of Michigan: Center for the Study of Higher and Postsecondary Education, 2002.
7. Ibid.
8. Baum and Ma, "Education Pays."

Informative Speech: "Black Friday"

This is a solid attention-getter because it uses material an audience can relate to in order to draw them in to listen.

To all of us, Thanksgiving means time with family, watching football, eating good food, and sleeping off turkey-coma. To companies, it also means that Black Friday is right around the corner. We have all heard of Black Friday, the day that follows Thanksgiving, but have you ever wondered where its nickname comes from and what it actually means? That is, what it means beyond lots of shopping! Well, as a general manager of a major retail store here in town who depends on Black Friday,

This is the speaker's credibility statement that tells the audience why s/he is qualified to speak about the topic.

I want to help explain both how Black Friday earned its dark moniker and why it is important to you and me. First, I will

Here is the speaker's thesis statement that clearly lays out the goal of the speech.

discuss what the term "black" means in relation to this specific date. Then, I will discuss why the day is so popular for retailers and stores around the country. Finally, I will discuss what Black Friday typically means for the holiday season to you, me, and the

Here is a clear preview of the main points of the speech and the order in which they will appear. It also indicates the main points will be conveyed in a topical order.

country. That meaning, however, begins with understanding the date's dark designation.

The date's dark designation" is a good example of alliterative language in that three words in a row start with the same consonant sound.

Here is a solid transition from the introduction to the body of the speech.

The term "black" has either a racial meaning or a negative association in most uses; however, it has an altogether different meaning when it comes to Black Friday. "Black" is often crudely used to denote someone who is African American in descent; however, Black Friday is not an ethnic holiday or celebration. "Black" also can mean dark, or evil, as in "black magic" or "black stain," but Black Friday is neither evil nor dark . . . unless of course you get up at 3 a.m. to wait in line for Best Buy to open! "Black" as it is used in Black Friday actually has its origins in accounting. When companies are in debt they are said to be "in the red," but when they are making money then they are "in the black." Black Friday is called "black" because it is the day that signals the largest sales period for companies around the country. Essentially, it is the day they start to move from the red on the balance sheet to the black. But why is the Friday following Thanksgiving the day that is most important to retailers for sales? The answer is simple, really.

This is an example of a rhetorical question, where even though the speaker is asking something, s/he is not waiting for the audience to answer. Rather, the speaker answers the question for the audience.

The largest retail shopping period of the year occurs before the Christmas holiday in December, and the Friday after Thanksgiving is the kick-off to the holiday shopping season. For many workers, the day after Thanksgiving is the last holiday they have before Christmas, so they take advantage of it by getting most of their holiday shopping out of the way early. People purchase toys, clothes, books, music, and electronics to give away to family and friends as holiday gifts. Heck, we even buy ourselves holiday gifts on Black Friday. In fact, according to the National Retail Federation, from 1999–2008 holiday retail sales during this period accounted for between 18.49% and 20.51% of the entire retail sales for the year.[1] That's roughly 9% of the year accounting for 20% of the sales for the year. Black Friday, as the first official day of the holiday season, is often seen as a barometer for how well retailers will do in the days leading up to Christmas. Now that I have illustrated where Black Friday gets its name and why it is deserved, I will next explain why this date is an important one for all of us.

As many of us know, our governments are funded by taxes, and one type of tax that generates revenue for our cities, towns, counties, and states is a sales tax. Sales taxes are used to fund things like education, road repairs, health services, and other such essential social programs, and thus they are very important for all of us as we all use them at one time or another. Sales taxes are generated when we purchase most products, with the exception of things like food and prescription medicine. The more retailers sell, the more taxes the government generates, the better the services it can provide for the community. So given the high percentage of sales in late November and December, having a strong holiday shopping season indicated by a strong showing on Black Friday is essential for the year-round operations of government. Black Friday, then, is an important day to watch for all of us, and not just because of the great sales and deals that appear in stores everywhere!

The word barometer in this context is actually an example of a metaphor. A barometer measures atmospheric pressure, but here it is used to mean something different.

This is a topic sentence indicating the main point of this section of the speech.

Here the speaker provides evidence that supports the main point about Black Friday as the beginning of the largest shopping period of the year.

This is an example of an internal summary because it lays out what has already been covered in the speech.

This is a signpost that is used by the speaker to indicate the beginning of the conclusion.

Finally, it is important to understand that Black Friday is more than just a day at the mall. It is the day that begins the period where retail stores return to making a profit thanks to large numbers of holiday shoppers and their purchases. It also gives an indication of how much in sales taxes our government will collect, thereby helping us see what social services they will be able to provide. Black Friday is perhaps the most important shopping day of the year for all of us. So, once you wake up from your turkey-coma, remember all those big sales you saw in the paper while eating gobs of pumpkin pie were not dreams, but vital attempts to drum up business.

Here is the summary of the main points provided within the body of the speech.

This is a simple restatement of the thesis for the entire speech, just to remind the audience again what they were supposed to learn from the speech.

Here is an example of a simple, yet effective, clincher for an informative speech. It relates back to the attention-getter at the start of the speech through the reference to turkey-coma, providing nice closure for the entire speech.

ENDNOTES

1. National Retail Federation, "2009 Holiday Survival Guide," http://www.nrf.com/modules.php?name=Pages&sp_id=1142 (accessed December 2, 2009).

Key Terms

A

abstract
words are not concrete or tangible items; they are only representations

accent
nonverbal behaviors that augment a verbal message

acceptance
the third step in the persuasive process where the audience decides whether or not to agree with the position advocated by the speaker

accuracy
the truthfulness or correctness of a source

achievers
people who are motivated by success, politically conservative, and work-oriented; they value the familiar

acoustics
the way sound travels in a room

active listening
listening to understand a message by processing, storing, and potentially evaluating a message; it also involves reactions by the listener in some form

ad hominem fallacy
when speakers attack the person making the argument and not the argument itself

ad populum fallacy
when we attempt to persuade people by arguing our position is reasonable because so many other people are doing it or agree with it

ad verecundium fallacy
an appeal for persuasion based on higher authority or tradition

alliteration
repeating the same consonant or vowel sound at the beginning of subsequent words

ambiguous
language that does not have precise, concrete meanings

ambushing
selective listening where the audience ignores the strengths of a message and hears only the weaknesses

American Psychological Association (APA)
preferred reference manual for social scientific communication scholars

antecedent
the hypothetical condition in the major premise of a conditional syllogism

antithesis
two ideas that sharply contrast with each other and are juxtaposed in a parallel grammatical structure

anxiety disorder
abnormal mental outlook where individuals experience high levels of apprehension that keep them from living life

apologia
a forensic speech that makes a defense against an accusation

arbitrary
symbols used to represent things that are not intrinsically connected to those things

argument
also called the proof or confirmation; the portion of the speech that validates your position on the issue laid out in the statement of facts

arguments from the past
appropriating historical events, facts, or people to justify present or future actions or explain events in the here-and-now

arrangement
the second canon of rhetoric where you determine the most effective way to organize your case for the topic and the audience

articulation
physically producing the sound needed to convey the word

artistic proof
constructed by the speaker for the occasion; concerns ethos, pathos, and logos

asymmetrical balance
emphasizes imbalance, thus creating an impression of stress, energy, and excitement

attention-getter
a device that immediately attracts the audience's interest to the subject that the speaker plans to discuss

axial balance
formal balance that strives for equal distribution of the elements of a visual so they do not appear tilted on one side of the image

B

background information
material that provides context for a topic

backing
the justification for a warrant

balance
the positioning of elements within the image

begging-the-question fallacy
when a speaker presumes certain things are facts when they have not yet been proven to be truthful

believers
people motivated by ideals, but who do not have a significant amount of resources

bias
presenting information in a way that unfairly influences someone's perception of something

bookend approach
a version of the moderator approach whereby the first speaker in a group presentation is also the last speaker, providing both the introduction and conclusion for the group

C

categorical syllogism
a syllogism in which the argument is based on membership in a group

cause and effect arrangement
orders your points first by discussing the cause of something that occurred and then moving to an explanation of the impact of its occurrence

central claim
the main point of which you seek to convince the audience

channel
the mode through which the message is conveyed to another party

chart
a visual device that helps you summarize and/or list blocks of information

Chicago Manual of Style (CMS)
preferred reference manual for rhetorical studies

chronological order
arranging points in the order in which they occur, or occurred, from start to finish

civic engagement
acting upon a sharp awareness of one's own sense of responsibility to his or her community

claim
the idea that you are seeking to convey

clarity
the ability of speakers to clearly articulate what they wish to say

classroom response systems
devices that allow students to answer questions posed during a lecture and provide tabulated results of the poll for everyone in the room in a timely manner

clincher
the final statement of your speech

coercion
the use of force or threats to make someone do something against his or her will

color pattern
collection of hues in your presentation aids

communication apprehension
the fear or anxiety associated with real or anticipated communication with another or others

Communication/Mass Media Complete
an electronic database for academic journals and popular sources related to communication and journalism

comparative advantage
an organizational pattern that uses each main point to explain why the speaker's solution is better than another proposed solution

complement
when the action demonstrates the message contained in the verbal content

comprehension
the second step in the persuasive process in which the speaker provides context for the issue in dispute so the audience understands what the speaker is talking about

condensation symbol
an element that evokes emotions by condensing them into one symbolic event

conditional syllogism
a syllogism in which the major premise contains a hypothetical condition and its outcome

conference call
use of the telephone to connect more than two parties on the same phone call

conflict
nonverbal cues that convey a message that contradicts the verbal statements of the speaker

conjectural stasis
when the issue in dispute is whether something occurred or not

consequent
the outcome of the hypothetical condition in the major premise of a conditional syllogism

context
the conditions surrounding the event

contrast
how objects and letters stick out from the background

coordination
all information on the same level has the same significance

correctness
the accuracy of information presented and the honest representation of the speaker

crescendo
an organizational pattern where the strongest point is placed at the end and is built up to by smaller main points

critical thinking
the ability for students to evaluate on their own the material they learn

D

dais
the area a speaker speaks from

decoding
the process of taking a message that has been sent and using one's own experiences and knowledge to give it meaning

deductive reasoning
an argument that reasons from known premises to an inevitable conclusion

definitive stasis
when the issue in dispute is the meaning of a term

dehumanization
making people seem less than human in order to more easily motivate action against them

deliberative speech
one of two forms of persuasive speech proposed by Aristotle; it often takes place in legislative settings and focuses on discussing policies and actions to be taken

delivery
the fourth canon of rhetoric; the manner in which you physically and vocally present the speech

demagoguery
speech that attempts to win over an audience through appealing to their prejudices and emotions, particularly those of fear, anger, and frustration

demographic data
information on selected population characteristics used by the government, market researchers, and speech writers

depth
the graphic nature of an item; involves both level of detail and the amount of background provided for the image

derived credibility
your level of credibility during a speech that comes from what you say and how you say it

Dewey Decimal Classification System
the coding system for books, magazines, and journals used in libraries

dialect
aspects of articulation, grammar, vocabulary, and pronunciation that differ from Standard English

disjunctive syllogism
a syllogism in which the major premise includes two or more mutually exclusive alternatives

division
in order to divide a point you need to end up with two or more items

dynamism
a social science term for strong delivery that creates the impression with the audience that the speaker has practiced and thus cares about what he/she is talking about

E

efficacy
the ability to produce a desired result

either-or fallacy
an argument in which you present two options and declare that one of them must be correct while the other must be incorrect

encoding
the process of attaching symbols to ideas and feelings so that others may understand them

enkyklios paideia
rounded education spread under the reign of Alexander the Great

enthymeme
a syllogism missing one or two of its parts

episteme
universal knowledge, or understanding about the common characteristics of like materials

ethos
the credibility of the speaker

eulogy
a speech that pays tribute to the life of the deceased

evidentiary information
information that supports main points within a speech and is directly related to the topic

exigence
a decisive point where a response is invited or required

exit poll
questions asked following an election that measure election results in terms of demographic categories

exordium
the place in the speech where you convince an audience to listen to your position; Latin label for the introduction of a speech

experiencers
people motivated by image who have the capability to express and improve it

extemporaneous speech
a speech delivered with notes but not the entire speech in front of the speaker

F

famous quotation
actual statements closely related to the topic of the speech made by individuals the audience will easily recognize

feedback
the responses and reactions to the messages transmitted by the sender; is itself a new message sent back to the original sender

figurative analogy
when the two cases being compared are from completely different classifications

fixed-response questions
items on a survey that allow only for prescribed answers

forensic speech
an argument where speakers debate the facts of a case and attempt to answer questions of justice

form
how an item appears in terms of its representation, size, and texture

formal survey
time-consuming way of gathering data on a population that employs randomized sampling to ensure reliability and validity

frame of reference
our own singular perspective of the world around us

G

general purpose statement
a brief statement representing what you aim to do with the speech; there are three types

gesture
a physical movement used to convey a message

ghostwriting
to write for and in the name of another person

glazing over
daydreaming instead of hearing the message

global plagiarism
taking an entire speech from a single source and pawning it off as your own

graph
a presentation device that indicates relationships found in numerical data

gravitas
importance

grounds
evidence in the Toulmin model

H

harmony
when all parts and aspects of the presentation aid complement one another within the aid's framework

hate speech
rude and crude speech that attacks or demeans a particular social or ethnic group, many times with the intent of inciting action against that group

hearing
the physiological process of processing sounds, conducted by one's ears and brain

heckler
a self-aggrandizing member of the audience who tries to distract from the speech by confronting the speaker in the middle of a presentation

hierarchical
language that is structured according to more or less, higher or lower

I

ideograph
an ill-defined, politically powerful term or phrase that can push people to action

impromptu speech
a presentation done with little or no preparation

inartistic proof
all the evidence, data, and documents that exist outside of the speaker and the audience, but nevertheless can aid in persuasion

incremental plagiarism
failure to give proper credit for parts of a speech that are borrowed from others

inductive reasoning
an argument that comes to a probable, instead of an absolute, conclusion

informal survey
polling a few people based on convenience

information literacy
the ability to figure out the type of information you need, find that information, evaluate it, and properly use it

informative speech
provides information in as neutral an environment as possible, where the speaker and the audience typically seek to teach and learn

initial credibility
the level of believability a speaker has before beginning his or her speech

innovators
people involved in change, who have high self-esteem and plenty of personal resources

insinuation
a form of exordium reserved for cases made about disputed topics to audiences with animosity toward the topic or the speaker

integration
the fourth stage in the persuasive process in which the audience makes the speaker's position a part of its own personal philosophy and worldview

intermediate knowledge
knowing what does not reflect an excess or a defect but instead what is intuitively correct to the persona

internal preview
serves as an outline of what is to come next in a speech and is often combined with transition statements

internal summary
a statement that summarizes what you already have covered and precedes transitions

interviewing
a direct method of gathering information from a human source that allows for questions to adapt to responses

introduction
one form of exordium where speakers use plain language to lay out their case in an effort to get a confused and ill-informed audience to pay attention

invention
the first canon of rhetoric where you choose the best possible arguments for your case

issue awareness
the first step in the persuasive process whereby the speaker alerts the audience about the issue requiring its attention

J

jargon
terminology that relates to a specific activity

JSTOR
an electronic database for political journals

K

kairos
Greek term meaning timing and recognition of the needs of the occasion

kategoria
a forensic speech that makes an accusation

kinesics
nonverbal behaviors related to movement

L

lectern
a reading desk affixed to a stand

Lexis-Nexis
an electronic database for newspapers and magazines

Likert scale
a way of measuring how strong a person's beliefs, attitudes, and values are; they usually consist of 3–7 possible answers

linear model of communication
communication process that involves a sender who encodes a message and sends it through a channel where it competes with distracting forces called noise while on its way to a receiver who then decodes the message

listening
the psychological process of making sense out of sounds

listening for appreciation
listening for enjoyment; not high in cognitive commitment

listening to comprehend
listening to understand a concept or message

listening to criticize
listening to make a judgment about a message; involves a high level of cognitive commitment on the part of the audience

literal analogy
when the two cases being compared are classified the same way

logos
the logical dimension of the appeal

lying by commission
when a speaker willfully makes untrue statements to an audience

lying by omission
when a speaker willfully chooses not to acknowledge facts about his or her argument that might damage its effectiveness

M

major premise
the first part of a syllogism, consisting of a general statement about the subject of your argument

makers
a low resource group that values self-sufficiency and the familiar

manipulation
the deliberate misrepresentation of facts and evidence to an audience

manuscript speech
when a speaker has an entire speech written out word-for-word in front of him/her as s/he speaks

medium
the channel through which the message travels (note: medium is singular for the plural term "media")

memorized speech
when a speaker commits an entire speech to memory and delivers with no notes in front of him/her

memory
the fifth canon of rhetoric; refers to one's ability to recall names and important information in the middle of a speech as well as to deliver a cogent speech without notes

message
the actual content you send to an audience, both intentional and unintentional

metaphor
comparisons that show how two things are alike in an important way, despite being quite different in most ways

minor claim
connects evidence within the speech to a particular point

minor premise
a statement about a specific case related to the general characteristics of the major premise

model
a to-scale device that depicts an actual object

moderator approach
a way of delivering a group presentation whereby one person acts as the coordinator of the discussion flow and ensures a civil, organized, and complete delivery of information to the audience

Modern Language Association (MLA)
a citation style used in disciplines within the liberal arts and humanities

Monroe's Motivated Sequence
a five-step organizational pattern that combines psychological elements with speech persuasion to move an audience to action

movement
appearance of or actual activity depicted with an image

multimedia presentation
a presentation aid that combines and integrates video, audio, pictures, and notes into one medium

myth
a rhetorical construction that tries to explain natural events or cultural phenomena and is used to identify with a group and justify actions or beliefs

N

narrative coherence
the degree to which a story makes sense in the world in which we live

narrative fidelity
the degree to which a story matches our own beliefs and experiences

narrative paradigm
humans are storytelling beings by nature

necessary cause
a condition that must be present for the effect to occur

noise
anything that interferes with the encoding, transmission, and reception of a message

nonlistening
providing the appearance of listening without actually paying complete attention to the message

non sequitur fallacy
when you make an unwarranted move from one idea to the next

O

object
a tangible item used in conjunction with a speech

Occam's Razor
one should not increase, beyond what is necessary, the number of entities required to explain anything

open-ended questions
items on a survey that allow room for the person taking the survey to answer in his/her own words

P

parallelism
similarly structuring related words, phrases, or clauses

passive listening
listening without reacting

patchwork plagiarism
stealing ideas from two or three sources without referencing them

pathos
the emotional dimensions of the appeal that can influence an audience's disposition toward the topic, speaker, or occasion

peroration
speech conclusion

plagiarism
to present another person's work or ideas as your own

podium
a platform used to raise the speaker higher

post hoc, ergo propter hoc fallacy
from the Latin for "after this, because of this"; assumes that because one event happened after another, then the preceding event caused the event that followed

posture
the position of your body

potential rebuttal
a statement that outlines the conditions which would make your central claim untrue

practicality
the proper places within the speech (the where, when, and how) you can and should make use of presentation aids

prejudging
entering into a presentation with a judgment already formed about the message being delivered

preparation outlines
detailed outlines that use full sentences next to symbols in an effort to help you organize the speech

presentation aids
visual devices used to assist a speaker in communicating ideas to the audience

principle of recency
the idea that the last message you heard is most likely to be the one you remember

prior ethos
credibility before the speech

problem-cause-solution order
a means of organizing a persuasive speech in which you discuss the problem first, then its root cause, and then your preferred solution that addresses both the problem and its inherent cause

problem-solution arrangement
orders points by first discussing a problem and then how it was addressed; a subset of chronological order

problem-solution order
a means of organizing a persuasive speech in which you discuss the problem first and follow with a discussion of your preferred solution

profanity
coarse and irreverent language

pronunciation
the accepted standard of how a word sounds when spoken

propriety
good behavior and faithfulness to what one considers moral and just

pseudolistening
when someone attempts to hide their inattention to the speaker's message

psychographics
data that measures attitudes, beliefs, behaviors, and motivations

Q

quadrivium
arithmetic, geometry, music, and astronomy

qualifier
a statement that establishes the boundaries in which the argument is true

qualitative stasis
when the issue in dispute involves the morality, ethicality, or value of an action

question of fact
when a speaker seeks to persuade people about how to interpret facts

question of policy
when a speaker takes a position on whether an action should or should not be taken

question of value
a persuasive speech about the rightness or wrongness of an idea, action, or issue

R

reasoning by analogy
when you compare two similar cases in order to argue that what is true in one case is also true in the other

reasoning by cause
arguments that claim one event or factor produces an effect

reasoning by example
the process of inferring general conclusions and making general claims from specific cases

rebuttal speech
a speech that involves overcoming the opposition's argument by introducing other evidence that reduces the appeal of the opposition's claims

receiver
the person or persons who receive the encoded message sent by the sender

red herring fallacy
when a speaker introduces an irrelevant issue or piece of evidence to divert attention from the subject of the speech

referential symbol
an element in objects or events that refers to a specific message or aspect of a message

refutation
response to potential opposition to your argument

regulate
nonverbal actions that help govern the course of a speech or interaction

reinforcement statement
an expression of the connection between the event and the social value it represents

repeat
when physical actions restate verbal messages

repetition
repeating either the same phrasing pattern for main points, or a phrase you just stated, in order to maximize the audience's ability to receive the information

research question
the question about your topic you seek to answer

rhetorical history
the appropriation and redefinition of historical events to augment an argument

rhetorical question
asking the audience a question related to the subject that does not require an answer from them

rhetorical situation
moments that call for a rhetorical response

rhetors
speakers

rostrum
the area a speaker speaks from

S

self-fulfilling prophecy
believing that something will happen before it actually does, and then when it does come true reinforcing the original expectation

sender
the person who desires to deliver a message to another person or group of people

shorthand
the process of shortening words or eliminating word clutter in the transcription process

signpost
a connective that lets the audience know what is next; most effective form of connective for moving from the last main point to the conclusion

simile
a comparison between two objects that allows each object in the comparison to retain its unique differences

single-word approach
meaning is derived from individual words used in a strategic way

slang
words derived from dialects that most people understand but do not use in professional writing or speaking

slippery slope fallacy
a logical fallacy that assumes once an action begins it will lead, undeterred, to an eventual and inevitable conclusion

sociophobia
the fear of social situations and/or people

Socratic questioning
the process of asking questions of a speaker focused on the responses to previous questions; its ultimate goal is to uncover the truth

Sophists
itinerant teachers who traveled from city-state to city-state in Classical Greece, training people in public speaking

spare brain time
the time available for your mind to wander due to your ability to process messages faster than the time it takes to construct them

spatial order
arranges points according to geography or logical movement through an area

speaking outline
a truncated form of your full-sentence preparation outline that does not include complete sentences

specific purpose statement
a narrower version of the general purpose statement that identifies what you will talk about, what you will say about it, and what you hope the audience will take away from the speech

spectacle
a symbolic event where the details send a deeper meaning

speech of refutation
a speech that seeks to prove the opposition's argument is wrong or false

speech of self-presentation
a speech where the speaker's topic is introducing himself or herself to the audience

spotlight syndrome
the belief encouraged by the room setup that all eyes are focused on you as the speaker

stasis
the basic issue in dispute between one or more speaking parties

statement of facts
an explanation of what the audience needs to know in order to appreciate the main argument of the speech

straw man fallacy
when a speaker ignores the actual position of an opponent and substitutes it with a distorted and exaggerated position

strivers
people who are low in resources, but motivated by achievement

style
the third canon of rhetoric; involves word choice, phrasing, and the level of formality in the language you use to present your case to the audience

subordination
the organization of a hierarchy of ideas where the most general appear first, followed by subsequently more specific ideas

substitute
physical actions that take the place of verbal messages

sufficient cause
a condition that automatically produces the effect in question

summary
the central part of the conclusion; it is where you reiterate the speech's thesis statement and recap the main points you addressed throughout the body

survivors
the lowest income bracket and the oldest median age of any VALS category

syllogism
basic structure of a deductive argument that comes to an absolute conclusion

T

tangential information
evidence used to provide color and capture an audience's interest

techne
experiential knowledge; knowledge of particular events in the world around us; the least reliable form of knowledge

terminal credibility
the credibility with which you end the speech

thesis statement
the verbalized foundation of your entire speech in a single sentence which presents your topic, main points, and goal to the audience in an explicit and understandable way

thinkers
mature, responsible, well-educated professionals who are motivated by ideals

tone
the syllabic emphasis on a sound that expresses emotion or meaning

topical arrangement
the organization of main points by subpoints that do not naturally fit together in another way

traditional aids
aids that do not apply electronic means to communicate ideas to the audience

transactional model of communication
recognizes that we simultaneously send and receive messages; a cyclical model of the communication process

transition
a connective statement that signals you are finished with one point and moving on to another

transitions
connective statements that signal you are finished with one point and moving on to another

translative stasis
when the issue in dispute is the competency of the judge or arbiter

transparencies
clear sheets containing information illuminated by a projector

travel spectacle
when the act of going somewhere sends a message

trivium
grammar, rhetoric, and logic

U

undercover interviewing
when the interviewer disguises either himself or his purpose in an effort to trick someone into sharing more information than they may have if the interviewee knew to whom he or she was speaking

V

Values, Attitudes and Lifestyles (VALS) framework
a tool used for categorizing individuals and groups according to their psychographic traits

verifier
provides the credibility for the grounds and backing provided in the speech

video conferencing
live transmission of the video and audio of a presenter who is in one place to an audience in another place

vocalic
anything that contributes to the creation or maintenance of sound in a person's voice

vocalized pauses
utterances that are not words and have no place in a speech, but are done instead of pausing the delivery of the speech

W

warrant
explains why the grounds support the claim and makes that connection clear to the audience

word-cluster approach
meaning is conveyed through more complex structures such as stories

Appendix B:
Exercises

McCroskey's Willingness to Listen

Everyday we are assaulted with noises. We hear sounds, but the sounds are meaningless unless we consciously interpret them. This of course is called listening. Often, it boils down to "Selective Listening." In other words we hear what we want to hear. Of course, every situation is different, but this instrument will give you an idea of your willingness to listen.

The following twenty-four statements refer to listening. Please indicate the degree to which each statement applies to you by marking whether you:

Strongly Disagree = 1; Disagree = 2; Neutral =3; Agree = 4; Strongly Agree = 5

_____1.   I dislike listening to boring speakers.

_____2.   Generally, I can listen to a boring speaker.

_____3.   I am bored and tired while listening to a boring speaker.

_____4.   I will listen when the content of a speech is boring.

_____5.   Listening to boring speakers about boring content makes me tired, sleepy, and bored.

_____6.   I am willing to listen to boring speakers about boring content.

_____7.   Generally, I am unwilling to listen when there is noise during a speaker's presentation.

_____8.   Usually, I am willing to listen when there is noise during a speaker's presentation.

_____9.   I am accepting and willing to listen to speakers who do not adapt to me.

_____10.   I am unwilling to listen to speakers who do not do some adaptation to me.

_____11.   Being preoccupied with other things makes me less willing to listen to a speaker.

_____12.   I am willing to listen to a speaker even if I have other things on my mind.

_____13.   While being occupied with other things on my mind, I am unwilling to listen to a speaker.

_____14.   I have a willingness to listen to a speaker, even if other important things are on my mind.

_____15. Generally, I will not listen to a speaker who is disorganized.

_____16. Generally, I will try to listen to a speaker who is disorganized.

_____17. While listening to a non-immediate, non-responsive speaker, I feel relaxed with the speaker.

_____18. While listening to a non-immediate, non-responsive speaker, I feel distant and cold toward that speaker.

_____19. I can listen to a non-immediate, non-responsive speaker.

_____20. I am unwilling to listen to a non-immediate, non-responsive speaker.

_____21. I am willing to listen to a speaker with views different from mine.

_____22. I am unwilling to listen to a speaker with views different from mine.

_____23. I am willing to listen to a speaker who is not clear about what he or she wants to say.

_____24. I am unwilling to listen to a speaker who is not clear, not credible, and abstract.

SCORING:

Scores can range from 24 to 120. To compute the score on this instrument complete the following steps:

Step 1: Add scores for items 2, 4, 6, 8, 9, 12, 14, 16, 17, 19, 21, and 23

Step 2: Add scores for items 1, 3, 5, 7, 10, 11, 13, 15, 18, 20, 22, and 24

Step 3: Total score = 72 - Total from Step 1 + Total from Step 2.

Scores above 89 indicate a high willingness to listen. Scores below 59 indicate a low willingness to listen. Score between 59 and 89 indicate a moderate willingness to listen.

Source: Richmond, V. P., & Hickson, M. III. (2001). *Going public: A practical guide to public talk.* Boston: Allyn & Bacon.

COMMUNICATION APPREHENSION (PRE-TERM ASSESSMENT)

Communication Apprehension (CA) measures how much an individual is afraid or anxious about speaking in public. Knowing what your CA is can help you work on the areas where you are most apprehensive.

Below you will see the Personal Report of Communication Apprehension, or the PRCA-24. This is an instrument used to calculate one's personal level of communication apprehension.

This instrument is composed of twenty-four statements concerning feelings about communicating with others. Please indicate the degree to which each statement applies to you by marking whether you:

Strongly Disagree = 1; Disagree = 2; Neutral = 3; Agree = 4; Strongly Agree = 5

_____1.   I dislike participating in group discussions.

_____2.   Generally, I am comfortable while participating in group discussions.

_____3.   I am tense and nervous while participating in group discussions.

_____4.   I like to get involved in group discussions.

_____5.   Engaging in a group discussion with new people makes me tense and nervous.

_____6.   I am calm and relaxed while participating in group discussions.

_____7.   Generally, I am nervous when I have to participate in a meeting.

_____8.   Usually, I am comfortable when I have to participate in a meeting.

_____9.   I am very calm and relaxed when I am called upon to express an opinion at a meeting.

_____10.   I am afraid to express myself at meetings.

_____11.   Communicating at meetings usually makes me uncomfortable.

_____12.   I am very relaxed when answering questions at a meeting.

_____13.   While participating in a conversation with a new acquaintance, I feel very nervous.

_____14.   I have no fear of speaking up in conversations.

_____15.   Ordinarily I am very tense and nervous in conversations.

_____16.   Ordinarily I am very calm and relaxed in conversations.

_____17.   While conversing with a new acquaintance, I feel very relaxed.

_____18.   I'm afraid to speak up in conversations.

_____19.   I have no fear of giving a speech.

_____20.   Certain parts of my body feel very tense and rigid while giving a speech.

_____21.   I feel relaxed while giving a speech.

_____22.   My thoughts become confused and jumbled when I am giving a speech.

_____23. I face the prospect of giving a speech with confidence.

_____24. While giving a speech, I get so nervous I forget facts I really know.

SCORING:

Group discussion: 18 - (scores for items 2, 4, & 6) + (scores for items 1,3, & 5)

Meetings: 18 - (scores for items 8, 9, & 12) + (scores for items 7, 10, & 11)

Interpersonal: 18 - (scores for items 14, 16, & 17) + (scores for items 13, 15, & 18)

Public Speaking: 18 - (scores for items 19, 21, & 23) + (scores for items 20, 22, &24)

Group Discussion Score: _____

Interpersonal Score: _____

Meetings Score: _____

Public Speaking Score: _____

To obtain your total score for the PRCA, simply add your sub-scores together.

_____

Scores can range from 24-120. Scores below 51 represent people who have very low CA. Scores between 51-80 represent people with average CA. Scores above 80 represent people who have high levels of trait CA.

NORMS FOR THE PRCA-24: (based on over 40,000 college students; data from over 3,000 non-student adults in a national sample provided virtually identical norms, within 0.20 for all scores.)

	Mean	Standard Deviation	High	Low
Total Score	65.6	15.3	> 80	< 51
Group:	15.4	4.8	> 20	< 11
Meeting:	16.4	4.2	> 20	< 13
Dyad (Interpersonal):	14.2	3.9	> 18	< 11
Public:	19.3	5.1	> 24	< 14

Source: McCroskey, J. C. (1982). An introduction to rhetorical communication (4th Ed). Englewood Cliffs, NJ: Prentice-Hall.

After completing and scoring the PRCA-24, write a paragraph or two explaining what you found. Did the results surprise you? Discuss the results with a friend. Do they feel it reflects the you they know? What were your weak points? Strong points? How do you think that this class will help you get over your fears and anxiety about public speaking?

-Submitted by Vernon Humphrey

COMMUNICATION APPREHENSION (POST-TERM ASSESSMENT)

Communication Apprehension (CA) measures how much an individual is afraid or anxious about speaking in public. Knowing what your CA is can help you work on the areas where you are most apprehensive.

Below you will see the Personal Report of Communication Apprehension, or the PRCA-24. This is an instrument used to calculate one's personal level of communication apprehension.

This instrument is composed of twenty-four statements concerning feelings about communicating with others. Please indicate the degree to which each statement applies to you by marking whether you:

Strongly Disagree = 1; Disagree = 2; Neutral = 3; Agree = 4; Strongly Agree = 5

_____1.   I dislike participating in group discussions.

_____2.   Generally, I am comfortable while participating in group discussions.

_____3.   I am tense and nervous while participating in group discussions.

_____4.   I like to get involved in group discussions.

_____5.   Engaging in a group discussion with new people makes me tense and nervous.

_____6.   I am calm and relaxed while participating in group discussions.

_____7.   Generally, I am nervous when I have to participate in a meeting.

_____8.   Usually, I am comfortable when I have to participate in a meeting.

_____9.   I am very calm and relaxed when I am called upon to express an opinion at a meeting.

_____10. I am afraid to express myself at meetings.

_____11. Communicating at meetings usually makes me uncomfortable.

_____12. I am very relaxed when answering questions at a meeting.

_____13. While participating in a conversation with a new acquaintance, I feel very nervous.

_____14. I have no fear of speaking up in conversations.

_____15. Ordinarily I am very tense and nervous in conversations.

_____16. Ordinarily I am very calm and relaxed in conversations.

_____17. While conversing with a new acquaintance, I feel very relaxed.

_____18. I'm afraid to speak up in conversations.

_____19. I have no fear of giving a speech.

_____20. Certain parts of my body feel very tense and rigid while giving a speech.

_____21. I feel relaxed while giving a speech.

_____22. My thoughts become confused and jumbled when I am giving a speech.

_____23.   I face the prospect of giving a speech with confidence.

_____24.   While giving a speech, I get so nervous I forget facts I really know.

SCORING:

Group discussion: 18 - (scores for items 2, 4, & 6) + (scores for items 1,3, & 5)

Meetings: 18 - (scores for items 8, 9, & 12) + (scores for items 7, 10, & 11)

Interpersonal: 18 - (scores for items 14, 16, & 17) + (scores for items 13, 15, & 18)

Public Speaking: 18 - (scores for items 19, 21, & 23) + (scores for items 20, 22, &24)

Group Discussion Score: _____

Interpersonal Score: _____

Meetings Score: _____

Public Speaking Score: _____

To obtain your total score for the PRCA, simply add your sub-scores together.
_____

Scores can range from 24-120. Scores below 51 represent people who have very low CA. Scores between 51-80 represent people with average CA. Scores above 80 represent people who have high levels of trait CA.

NORMS FOR THE PRCA-24: (based on over 40,000 college students; data from over 3,000 non-student adults in a national sample provided virtually identical norms, within 0.20 for all scores.)

	Mean	Standard Deviation	High	Low
Total Score	65.6	15.3	> 80	< 51
Group:	15.4	4.8	> 20	< 11
Meeting:	16.4	4.2	> 20	< 13
Dyad (Interpersonal):	14.2	3.9	> 18	< 11
Public:	19.3	5.1	> 24	< 14

Source: McCroskey, J. C. (1982). An introduction to rhetorical communication (4th Ed). Englewood Cliffs, NJ: Prentice-Hall.

After completing and scoring the PRCA-24, write a paragraph or two explaining what you found. Did the results surprise you? Discuss the results with a friend. Do they feel it reflects the you they know? What were your weak points? Strong points? How do you think that this class will help you get over your fears and anxiety about public speaking?

-Submitted by Vernon Humphrey

OUTSIDE OF THE BOX

Despite some of your best efforts, many of you may still be extremely apprehensive about the prospect of speaking in front of the class. What you do not realize is that you participate in speech communication every single day, even though you do not realize it.

Let's analyze some of your daily or weekly rituals to give you a better idea of how much you speak publicly already. Just answer the questions below and you will begin to see how much practice you have at giving speeches.

1. Do you work with the public? _____
   a. If you answered yes, what type of interaction do you have with them?

   _____

   _____

   b. Does this interaction require you to speak with people on a daily basis?

   _____

   _____

2. Do you go to church? _____
   a. If you answered yes, do you participate in the liturgy by responding aloud with the congregation?

   _____

   _____

   b. Are you a reader or in a choir at your church?

   _____

   _____

3. Do you go out to eat with friends or family often? _____
   a. If you answered yes, do you actively engage in conversation?

   _____

   _____

   b. Do you call these same people on the phone to make plans or do you rely on other virtual communication to set up your plans?

   _____

   _____

4. Do you have any children? _____

    a. If you answered yes, do you read to them or help explain things to them that they might not ordinarily understand?

_____

_____

    b. Do you instruct them in day-to-day activities?

_____

_____

5. Do you have a spouse or significant other? _____

    a. If you answered yes, do you converse with them on a daily basis about day-to-day activities and interests?

_____

_____

    b. Do you tell them what your wants, needs, and expectations are in the relationship?

_____

_____

6. Do you still live at home with your parents or see them often? _____

    a. If you answered yes, do you tell them about what you are working on in school?

_____

_____

    b. Do you ask them for advice or tell them about some of the problems you may be experiencing at work or school?

_____

_____

If you answered yes to many of these, then you are already a seasoned public speaker. You should start to think of public speaking and the speech-giving process in small terms. For example, if you are a waiter or waitress, every time you walk up to a table to take an order or tell customers about the day's specials, you are giving a speech of sorts. When you think about public speaking in this manner, it makes it much easier to overcome the phobia and anxiety you may be feeling.

Just remember – take a deep breath! You are doing great!

WHAT ARE YOUR CLOTHES SAYING TO ME?

Often times, we forget that the nonverbal signals that we are giving the public speak volumes louder than anything we can communicate verbally.

Take the outfit that you have on today. What is it saying about your personality and who you are as a person? Are you dressed sloppy because you had a big paper due today that you waited to start at the last minute? Are you dressed up to impress that certain someone you have had your eye on for a while? Perhaps you simply do not care what your outward appearance looks like and put on anything lying on the floor that doesn't stink to high heaven, even though that fact does communicate something in and of itself. Even the type of car you drive and cell phone you use communicates some idea or message about you.

For this exercise, go through a series of images or advertisements (online or in a magazine) and find images that convey each of the character traits listed below. Explain how the images you find demonstrate each characteristic. Once you are done, answer the questions at the end of the exercise.

Preppy _____

_____

_____

Sloppy _____

_____

_____

Snobby _____

_____

_____

Intelligent _____

_____

_____

Wealthy _____

_____

_____

Creative _____

_____

_____

Stylish _____

_____

_____

Clueless _____

_____

_____

Promiscuous_____

_____

_____

Prudish _____

_____

_____

1. What do these nonverbal messages hinge upon in order to be so powerful?

_____

_____

_____

_____

_____

_____

2. How much stress should be placed on nonverbal cues and communication?

_____

_____

_____

_____

_____

_____

_____

APA: A STYLE EXERCISE

Knowing how to cite a work used in your research properly is just as important as knowing how to use the work itself. In the Communication discipline, APA, or the American Psychological Association, citation style is used.

Below are two websites that give examples as to how to cite works in your research properly.

http://owl.english.purdue.edu/owl/resource/560/01/

http://www.apastyle.org/

Using these as guides, find a source that fits each of the following descriptions. Put them into proper APA style on a reference page. Make sure to do this exercise on your computer and print out a copy to bring with you to class. **You may not cut and paste examples from Web sites!**

1. Journal article with one author _____

_____

_____

2. Journal article with multiple authors _____

_____

_____

3. Book with one author_____

_____

_____

4. Book with multiple authors _____

_____

_____

5. Edited book _____

_____

_____

6. Magazine article _____

_____

_____

7. World Wide Web article _____

_____

_____

8. Weekly newspaper article _____

_____

_____

9. Chapter in a book_____

_____

_____

10. Dictionary _____

_____

_____

It's Storming Brains!

Where are you in your speech-writing process? Are you preparing for an informative speech or a persuasive speech? Have you chosen a topic yet? If so, have you thought about what main points you are going to make? What kinds of things will you say about these points? What is the overall feeling that you want to leave your audience with?

Feel a little overwhelmed? Well, you shouldn't because these are things that we all go through when preparing and giving a speech. Brainstorming is an activity that can help you clear your head and organize your thoughts to put together your speech.

Answer the questions below as quickly as possible, jotting down the first answer that pops into your head. You can list several if you come up with more than one. After you have finished, go back through your answers and highlight the ones that you would like to use for your speech. Remember, the ideas that you do not use for one speech can be used in the future.

Let the brainstorming begin!

1. What topic do you want to talk about?

_____

_____

_____

_____

_____

2. What is one idea that comes to mind when you think about this topic?

_____

_____

_____

_____

_____

3. What are some words that you can use to describe this topic?

_____

_____

_____

_____

_____

4. What is the most important thing about this topic?

_____

_____

_____

_____

_____

5. What makes this topic something of interest?

_____

_____

_____

_____

_____

6. What experience do you have with this topic?

_____

_____

_____

_____

_____

7. Repeat this exercise with each speech for best results.

_____

_____

_____

_____

BODY BUILDING

The body of a speech is your biggest section, which makes it a little more tedious to write. We are going to look at this section first, because it has a great deal of influence over what you are going to say in your introduction and conclusion.

For each speech it is important to make multiple points, each supported with sub-points, or material that support and expand on your point. This exercise is designed to help you build the body of your speech.

Answer each of the questions below. Make sure to keep these answers because they will be used in the outlining chapter.

I. What is the first point you would like to make about your topic? _____

_____

    A. What is something that everyone should now about this point?_____

    _____

        1. Why is this important?_____

        _____

        2. How did you find out about this? What is your source? _____

        _____

    B. What is another fact about your point that everyone should know?____

    _____

        1. Why is this important?_____

        _____

        2. How did you find out about this? What is your source? _____

        _____

II. What is the second point you would like to make about your topic? _____

_____

    A. What is something that everyone should now about this point?_____

    _____

        1. Why is this important?_____

        _____

2. How did you find out about this? What is your source? _____

_____

B. What is another fact about your point that everyone should know?____

_____

    1. Why is this important?_____

    _____

    2. How did you find out about this? What is your source? _____

    _____

III. What is the third point you would like to make about your topic?_____

_____

A. What is something that everyone should now about this point?_____

_____

    1. Why is this important?_____

    _____

    2. How did you find out about this? What is your source? _____

    _____

B. What is another fact about your point that everyone should know?

_____

    1. _____

    _____

    2. Why is this important?_____

    _____

    3. How did you find out about this? What is your source? _____

    _____

INTRODUCTION PRODUCTION

Now that you have the body of your speech taken care of, let's work on what's left.

The first part of your speech, the introduction, is important for a multitude of reasons. First, this is when you have to gain your audience's attention. Second, it is within this part of your speech that you establish your credibility as a speaker. Third, the introduction offers your audience a preview of the main points to be made in your speech. Finally, your introduction is where you give your thesis statement, which tells your audience what your speech is about. This exercise is designed to help you put together your introduction.

Answer each of the questions below. Make sure to keep these answers because they will be used in the outlining exercise.

1. What is the topic of your speech?

_____

_____

_____

_____

_____

2. How do you intend to get the attention of your audience? Do you plan on telling a brief story or a joke? Do you plan on asking your audience a question to engage them and get them involved in your speech?

_____

_____

_____

_____

_____

3. What makes you a credible source for this speech? How did you become an expert to talk about this topic? Have you had experience with this topic before?

_____

_____

_____

_____

_____

4. What main points do you plan on making in your speech?

_____

_____

_____

_____

_____

5. What is your thesis statement? What is the purpose for your entire speech? What do you intend on happening as a result of this speech? Are you trying to persuade or inform your audience?

_____

_____

_____

_____

_____

FINAL THOUGHTS

   Your conclusion is full of the final thoughts that you want to leave with your audience. It should be filled with an overview of the speech that they just heard as well as a look to the future and what they can do with the speech that they just heard. This exercise is designed to help you put together your conclusion.

   Answer each of the questions below. Make sure to keep these answers because they will be used in the outlining exercise.

1. What was the purpose for your entire speech? What was your thesis statement?

_____

_____

_____

_____

_____

_____

_____

2. What were the main points that you made in your speech?

_____

_____

_____

_____

_____

_____

_____

3. How can you use this information in the future?

_____

_____

_____

_____

_____

_____

_____

_____

4. What final thought would you like to leave your audience with? Is there a story or joke that would best tie together everything that you have said today?

_____

_____

_____

_____

_____

_____

CRITIQUE CHIC

Now that you have had the chance to view numerous speeches and give several speeches of your own, you should have a pretty good idea of what is expected of you when you deliver a speech. Just to be certain though, let's try the following exercise.

1. List **ten things** that you should be aware of when PREPARING your speech.

_____

_____

_____

_____

_____

_____

_____

_____

_____

_____

2. List **five things** that you should do when GIVING your speech.

_____

_____

_____

_____

_____

_____

_____

_____

_____

_____

3. List **five things** that you should AVOID doing when GIVING your speech.

_____

_____

_____

_____

_____

_____

_____

_____

4. Out of all of these lists, what is the toughest for you to do? Why?

_____

_____

_____

_____

_____

_____

_____

_____

5. What can you do to make this easier to do in the future?

_____

_____

_____

_____

_____

_____

_____

_____

MONROE'S MOTIVATED SEQUENCE

As a presenter, there are many things that you must consider when writing a speech. One thing that you must determine is the kind of pattern of organization you are going to implement in your speech. One pattern that works particularly well for persuasive speeches is known as Monroe's Motivated Sequence.

Monroe's Motivated Sequence follows the following five steps to organizing a persuasive speech:

1. Gain the ATTENTION of the audience
2. Establish a NEED
3. Create SATISFACTION
4. Offer VISUALIZATION
5. Call for ACTION

-Source: Pearson, J., Nelson, P., Titsworth, S., & Harter, L. (2008). *Human Communication* (3rd ed.). Boston: McGraw-Hill.

Now, let's put Monroe's Motivated Sequence to work for you and your persuasive speech. Fill out the questions below. Once you are done, you should have a better grasp on persuasive speaking and be better prepared to give a speech of your own.

1. What is the topic of you persuasive speech?

2. Step One – ATTENTION
    a. How do you plan on gaining the attention of your audience? (Hint: Often, a joke, a surprising statistic, or a personal story works well here.) _

    _____

    _____

    b. Once you have their attention, how can you ensure that you maintain it?

    _____

    _____

3. Step Two – NEED

    a. What problem are you identifying that needs to be fixed? _____

    _____

    _____

    b. How does this problem affect your audience? (It is important to make your audience consider important facts and ideas that they might not have considered prior to hearing your speech.) _____

_____

_____

4. Step Three – SATISFACTION

a. How do you propose that your audience solve the problem that you identified? _____

_____

_____

b. Is the solution something that the audience members can do themselves or is it something that they can help make happen in other way (i.e., voting, etc.)? _____

_____

_____

5. Step Four – VISUALIZATION

a. How will you help your audience visualize the way in which your solutions will help to satisfy the need that you identified? _____

_____

_____

b. What kind of images are you going to create in order to aid in this visualization? _____

_____

_____

6. Step Five – ACTION

a. How will you ask you audience to take action? _____

_____

_____

b. What suggestions can you make to help them feel like they can be part of the solution? _____

_____

_____